BURT FRANKLIN: RESEARCH & SOURCE WORKS SERIES 802
American Classics in History and Social Science 203

THE

LIFE AND PUBLIC SERVICES

OF

MILLARD FILLMORE

Millard Fillmore

THE

LIFE AND PUBLIC SERVICES

OF

MILLARD FILLMORE

BY

W. L. BARRE, OF KENTUCKY

BURT FRANKLIN
NEW YORK

Published by LENOX HILL Pub. & Dist. Co. (Burt Franklin)
235 East 44th St., New York, N.Y. 10017
Originally Published: 1856
Reprinted: 1971
Printed in the U.S.A.

S.B.N.: 8337-46340
Library of Congress Card Catalog No.: 70-170962
Burt Franklin: Research and Source Works Series 802
American Classics in History and Social Science 203

CONTENTS.

CHAPTER I

Birth of Millard Fillmore — Family reminiscences — Early propensities — Is started to a primary school — Makes rapid progress — Enters a higher school — Studies grammar and mathematics — Is apprenticed to a clothier — His thirst for knowledge — Returns home — Again apprenticed to a clothier — His assiduous application — Masters his trade — He teaches school — Studies surveying — Personal appearance — Manners, etc., ... 11

CHAPTER II.

He resumes his trade — Determines to study law — Reflections upon the importance of the step — Reads with Judge Wood — Sketch of that gentleman — Goes to Buffalo — Lives within his means — State of society — Political matters — Is admitted to the bar — Goes to Aurora, and engages in practice — His first case — Teaches school — Is married — Is regarded as a lawyer of ability — Nature of his eloquence — Prospects brighten, ... 25

CHAPTER III.

At the head of his profession — Is offered an excellent connection in Buffalo — Admitted to the supreme court — Individual sketches — Legal profundity — Is elected to the Assembly — Sketch of that body — Evinces legislative capacities — Party politics — Adherence to his principles — His nature as a debater — Adjournment of the

Assembly — His devotion to his profession — Re-elected to that body — On the committee on Public Defence — The law of imprisonment for debt — Governor Throop — Mr. Fillmore's active endeavors for the repeal of the imprisonment law — His success — Important measures in the Assembly — Close of the session — Sketch of Mr. Fillmore in that body — Remarks thereon, . 85

CHAPTER IV.

Mr. Fillmore as a lawyer — Brief review of his legal career — His view of the law as a science — Advantages of his connection — Spurns all artifice and chicanery— Responsibilities of the law — His views of its morality — His capacities as a lawyer — His ardent desire to promote justice — His weight of character — His faithfulness to his clients — In speaking, not a Patrick Henry— Examples of his success in civil cases — The Cattaraugus Reservation — The great importance of that case — The remarkable Ontario Bank case — His argument before the Supreme Court— His success in both, 130

CHAPTER V.

State politics — Political Anti-masonry— The Morgan outrage — The Clintonians and Bucktails — Anti-masonic convention — How the action of the Anti-masons should be construed — National politics of 1832 — Leading measures of the Whig party — Mr. Fillmore is elected to Congress — Sketch of that body— Jacksonism and its effects — Mr. Fillmore's view of the U. S. Bank, and the removal of the deposits — Mr. Clay's Compromise Tariff of 1833 — Excitements occasioned by the removal of the deposits — Internal improvements — Mr. Fillmore's efforts to reduce high salaries — Mr. Fillmore and Mr. Polk— Mr. Fillmore's qualities as a legislator — Other measures of Congress— Its adjournment, . . 166

CHAPTER VI.

Reëlected to Congress —Van Burenism — Distinguished characters — Polk elected speaker— Fourth installment of the Deposit Act —A bill to postpone the payment of the installment — It passes the senate — Mr. Fillmore's opposition — His able speech against the bill — Mr. Fillmore gives his views of the U. S. Bank — The passage of the bill — Mr. Fillmore and Mr. Clay — Slavery in the District of Columbia — The right of petition — Mr. Clay its champion in the senate, and Mr. Fillmore in the house — His views on the subject of slavery at that time — The North and the South — Mr. Fillmore's conciliatory nature as a statesman — His patriotism, ... 212

CHAPTER VII.

His views on the subject of public defence — The outrageous conduct of British officers —Awful fate of the Caroline — Mr. Fillmore's resolution urging redress — A committee reports upon the outrage — He opposes the report — Prompt, but not excitable — His solicitude for the northern frontier— The celebrated Jersey case — Its importance — Mr. Fillmore's determination to investigate it fairly— Proceedings of the committee on elections — Foul play— Democratic contestants successful — Letter to his constituents — Twenty-seventh Congress — Great change — Party politics— Harrison and the Whig party— The nominal president — John Tyler's treachery— Committee of ways and means — Distress of the country— Giant efforts of the twenty-seventh Congress — Equal to the emergency— Great innovations, . . 244

CHAPTER VIII.

Tariff of 1842 — A remedy for an existing evil — Protective tariff as a feature in politics— Tariff men in all parties —Jackson's views — Early statesmen's views — Clay calls it the American system — Mr. Fillmore's speech on the Tariff — Conclusions to be drawn from his course in regard to the Tariff — His high position in Congress — The Morse Appropriation — Cave Johnson — Close of his congressional career—J. Q. Adams and Mr. Fillmore—Campaign of 1844 — Prospects of the whig party — Mr. Fillmore urged as a candidate for the vice-presidency— Defeat of Clay— Causes which led to that result — Mr. Fillmore nominated for governor — Letter to Thurlow Weed — Foreign influence — Letter to Henry Clay— Extracts showing the cause of defeat — The Comptroller-ship — Its arduous duties — His report to the state — Its ability— His sympathy for the sufferers of the Emerald Isle, . . . 273

CHAPTER IX.

Another national convention — Great changes — Military glory — General Taylor nominated for the presidency— Millard Fillmore for the vice-presidency — Their election — Sketch of the U. S. Senate — Illustrious names — California asks admission — Sectionalism in the senate — ONE MAN at the head — The " omnibus bill "— Death of President Taylor — Mr. Fillmore communicates the fact to the senate — Proceedings of the two houses — Mr. Fillmore takes the oath — Assumes the chief magistracy — Funeral obsequies, ... 305

CHAPTER X.

MR. FILLMORE'S ADMINISTRATION — He selects a cabinet — Wisdom of his selection — Excitement in the senate — Defeat of the omnibus bill — The North and the South — Struggle for supremacy — Three parties in the senate —Wisdom and patriotism — The great crisis — Mr. Fillmore's firmness and patriotism — Difficulties in New Mexico and Texas — Passage of the compromise measures — Their submission to the president — A civic Callimachus — Fugitive Slave Law— Attorney General — Mr. Fillmore signs the compromise measures — Is violently assailed in consequence — Judge McLean's opinion — First annual message — Its ability, 321

CHAPTER XI.

Fillibustering — The Cuban movement — Proclamation of the president — Progress of the adventurers — Their delusion — General Quitman — The Lopez expedition — Condensed history of that movement — Its disastrous termination — The Crescent City and Captain General of Cuba — European interference — Their proposals in regard to Cuba — Mr. Fillmore's views — A second Hulsemann letter — Mr. Fillmore's course in regard to Cuba — Kossuth — His mission — His interviews with Mr. Fillmore and Mr. Clay — Their views of his mission — Sound views in regard to foreign and domestic policy—Wisdom of Mr. Fillmore's administration —The American party—Its rise and progress —Causes that led to the defeat of the whig party— Mr. Fillmore's Americanism — His tour to Europe — Reflections, etc.— His nomination for the Presidency— Mr. Fillmore at home, ... 352

CHAPTER XII.

Character of Mr. Fillmore as a domestic man — His adaptation for the family circle —Amiability and industry of Mrs. Fillmore — Mr. Fillmore as a philanthropist — As a neighbor — His love of home — Mr. Fillmore as a husband — As a parent — His residence and its sociabilities — His manners — His order and regularity—His industry—His temperance—His morality—Mr. Fillmore as a statesman —As a patriot —And as a man — Conclusion, 386

PUBLISHERS' PREFACE.

In presenting to the public the life of so distinguished a man as the subject of this memoir, the publishers deem it unnecessary to offer any apology for its appearance, either politically or generally, as it is not the object of this publication to inculcate the peculiar principles or views of any party.

The subject matter has been carefully and thoroughly prepared by the author, after having had free access to every aid necessary to render the work authentic and reliable.

American citizens have always evinced much interest in the history of those men whose public course has reflected credit on the times in which they have lived, and especially when such men have risen from the humble walks of life to the highest and most honorable position in the gift of an intelligent and enterprising people.

The author knows full well how to present a truthful and interesting record of one, whose early life, untar-

1*

nished character, and public career, have created a bright example for the encouragement of American youth.

This work is designed especially for young men, and, with the hope that many may find in its pages an incentive to just ambition, we cheerfully submit it to the consideration of the reading public.

WANZER, MᶜKIM & CO.

BUFFALO, August 20, 1856.

LIFE OF MILLARD FILLMORE.

CHAPTER I.

Birth of Millard Fillmore — Family reminiscences — Early propensities — Is started to a primary school — Makes rapid progress —
Enters a higher school — Studies grammar and mathematics —
Is apprenticed to a clothier — His thirst for knowledge — Returns
home — Again apprenticed to a clothier — His assiduous application — Masters his trade — He teaches school — Studies surveying — Personal appearance — Manners, etc.

MILLARD FILLMORE, the oldest son of Nathaniel and
Phœbe Fillmore, and one of nine children, was born on
the seventh day of January, in the year 1800, at the town
of Locke, Cayuga county, in the state of New York.

For a number of years, his parents remained the
residents of his birth-place, and here he received the
rudiments of his education. His parents, though very
poor, and obliged to combat the fierce elements of adversity in their darkest aspects, were universally esteemed
as among the most respectable inhabitants of the country.

His father, Nathaniel Fillmore, was a native of Bennington, in the state of Vermont, and well recollects the
victory gained by the immortal Starke, at that place, in
1776. The grandfather of Millard Fillmore was one of

the early settlers of the New England States, and hero-
ically participated in all the hardships and privations
incident to the pioneers of western civilization. With a
strong arm, and a stronger heart, he endured all the back-
woods' privations of pioneer life, undismayed by the difficulties that surrounded him. A family growing up
around him, of whom he was the head — a devoted wife,
who shared all his toils, and to whom he was ardently
attached, appealing to him for legitimate protection, and
nothing but a wilderness before him, where that protection
was to be sought, in the peaceful asylum of a home, it
must be confessed the prospects were gloomy indeed.

But his was not the heart to quail before such difficulties as these. With that energetic perseverance and
prompt decision that characterized the early settlers of
the New England States, and has ever been a marked
development of his family, no difficulty was too great to
be overcome, no obstacle too great for him to surmount.
At length, the footprints of civilization began to impress
the soil of his adoption, farms opened in the wilderness,
cottages supplanted the rude wigwam of the savage,
abundant crops and well-stored granaries began to reward
the husbandman for his labor. But scarce had these indications of peaceful prosperity received the acclaim of
welcome from the grateful colonists, when, from across
the Atlantic, the news of the infamous Stamp Act
announced the commencement of new troubles. The
call to arms met a response in the breasts of many brave
New Englanders. Among these was the grandfather of
Millard Fillmore.

Seeing the jewel of Colonial Independence in danger of extermination, and fearing the triumphant exactions of tyranny upon the fields of his virgin home, he needed no other incentive. In obedience to the dictates of a patriot heart, he espoused the cause of the colonists, and rendered efficient service in their resistance to the encroachments of foreign aggression. Gallantly did he defend his country's flag, at the battle of Bennington, and other ensanguined fields, consecrated by the hero dust of the Revolution. He lived, I believe, to see victory perch upon the banners of his country, and to reap the rewards of his labors. He lived to see a numerous offspring growing up around him, universally esteemed as ornaments to society. He died at an advanced age, beloved by all, leaving to his descendants the rich legacy of a name without a blemish.

Nathaniel Fillmore, the father of Millard, inheriting all the noble qualities of his ancestry, commenced life with nothing but an inflexible determination to succeed for his heritage. He spent his early years in the place of his nativity; acquiring what knowledge his limited means would permit, and following the industrial pursuits to which he had been carefully reared. His vocation being that of a farmer, wholly dependent upon his own resources for whatsoever he acquired, he was in a position admirably calculated to develop a naturally good physical organization. His habits, from early youth, were exceedingly regular and temperate — so much so that he refrained entirely from the use of all stimulants. So early, indeed, were the formation of his strictly tem-

perate habits, that in his boyhood he was designated as
a model for the boys of his neighborhood.

At the age of sixteen, he evinced considerable judgment, in regard to the future value of New York lands,
by persuading his father to go to Syracuse, and purchase
lands which were then selling at ten shillings per acre.
His father declined this good advice, assigning as a reason, that "it was too far from market."

He continued the industrial pursuits of his vocation
in his native county, without that accumulation of wealth
he desired, for a number of years. By pursuing a course
of scrupulous integrity toward his fellow men, and cherishing the nicest sense of honor, with an ardent desire to
render himself agreeable and useful, he won the confidence and esteem of all with whom he mingled in the
intercourse of every day life. Though possessing but a
limited education, with naturally a good practical mind,
he had been especially careful to avail himself of every
facility within his reach to improve it, and to acquaint
himself, as far as possible, with the institutions of
his country and the history of the times. Born on the
eve of the Revolution, and cradled amid the thunders of
an enemy's cannon, he learned the lessons of patriotism
on the very battle-fields of liberty. Peace had perched
upon the American banner, and prospects more brilliant
were then before the youth of the land than had hitherto
been known on the continent. Surrounded by the vast,
fertile fields of North America, free to make his own
selection for a home, at the age of twenty-five, Nathaniel

Fillmore began to look around him with a view to a permanent settlement.

Consequently, in his twenty-sixth year, he married Miss Phœbe Millard, daughter of Dr. Millard, of Pittsford, in the state of Vermont. He in his twenty-sixth and she in her seventeenth year, unknown to fortune or to fame, possessing nothing but honest, determined hearts, rich in the possession of each other's love, they commenced the journey of life — the destined parents of: MILLARD FILLMORE.

After marriage, he remained in his old county but a short time. In February, 1798, in company with his brother, he left his native home, and went to Cayuga county, New York, in quest of that independency which seemed so difficult to procure at the home of his youth. Here, from February, 1798, to January, 1799, he and his brother lived, alone and almost in the woods, enduring many hardships and privations in making preparations for the reception of their families, whom they designed removing the ensuing spring. Scarcely awaiting the coldest of winters to abate its rigor, he commenced the difficult process of his family's removal from the state of Vermont to Cayuga county, New York. Through many difficulties, however, and after much labor, the task of removal was accomplished, and the parties installed in their new home.

Here, active measures were early taken, to perform the varied duties of practical life, in procuring a competency, which they required as heads of a young and growing family. Mr. Fillmore, as he had ever been, by his kind and courteous demeanor, and irreproachable integrity, was eminently successful in getting the entire confidence of his fellow citizens. With such undeviating rectitude did he pursue the course marked out by virtuous honor, that his words were regarded as bonds by all who knew him.

As a proof of the high appreciation on the part of his fellow citizens for his sound judgment and exalted moral worth, I will state that he was created a justice of the peace for Cayuga county, the duties of which office he discharged to the satisfaction of all, and to the promotion of public justice, for the period of eleven years. The incumbents of those offices were then invariably selected from the best men of the country. He held the scales of justice with an even hand, and often evinced a sound judgment and a nice discrimination rarely excelled even by those gifted in the elucidation of legal technicalities.

His early friends in Cayuga county were among the first citizens, possessing those high traits of character for which the early fathers of the New England States were so proverbial. His interests being identified with theirs — his love of virtue being in common with theirs — he early became domesticated in their families, and had a place assigned him in their affections. He had been, as he thought, successful, too, in accumulating a portion of that property which the wants of a growing family required. He had, in fact, by investing the proceeds of his labors in Cayuga county lands, become the proprietor of quite a handsome property ; but a deficiency in the title by which those lands were held being subsequently discovered, it was seen that the means which he thought judiciously appropriated were a total loss: and the lands passed into other hands. About a year after his removal to Cayuga county, Millard was born. Like Washington and Clay, he was born with no silver spoon in his mouth— and like them, he was destined to become an enduring monument of his own architectural genius. Nathaniel Fillmore continued a resident of Cayuga county for a number of years, but being deprived of his lands by the deficiency of title before alluded to, and having quite a large family to support, he resolved on removing to Erie county, in the more western portion of the state. He reached the city of Buffalo with his family, on the tenth of March, 1820. Buffalo was then becoming a place of commercial importance, and offered excellent inducements to the settlers in every department of business. He resided near Buffalo for a number of years, universally beloved and respected. He now lives at the beautiful village of Aurora, twenty miles from Buffalo, regarded by all as an embodiment of virtuous integrity. Though he has reached the advanced age of eighty-six years, he is in the vigorous possession of his mental faculties, is in excellent health, and never feels a pain, though somewhat enfeebled by age. Thus, in the peace and quiet of healthful old age, as he approaches the grave of his fathers, he

> " Looks back upon life from its dawn to its close,
> Nor feels that he's squandered its treasures away."

Phœbe Fillmore was a lady of prepossessing appearance, and richly endowed with the amiable qualities of

soul for which the ladies of New England were proverbial in the early days of the republic.

Her father, Doctor Millard, was, in that day, regarded
as an able physician, and a man of considerable attainments in various departments of useful knowledge.

A sympathizer with the colonial sufferers through the
scenes of the Revolution, after a peaceful adjustment of
the difficulties between the two countries, he was anxiously solicitous that his children should receive all the
blessings of our free institutions.

Phœbe Millard, was, therefore, blessed with all the
educational facilities the country could afford, and received the kindness of the best of parents.

Thus, in early girlhood, she evinced an amiable disposition, a spirit of meek forbearance, and a richly stored
intellect, that eminently qualified her for the position she
was destined to occupy.

At the age of sixteen, she became the wife of Nathaniel
Fillmore, and left the paternal home to share the fortunes of the young pioneer. Though young in years,
she fully understood the duties and responsibilities of a
wife. Devotedly attached to her husband, she was ever
careful to promote his happiness. With clear conceptions of her responsibilities as a mother, she was tenderly
careful to instill into the minds of her children lessons of
virtuous wisdom for their guidance. How much influence the examples of such parents have had in shaping
the career of their distinguished son eternity alone can
tell. It is a remarkable fact, that, in the perusal of our
great men's early histories, we find they all had excellent

mothers. Nathaniel Fillmore was peculiarly a domestic man; he knew no joys to compare with those that eradiate around the green vales of home. He was ever gratified, therefore, to find his wife endeavoring to make happiness the inmate of his humble abode. She shared his fortunes with the changeless devotion of a faithful wife, gladdened his path with the sunshine of her smiles, and gave into his arms a son, the glory of whose name will live forever.

In company with her husband, she arrived at the city of Buffalo on the 10th of March, 1820, where she continued, zealous in the discharge of every duty, smoothing the cares of her husband with devotional kindness, and impressing upon the minds of her children the deathless example of a virtuous life.

At the time of their arrival in Buffalo, the family had become quite numerous, and required all the efforts their parents could bestow. Mrs. Fillmore, by the zeal with which she guarded the welfare of her children, proved herself worthy the position she occupied.

During her residence in the vicinity of Buffalo, she won the esteem of all with whom she became acquainted. She lived to see her children the recipients of public confidence. She died on the 2nd day of April, 1831. Heavily, indeed, did this bereavement weigh upon the minds of her husband and children — he lost the best of wives, they the best of mothers. Mrs. Fillmore had five brothers and four sisters: her brothers are good citizens, and her sisters beloved by those who knew them. Nathaniel Fillmore has several brothers, who are regarded as excellent citizens in their respective neighborhoods. Colonel Calvin Fillmore was a captain under General Scott, in the war of 1812.

The family of Mr. Fillmore are remarkable for their strictly temperate habits, and great physical vigor and longevity. I have deemed it necessary to say this much of the parentage and relations of Millard Fillmore. I presume it will be thought quite sufficient to say of a man's parentage, who owes no part of his fame to an illustrious ancestry, who plucks no laurels from the "lineal tree," but who is essentially the architect of his own fortunes — the builder of his own temple. True, the ancestry of Mr. Fillmore vies with the oldest and most respectable of the early New England settlers, but still their brows are circled with the chaplets of no civic or military fame. They present themselves to our view panoplied in the gorgeous drapery of no illustrious deeds, wherewith to decorate the page of history. Yet, as impersonations of the purest virtue and patriotism, as men who strictly abstain from all vicious habits, and, by an adherence to the principles of temperate morality, live a life of irreproachable rectitude, and reach an old age in the full possession of all their faculties, they should elicit our esteem and emulation.

Men who thus live, careful to leave upon the minds of their posterity the impress of virtuous example, are the true noblemen of the country.

Millard Fillmore, in early childhood, possessed a sedate gravity of manners and a peaceful quietude of disposition that was extraordinary in a child of his age.

Possessing little taste, in common with other children, for the amusements incident to that age, he was rarely seen engaged in the sports which were a source of enjoyment to the other boys in the neighborhood. He loved his young associates, but had no desire to participate in their frolicsome pastimes. The quality of his disposition was steady and earnest, yet mild and gentle. These traits of character, thus indicated at so early an age, have, to a great extent, grown with his growth, and become marked developments of his maturer manhood. In childhood, he doted on his parents with an ardor that knew no abatement, and loved to render implicit obedience to their commands. He was industriously assiduous in the performance of every duty, and evinced, at a very early age, a determined spirit of energy, whose restless activity no discouragement could suppress.

Prompted in his earliest undertakings by an emulative ambition to excel, his efforts were characterized by such a spirit of vigilant perseverance, that he seldom knew such a word as " failure," in childhood. His intercourse with his playmates was quiet, kind, and agreeable. The acknowledged favorite of his young companions, he was often chosen arbiter of their little disputes, which he seldom failed to settle in a manner entirely satisfactory. From his earliest childhood, he was remarkable for these peaceable traits of disposition.

He was never known to quarrel with other boys, or to use language in the least exceptionable to any one. At six years of age, he was sent to school, in the immediate neighborhood of his father's, where he commenced learning to read and write. At this school he began to manifest a love for books, and to evince a thirst for useful knowledge, that has been characteristic of his whole subsequent life.

At the time of which I am now speaking, there existed in the New England States no efficiently organized school system, as at the present day, possessing all the facilities to rapid advancement in every department of useful knowledge; and even had such advantages existed, the father of young Fillmore was too poor to avail himself of them. The name of the first teacher to whom young Fillmore was sent was Amos Castle, who, I believe, was a native of Connecticut. Mr. Castle was a very religious man — observing the strictest principles of the early Puritans — but was a man of no extraordinary attainments as a scholar. He had a good school, and was careful to advance his pupils as fast as possible; he was especially careful in the rigid enforcement of his rules regulating the morals of his school. He was beloved as a teacher of a primary school, and as a Christian of exemplary piety. At this school, young Fillmore made such rapid progress in the elementary branches of learning, that all the scholars, and even his teacher and father, were surprised at the ease and facility with which he mastered his lessons. In a very short time, so rapid had been his progress, that he was enabled to stand at the head of his classes, and compete for the prize with the best scholars in the school. His rapid progress soon became manifest to the whole school, and though it excited the envy of some, with the encouragement of his father and his teacher, the spark of ambition was kindled in his breast, that was destined to blaze its light across the world.

Under the parental direction of his father, who had opened his young mind, thus early, to the importance of mental culture, and filled his soul with exalted conceptions of future success, he soon learned to read and write, and acquired a superficial knowledge of many things that were eminently useful. He made considerable proficiency in the different branches of his primary school, displaying in childhood a strong predilection for whatever pertained to books. He was extremely careful to avail himself of all the advantages thrown in his way, and, passionately addicted to the attainment of knowledge — so much so that it became the one absorbing desire of his soul, to which all others were subordinate. For the hardships of confinement in a school-room, he regarded himself richly remunerated by the acquisition of knowledge as the fruits of such coercion. Hence, though very young, instead of the desultory, irregular efforts at progress, usual among boys of his age, his mind became engaged in its one absorbing idea, until the manner of his studies assumed the regularity of system. He did not engage in the prosecution of his studies as though it was a task imposed upon him : to him, study was a delightful occupation. He was never seen engaged in those frivolous occupations of fishing or hunting, so usual among boys when uncontrolled by coercive authority. Instead of participating in these boyish sports, he would pore for whole days over the pages of a book, with a taste that seemed increased rather than diminished by the perusal of his pages. His growing passion for books and ardent thirst for knowledge became a theme of observation and comment on the part of his acquaintances and associates. They perceived that his progress was unchecked by any desire to engage in the amusements of his companions, or by his assiduous application to his studies, and ultimately concluded he loved to study, as his greatest source of enjoyment. He was frequently, when very young, known to pore for whole days over the pages of a book, the perusal of which could scarcely be imposed upon most boys of his age as a task, and yet, to him its perusal was a source of gratification. This love of books and taste for reading, in his early boyhood, was often a subject of remark. No scenes of mirthful festivity or boyish sport could allure him from his favorite pursuit. If asked to participate in the amusements of his young companions, he preferred to remain at home, where, undisturbed and alone, he could enjoy the glorious luxury of reading. Not that he had an aversion to the society of his young friends at this early age; he had a species of zest for social intercourse, but never participated in the wild sports incident to that age. He was calm and social, but never gay and boisterous. This love of quietude has always been characteristic of Mr. Fillmore. It seems a part of his nature.

While young, his enjoyments were somewhat of a peculiar nature. Reading, and reflecting upon what he had read or seen around him, were for him enjoyments that far surpassed the transient gaieties of the festive throng.

When very young, he was a close observer, and loved particularly to study the traits of different characters with whom he came in contact, and form his own conclusions in regard to the same. Many of those early conclusions evince great justness and accuracy, while the correctness of many of his early delineations of character would have done credit to a moralist of an older growth.

These traits of close observation seemed peculiarly manifest in Mr. Fillmore at a very early age, and have doubtless contributed much to form that correct basis for his actions through life. At ten years of age, he was sent to school to a Mr. Western, in the village of Sempronius, Cayuga county, New York. Of this gentleman I have been able to learn but little, save that he was a man of correct habits, and was regarded there as a well educated man.

At this school, young Fillmore commenced the study of grammar and mathematics. He took the lead in his classes, and mastered his studies with an ease and facility that evinced an intellectual capacity of the first order, and an indomitable perseverance in overcoming obstacles to his progress, that would quail before no discouragements. Of young Fillmore it may be truly said, that he possessed in youth a mind eminently susceptible of an indefinite expansion in the various departments of scientific literature. Possessing no choice, particularly, for one branch of learning over another, he had only to see that it was knowledge and become convinced of its utility, when he mastered its intricacies as by the glance of intuition. About this time, his youthful predilection for

2

books developed itself in its true light. So great was this propensity that it seemed an inherent one — born with him; the moment a new subject presented itself for his investigation, his active mind exerted itself with the promptness of instinct, until its abstrusities were thoroughly understood.

The vigorous powers of his intellect thus cultivated by all the means of which he had been able to avail himself, became more and more incessant in its restless activity to acquire knowledge until those of an intellectual nature were, at length, the only pursuits in which he took delight.

From the career of Mr. Fillmore, let the youthful reader deduce an argument in favor of early application, to qualify himself for the exalted position of his destiny. Let him remember that obscure soever as may be his birth, that it is a distinguishing feature of our social and political organism to open the avenues to wealth, fame, and honor, to all who, by application, deserve being the recipients, irrespective of name, distinction, or birth. Let him remember when adverse circumstances darken around his young aspirations, and "chill penury freezes the genial current of his soul," how like a star young Fillmore arose from the gloom that enshrouded him, and gradually ascending, radiant with light, until he took his place among the brightest that constellate in the horizon of mind. Let him remember too, that the secret of his success and his immortality lies in the fact that the high-toned resolves of his early boyhood kept him entirely **free from the witching sorcery of evil habits — and that,** by close application, to qualify himself for the discharge of after duties, in the prosperity of subsequent life he never had to look back to the days of his youth, to commune with " the ghosts of his departed hours."

Up to this time, young Fillmore, by assisting his father on the farm during the spring and summer months, was enabled to attend school during the fall and winter months of each year ; and thus his thirst for knowledge had been partially supplied by the means offered for its gratification. But owing to the limited means of his father, who was unable to support so large a family as was accumulating upon his hands, he was compelled to quit school, and smother for a while his young ambition, except when opportunities presented themselves for its gratification in the sphere of an apprentice, of which he was sure to avail himself. It was a source of bitter regret to young Fillmore, to leave his school-room, where he had made such rapid progress, and to lay aside his books that had been his most delightful and familiar friends. He was the oldest son of a growing family, however, who had no resources for a support but the labors of his father, and saw clearly the imperative necessity of being early qualified not only to support himself, but to render his father assistance in supporting the younger members of the family. With this view, in his fifteenth year he was placed under the care of Mr. Hungerford, in the town of Sparta, Ontario county, (now Livingston,) New York, for the purpose of learning the clothier's business. Until about this age, he had been timid and diffident, with no indications of that buoyant health and physical vigor which he ultimately attained. Taking into consideration the destitute circumstances of his· father, and hoping he might be enabled to alleviate them, with a stout heart young Fillmore cheerfully submitted to the mandate of necessity, bade adieu to his school-room, left his companions and his home, to commence the arduous duties of an apprenticeship. Thus, at the tender age of fourteen, dependent entirely upon his own resources — an ancestry without a blemish his only legacy — the aristocracy of an honest heart that no evil influences could corrupt, his only guide — and an indomitable energy that no difficulties could subdue, his only capital, he commenced a career that was destined to become immortal. His connection with Hungerford, in the capacity of an apprentice, resulted in no abatement of his thirst after useful knowledge. Aided by the attainments he had subsequently made, with a mind whose conceptions became elevated and enlarged, as he advanced in years he seized those books he could procure best calculated to familiarize himself with examples of the great and the good, and devoured their contents with avidity. Carefully assiduous to appropriate every moment of his time not required by the duties of his apprenticeship to the cultivation of his mind, he accumulated a large amount of useful information in regard to his own and other times. One of his favorite pursuits at this time was the study of history. He loved to confer with the dead as well as the living, and upon the records of the past to see the imperishable impress of departed worth.

Though at times young Fillmore longed for better

opportunities to cultivate his mind than presented themselves as a clothier's apprentice, and wished relief from the coercive restraint under which his aspiring soul was fettered, he never uttered a murmur of discontent, or mourned at his lot. His was not a geuius whose spark of inspiration could be extinguished by adverse winds that assailed it. With a firm reliance upon the happy result of his continued efforts, and the ultimate triumph of virtuous perseverance, he pressed steadily forward to the consummation of his wishes. Many bright geniuses, situated under circumstances similar to those that surrounded the youth of Mr. Fillmore, have slumbered forever in obscurity. Many sensitive minds, gifted with all the natural endowments of talent requisite to success, have been crushed by difficulties of less magnitude than weighed upon the aspirations of young Fillmore. With struggling genius thus fettered, we can not sympathise too deeply. No condition of life is, perhaps, so fraught with mental suffering as that of a young student who aspires to a name and is conscious of his own inherent worth, but feels every energy palsied by the icy chill of poverty that binds him forever to his original sphere. Such commence their careers full of bright hopes for the future; they breast the storms of adversity for a while with true courage, but they have no influential friends to speak well of their efforts; they possess no combination of influences favorable to their advancement, and having to turn aside from their chosen profession to earn the necessities of life, they see those more favored of fortune outstripping them, and becoming the recipients of public confidence, and finally, depressed and discouraged, the word "failure" becomes impressed upon their minds — they pass into obscurity, or become votaries of dissipation.

This is the fate of hundreds — the history of thousands. The main cause of these disastrous results is a want of *moral courage* on the part of young students thus situated to press steadily forward, over all obstacles, and wait with patience the reward of merit. Herein consists an essential element of Mr. Fillmore's greatness; he was one of the immortal few who had the moral courage to combat every difficulty, to resist every temptation, and to await with patience the reward of his labors. He knew that success was not the creation of an hour, but the result of labor, of study, and of thought. For all young men thus situated, he stands a beacon light to immortality, enduring as the Pyramids. How worthy their emulation is his example for the American youth. The stay of our young apprentice with Hungerford was a very short one. That gentleman, not having sufficient work in his clothier's business to require the services of his apprentices more than half the time, would send them to other work, when not engaged in the business of the establishment. This did not suit young Fillmore. He had left home, and entered the establishment for the purpose of learning the trade, and when he found that his services, instead of being confined to that exclusively, were chiefly required in the labors of another vocation, he resolved on returning home. This resolution was not without good reasons — he was anxious to learn a trade, in order to render his father that assistance, in the support of his

family, which his limited means required, and to promote
his own advancement. The duties required at his hands,
by his employer, when not engaged in his regular business, were of the most onerous nature. Everything, therefore, being satisfactorily arranged with Hungerford, he
started for his home in Cayuga county, where he arrived,
after an absence of only a few months. It was in the
fall of the year when he reached home. During the ensuing winter he remained with his father, cheerfully
assisting him in his out-door labors, and contributing
much to the happiness of their humble home. The home
of Mr. Fillmore was, at this time, comparatively speaking, situated in little less than a wilderness. The country
was but sparsely inhabited, with few indications of the
subsequent prosperity it has attained. What improvements had been made were of a rustic nature, and upon
the strictest principles of economy and simplicity. Social intercourse was restricted to only a few families,
which were the entire community. Schools were few in
number, and not very well sustained. There were none
of those facilities, in fact, for the youthful student, that
are thrown so profusely around the young men of our
day. Books without number, school systems, libraries,
lyceums and Sunday schools, etc., that render such
efficient assistance to young men of the present day, were
advantages unknown to the youth of Mr. Fillmore. Yet,
unaided with these facilities, during the winter, while at
his father's, by applying his leisure moments to reading
what books he was enabled to procure, he added a large
amount of useful information to what he had previously

acquired. He had a great passion for reading, and a happy faculty of *thinking* on what he read. He thus treasured from the records of the historian, the leading events, the virtues and wisdom of other times. With Grecian and Roman history he became somewhat conversant, and thoroughly imbued with the sentiments of virtuous patriotism of the ancient sages. He was fond of perusing their history, he loved to treasure their deeds of renown, and read, with delight, the pages of their matchless oratory. He fully understood the advantages, in his youth, of reading; but as a distinguishing trait in his youthful character from that of most youths, he bestowed much thought upon what he read. In his reading, he would compare characters, and seek for the existence of analogy, or view the beauties of virtue, when contrasted with the deformities of vice. He loved to analyze the actions of those of whom he read, and trace the motives of their origin. By this course, he was seldom incorrect in the opinions he formed of different characters. He possessed, in youth, an extraordinary memory. The most casual occurrence he would never forget, while the details of all conversations in his presence were remembered with minute accuracy. Though his opportunities were limited, owing to the scarcity of books, his passion for reading and general observation, combined with these retentive faculties of memory, resulted in the accumulation of a vast fund of facts and information, embracing a portion of almost every department of useful knowledge.

Though deprived of those means of enjoyment so prized by youth and incident to thickly settled communities, the boyhood of Mr. Fillmore was not wholly without its pleasantries. With the youths of the neighborhood, when he could get time and his own consent to forego the pleasure of his studies, he would have considerable pastime. In their little excursions, the peaceable and quiet disposition of young Fillmore was always manifest. He never gave way to anger, nor permitted his associates to do so, if he could possibly prevent it. As illustrative of his peaceful disposition, I will insert the following incident, that occurred in his thirteenth year. The peculiar domestic habits of his father often induced him to have the children of the neighborhood around him, whose playful gambols were to him a source of delight, unknown to the morose and misanthropic. Living on terms of entire sociability with all his neighbors, he had frequent opportunities of getting all their children together at his house, for an evening's amusement. It was on one of those occasions, when quite a number of the neighbor boys and girls had assembled for the purpose of enjoying their sports; when at the height of their enjoyment, however, a sudden misunderstanding occurred among the juveniles, and a quarrel ensued. Young Fillmore, who had taken no active part in the amusements of the occasion, on seeing the disturbance, approached the parties with great gravity, and chided them in the mildest possible manner for their conduct, and gave them a moral lecture upon good behavior, telling them "it was unmanly,"—"it was not ladylike," thus to interrupt their evening's entertainment. In this way, he soon succeeded in restoring quiet, and making the quar-

2*

relsome parties heartily ashamed of their conduct. He thus, at a very early age, evinced the desires and capacities of "peacemaker" that have been eminently characteristic of his subsequent career.

So conspicuous, indeed, was his peaceable, quiet disposition, that the parents of the community, in correcting their children for any exhibition of rudeness or ill-temper, would refer to him as an example they should follow. He was quite a favorite, not only among those of his own age, but among the elder inhabitants of the neighborhood, who always felt happy in having him associate with their children. But the time was near at hand when again he had to quit his books and leave his friends, for the duties of an apprenticeship. A portion of the fall and winter had passed since he left his first employer, embracing a period of six months. His time had not been wasted or misapplied. With characteristic energy he had made use of it to the best advantage. In the spring of his sixteenth year, he was, for a second time, apprenticed to a clothier. For the business of a clothier young Fillmore expressed a preference, from the time he became convinced of the necessity of learning a trade, though he doubtless entertained intentions of a vocation beyond that at no distant day. As an available facility to promote his advancement, in the selection of his trade, he could not, perhaps, under the circumstances, have been more fortunate. If he expected to follow it, it was a business in which there existed but little competition; it was a business in the pursuit of which his physical powers were called into requisition, and his constitutional development and vigor promoted; then, withal, in learning the business, his application was only required during the spring and summer months of each year, while he could devote the fall and winter to other pursuits, and to the cultivation of his mind. These are the considerations, it is presumed, whereby he was actuated in his expressed preference of this for his trade. The most successful results have demonstrated the wisdom of the selection. The infinite utility of combining physical with mental labor, will scarcely be called in question by any one — certainly not by the intelligent, thinking reader.

The position now occupied by young Fillmore necessarily insured this successful combination. His application during the time required to the arduous duties of his trade, resulted in the expansion and development of his physical powers; while, during the fall and winter months, the same spirit of persevering application to his studies resulted in a still happier development of his mental powers: hence, though his mental capacities are entitled to superior claims, as being eminently preponderant, both are remarkable for their vigorous elasticity.

The name of the gentleman under whose charge he was this time placed was Cheney. He lived in the immediate neighborhood of his father's, so that the regret it was natural for him to feel on leaving home was not aggravated by the idea of a distant separation. Of this gentleman's traits of character I have not been able to acquaint myself in detail. So far as I have been able to learn, he was a man highly respected for his business habits, and many other good qualities of citizenship.

His business was somewhat extended in its nature, and required in its prosecution his personal care and supervision. In the pursuit of his vocation, he had amassed considerable property, and been strictly economical in husbanding his resources. Being ever watchful in guarding the interests of his establishment, the conduct of his apprentices came under his immediate observation. Whether he was naturally kind to his apprentices, or the dictates of feeling prompted him to give them encouragement, I cannot say. Certain it is, however, he became attached to young Fillmore immediately after his entrance into his service. There was, in fact, between Cheney and his father, an explicit stipulation, to the· effect that his labors should be confined exclusively to the duties of his trade. In a strict conformity to this stipulation on the part of his employer, young Fillmore was, of course, deeply interested. Not being discouraged by those drafts upon his time made by his former employer, he prosecuted his trade with an energetic determination to assume its complete mastery. Cheney was not repulsive and overbearing towards those in his employ, though he required at their hands a faithful discharge of every duty. Instead of assuming the haughty arrogance of a master, in his intercourse with those over whom he exercised control, he was uniformly kind and courteous. Far from being exacting and tyrannous toward young Fillmore, he held out to him every inducement, and manifested great willingness to do all in his power caculated to promote his advancement in a thorough knowledge of his business.

Young Fillmore, as he had ever done toward difficulties over which he assayed to assume the mastery, evinced a perceptive aptitude in understanding the peculiarities of his new vocation.   In the pursuit of his trade, he was as anxious to succeed as when in the pursuit of knowledge, and applied himself to the duties of his apprenticeship with the same spirit of assiduity that characterized his efforts in the school-room.

From his trade, as before indicated, he expected much assistance in the prosecution of his plans for the future, and through it, as a medium of support, hoped to reap the rewards of their effectual maturity.   For him to bend every energy, therefore, to its successful prosecution, the incentive was a very great one.   It was his boyhood ladder, whereby he was to climb from obscurity.   That he should be particularly careful in the construction of an article whereby he was to make an ascent so difficult should be no matter of suprise, when we take in consideration the laudable nature of his aspirations.   During this time, while making these exertions, he was not forgetful of his mind ; but whenever occasion offered, he would turn aside, and drink draughts from the fountain of knowledge.

These opportunities, however, did not often occur, except at night, when after a hard day's toil, instead of giving way to " tired nature's sweet restorer, balmy sleep," from his books, by the midnight lamp, he would cull the jewels of literature.   Nights were the only times he now had to indulge in these, his favorite pursuits ; for, while in the performance of his duties in the estab-

lishment, by day he made every thing subordinate to the
main desire of becoming master of his trade. Watchful
of his employer's interests as though they were his own,
he was always careful to promote them by all possible
means in his power. During his entire apprenticeship,
he was scrupulous in the observance of every regulation.
Conducting himself with the strictest propriety, in every
particular, he acted in accordance with every requirement,
and performed the tasks assigned him with cheerful fidel-
'ity. He very well knew that in promoting the interests
of employers he was paving the way to his own, and
that, in discharging his duties to them, he was discharging them to himself. From the dawning of his earliest
aspirations, he acted upon the principle that he had
something to do in life — some duty to perform — some
sphere to fill. He has always felt that, as a citizen of a
free country, he had something to do for that country —
as a member of society, he felt there was a debt due society from him : and in order to have just conceptions of
those relative duties, and to qualify himself for their
faithful discharge, he has left no means untried. Ambitious as he was to excel in his undertakings, it was not
that selfish, groveling ambition that glories in the elevation of self at the prostration of others, and exults at the
consummation of its ends, even though it be at the entire
sacrifice of all moral principle. His was an ambition of
a nobler stamp, whereon the Divinity has left the signet
of approval.

His ambition was of that laudable nature, to cultivate
the faculties that God had given him, to understand fully

the duties incumbent upon him, and be enabled properly
to discharge them — to make himself worthy the confidence of his fellow men, and be useful to his country.   Of
this nature was Mr. Fillmore's youthful ambition — of
this nature it still is.   It was this kind of ambition that
actuated the efforts of his boyhood, made him the con-
queror of every difficulty, and ultimately secured his
triumphant success.   By pursuing the praiseworthy course
he did during his apprenticeship, he won the unlimited
confidence, not only of his employer, but of every one
connected with the establishment, before the labors of
the first year were concluded.

At the expiration of the summer, the busy season of
his employer being over, he returned home, where he
spent the fall and winter pretty much as he had the preceding ones — dividing his time between his studies and
his labors on the farm with his father.   Than the father
of Mr. Fillmore, no one was ever more careful toward a
son.   He was gratified at his ambition, and did everything in his power to promote its gratification.   He encouraged his taste for books, and strengthened his virtuous
resolves by the strongest fortifications of precept and example.   Without the remotest idea of the future eminence
foreshadowed in his son's ardent thirst for knowledge,
he was careful to keep alive the spark of his ambition.
Seeing his strong inclination for books, he gave him
all the assistance his straitened circumstances would
allow, and watched with pride the development of his
young mind.   On one occasion, while his son was intently
absorbed in the contents of some book, he was known to

ask Mrs. Fillmore, with a degree of pleasantry, the following question : " Wife," he remarked, " who knows but Millard will some day be President ? "

Let us go, in thought, for a moment, to one of the most thinly populated portions of Cayuga county, New York, in the year 1813. There, amid almost a wilderness, surrounded with the fearful echo of the wolf's howl, in a rudely constructed cabin, we see a middle-aged man, clad in his home-spun, just from his work ; near him, busily engaged in her household duties, clad with equal simplicity, we see his wife : that rustic boy at the table, poring over the pages of a half-worn book, is their son. We hear the father ask his wife the question, " Who knows but our son will be President ? " and smile that the old man should have such a thought.

Yet, it was literally true — that rustic boy was destined to be President. It was young Fillmore ; those were his parents. From that rude cabin, he was destined to deal justice to his fellow men at the bar — from the pages of that worn book, he was destined to become the expounder of international law, and enlighten his countrymen in the congressional halls of the nation. From that rude cabin he was destined to be transferred to the presidential chair — the highest position on earth — and make the monarchs of Europe stand abashed in his presence. Henceforth, who can tell what cabin walls inclose our presidents ?

There is, in contemplating the lives and characters of such men as Mr. Fillmore, something sublime and ennobling, that teaches us man is immortal, and stamped with the impress of Deity. When emerging from the obscurity of his boyhood, we see him, with a bold hand, dash every obstacle from his pathway, as though they were but threads of gossamer, and advancing with the strides of an intellectual giant, from one post of honor to another, until he stands foremost in the galaxy of patriotic greatness, we are bound to endorse the sentiment that " there is a divinity that shapes our ends."

In the spring of his seventeenth year, he returned to his employer and resumed the labors of his apprenticeship. He devoted himself to business with the same assiduous application he had evinced the previous season, and manifested an anxiety in no way abated by the relaxation of his energies in that peculiar sphere. In the meantime, the same successful results that attended his efforts in the school-room began to be manifested in his new sphere. Like all of his other undertakings, he commenced learning his trade with " success " engraven upon his mind for his motto, and resolved by continued perseverance to win its valued insignia. So rapid, indeed, was his progress, that he outstripped his fellow apprentices, and was advanced to the position of master workman. In this position, he was relieved from that portion of the labor usually devolving upon apprentices in an establishment of this sort. The business of the master workmen, as they were called, was of a more particular nature, which none but experienced hands were allowed to perform. The advancement of young Fillmore to this position, before he had served anything like the time usually allotted to boys to attain it, certainly speaks well of the manner in which he had applied himself to business, and shows that he possessed the entire confidence of his employer. As a master workman, he was entitled to all the privileges, though not the wages, of journeyman. The business of finishing, that devolved upon his hands, though of a less arduous nature than the part of the labor in which he had been previously engaged, required the no less strict attention of his mind, nor permitted any cessation of his labors. Yet, he was highly pleased at his progress and good fortune, especially as it afforded a good opportunity to become thoroughly acquainted with the finer and more difficult part of the business.

But this was not the only good fortune attendant upon his labors during that season. His strict adherence to the principles of justice and honor resulted in such a high appreciation for the correctness of his character, on the part of his employer, that he was intrusted with the books of the establishment. The proper performance of these duties was a task of no small magnitude. In keeping a series of books, regulative not only of the finances but of every department of an extensive business in its minutest branches, there was, of course, a necessity for the strictest accuracy, on the part of the individual in whose hands they were intrusted.

When not engaged in the rendition of accounts or making entries of transactions upon his books, he was still expected to discharge the duties devolving upon him as a master workman. Young Fillmore proved himself equal to the tasks, and discharged the complicated duties of his combined capacities in a manner that reflected great credit to himself, and to the entire satisfaction of all concerned. His books were kept with an accuracy and nicety that evinced considerable financiering capacity, while his finishing work indicated a complete mastery of his business. The reviewal of his books by the employer resulted in the detection of no inacuracies, even of the smallest nature, until, thoroughly convinced of the correctness of his young book-keeper, he felt entirely satisfied that the financial department of his business was in safe and reliable hands. In keeping the books, he was obliged to keep a correct record of the transactions of each day, by making charges and entering credits upon his day-book, as they occurred, then drawing them off in his ledger, assigning to each its proper head. Thus, when wages were to be drawn, bills to be paid, or accounts to be collected, pertaining to any department of the establishment, at the clerk's desk, they were properly made out, with the nicest accuracy. In this, his employer was relieved from all anxiety in regard to the correct management of his business, while the whole department was conducted with regularity and system.

Thus, in a very short time, he not only gained the complete mastery of a trade that would insure him a competency through life, if called into requisition, but, by his regular habits and correct industry, was actually the financier of an extensive business establishment, possessing the unlimited confidence of every one connected therewith. Such men are born to success — their iron energy cannot be subdued. Be they placed in whatsoever capacity they may, though it be of the humblest nature, and though assigned to them be its most obscure position, by arousing their latent energies, they will make themselves known, and take the lead.

The capacities and energetic perseverance of young Fillmore would have advanced him to the head of any vocation. Regardless of the honors conferred upon individuals by rank or station, instead of expecting to be honored by his vocation, his ambition, in whatsoever enterprise he embarked, was to honor his calling. What intelligent reader will say this is not the true principle of action, to insure success ? That individual who aspires to a position, with a desire to honor it by the faithful discharge of the duties it involves, and to be useful to his country, if he succeeds in attaining it, and evinces a capacity in performing its responsibilities, that reflects credit upon the station, and proves the usefulness of the incumbent to the people, that individual finds but few impediments to his rapid advancement from one position of trust to another, by his fellow citizens. They see that the manner in which he guards the interests reposed in his keeping reflects credit to the station, and is ameliorative of its condition ; consequently, they are ready to endorse his aspirations as the offspring of a noble patriotism, that aspires to make itself useful to the country, in any and every shape. While, on the other hand, that individual whose aspirations to a station are actuated merely by a contracted desire for self-elevation, and the honors he expects to derive from the station, instead of those he expects to confer upon it, though he may, for a while, by a species of demagoguery, succeed in deluding his fellow citizens and reaching some post of honor, they will ultimately perceive that all his protestations of patriotism are but a glossy film, which he weaves for the concealment of his real character ; and such an one, instead of occupying a place in the affections of the people, and being endorsed, as the embodiment of his pretensions, finds himself subjected to the whims and caprices of unstable friends, who forsake him the moment fortune begins to wane, and leave him hopelessly wrecked upon the reefs of his own ambition.

Of the former nature have ever been Mr. Fillmore's aspirations. We have seen that, in his childhood, regarding obedience as heaven's first law, he was careful to honor his parents in the filial discharge of every duty. Afterward, when endeavoring successfully to master the branches of his primary school, we have seen his anxious solicitude to honor his teacher, by his own rapid progress. In the capacity of a clothier's apprentice, we have seen the ardent desire he manifested to honor his employer and his business, by assuming its complete mastery. Thus we have shown, that, up to this time, every situation in which he had been placed was honored by the faithful and correct manner in which he discharged his duties ; and to the reader who follows us through the pages of this book, we expect to show that every position he occupied, from the commencement of his alpha, at the wild-wood home, in Cayuga county, until he vacated the presidential chair of the United States, was essentially honored by his being the incumbent.

He is now about to be introduced to the reader in an entirely new sphere — one, however, that has been the starting point of many of our greatest men. In the fall of his eighteenth year, he opened a three months' school, in the town of Scott, about six miles from his father's residence, and assumed, at this early age, the responsible duties of a teacher. Among those of our great men who have figured conspicuously in the history of their times, and formed the brightest jewels of our national adornment, whose early vocation was that of school teaching, we may number a Cass, an Underwood, and a host of others who made this the commencement of a career that was to end in their being recipients of the highest offices in the gift of the people.

Alongside with such names as these, then, we find young Fillmore's, at their age. The town of Scott was but a small place, containing no great number of inhabitants. They had possessed but few educational facilities, and the manners and customs of the place bore unmistakable marks of rustic simplicity. The citizens of the place, as was the case of most places, in that day, were but illy prepared to appreciate the advantages of a good school. Yet for the high moral character, and indomitable energy of young Fillmore, in the prosecution of his undertakings, they entertained the highest respect. He opened his first school, therefore, under circumstances somewhat favorable to entire success. As a remuneration for his services as a teacher of this school, he received ten dollars per month, with the privilege of " boarding around "— it being the custom of teachers to board with the different patrons of their schools. His school was liberally patronized by the citizens of the town, and he as a teacher became universally beloved. As a teacher, he was fully aware that his position was one of no ordinary responsibility, and resolved on devoting his entire energies to the duties it required. Among his pupils there were but few who had made any considerable proficiency in the acquisition of knowledge, though many of them evinced a strong desire to advance themselves as fast as possible. His intercourse with his scholars was marked with a courteous amiability of temper, and a mild dignity of feeling well calculated to elicit their warm esteem. He set them an excellent example, and was careful to inculcate the necessity of its observance. Acting upon the principle that it "was better to rule by love than fear," in conducting his school, he uniformly manifested a gentleness of disposition which would infuse itself into the minds of his scholars, by unvarying principles of assimilation.

Though scrupulously strict in the enforcement of the rules he adopted for the regulation of his school, his reproofs to his pupils for their transgression were mild, yet firm and decisive. He was very careful to give them clear conceptions of the future duties devolving upon them as men, and to create a desire in their minds to become qualified for their discharge. Among the pupils attending his school, were several overgrown boys, much older than himself, who, notwithstanding his courteous demeanor toward them, but illy brooked their submission to one so much their junior in years, and resolved on creating a spirit of insubordination throughout the entire school. The manner by which this was to be accomplished was about this: one of the older boys was purposely to transgress the rules of the school, and instead of submitting to correction for the offence, was to refuse, and show resistance, when the other boys were to come to his rescue. Such a plan, however, was not matured without being detected by the vigilant observation of their teacher, who awaited patiently for them to put it into execution. Accordingly, during an afternoon, while engaged in recitation, the older boy who was designated for that purpose violated a positive rule of the school, in the grossest manner. His teacher called him forward, and the boy peremptorily refused to come. Mr. Fillmore approached him in the sternest manner, and demanded an apology, which the boy refused to grant. The infliction of a blow on the back of the refractory pupil was the preconcerted signal for action, among the boys who understood the secret. But instead of punishing him that way, he sternly placed one hand on the boy's shoulder, and gave him a cut across the knees with his switch in the other; then turning to the other boys, with a look of stern resolution, that told he knew all about it, and with a motion of his hand, he so awed them into submission that they dared not move, while their companion received a pretty severe castigation for his conduct.

After the excitement had subsided and the boys began to be ashamed of themselves, he took occasion, in a very firm, effective manner, to let them know that he would have order, and be obeyed, and was determined to punish all who refused obedience; but hoped that in future there would exist no necessity for the infliction of punishment. From this time, he saw no more exhibitions of insubordination. His patrons commended him very highly, for the prompt efficiency with which he had quelled the first indications of disorder in his school, which, had they been suffered to spread, would have infected the whole school, and resulted disastrously to its prospects of success.

Thenceforth, all his scholars became ardently attached to him; he taught a good school, and succeeded in getting the good will of all. In the town of Scott, he was universally beloved as a teacher, and as a young man of unexceptionable habits.

Let it not be supposed that while Mr. Fillmore was thus engaged in the vocation of teaching others he was forgetful of his own improvement. His active mind, ever restless in the acquisition of whatever would tend to its vigorous expansion, suffered no diminution in its desires to become decorated with the treasures of knowledge. About this time, he evinced a great taste for the pure mathematics, and, in the solution of the most difficult problems, gave evidences of a mind, strong, comprehensive, and analytic.

His aptitude in mastering the science of mathematics was, indeed, extraordinary. For in this department of scientific investigation, the reasoning, analytical faculties of his mind were brought into requisition. Among the mental attributes of Mr. Fillmore, these strong reasoning faculties and deep profundity of power have ever been to some extent, predominant. In reasoning from cause

3

to effect, and investigating perplexing subjects, where the powers of perceptive analysis are required, to understand their intricacies, he has had few equals, and no superiors. There was, perhaps, in this respect, a closer analogy in the mental organism of Daniel Webster to that of Mr. Fillmore's than any one else whom I can now call to mind. He studied the theory of surveying, at this time, under a gentleman by the name of Taylor Stowe. So completely did he master both the theory and practice of this useful branch of science, that in a very quick time he became the best surveyor in the county. This valuable acquisition to his previous attainments, to say nothing of its great utility to him in his future practice as a lawyer, was subsequently of eminent service to Mr. Fillmore; it was a safe medium to which he could resort to relieve his pecuniary difficulties. In personal appearance, at this time, Mr. Fillmore is described to have been rather slim, with his proportions undeveloped, and exceedingly awkward in his movements. The circumstances by which he had been all his life surrounded prevented him from mingling much in society, and he was, consequently, entirely destitute of those refined graces which are so much the result of social intercourse.

In a sparsely inhabited community of an interior county there was, in fact, no finely cultivated society with which to mingle, and even had there been, the temperament of Mr. Fillmore would not have adapted itself to it. His mind at that time was peculiarly sensitive, and somewhat averse to participating in the gaieties of fashionable life. He was poor, with nothing prepossessing in his appearance, ·and deprived of the means that were available to those with whom his associations were confined, he seemed to feel keenly the disadvantages of his position. These disadvantages, so far as personal appearance and capacities for society were concerned, were doubtless greatly magnified by the peculiar sensibility of his temperament. He was exceedingly modest and diffident, especially when in the presence of superiors, and the inclination of his sensitive nature was to assign to almost every one that position, though very far from deserving it. Another, and the main reason why he mingled so little in the social circle, and was so seldom a participant of its enjoyments, was the want of time. No youth ever had juster conceptions of the value of time, or made better use of it than did young Fillmore. The enjoyments he derived from his studies in his leisure moments he would sacrifice for no other. Save a lofty expression of feature that bespoke a consciousness of his own inherent worth, and a mild, steady eye, that beamed with a natural love for his fellow men, his countenance exhibited no extraordinary indications of the great man. Such is the appearance he presented to the casual observer; but I am told that the close and observant reader of human character with no great difficulty could then discover beneath that uncouth covering the workings of a mighty soul.

In manners he was at this time no Chesterfield. Spurning the mere show of exterior politeness, unadorned by good qualities of heart, the natural dictates of his feelings, while they have subdued all semblance of pride and ostentation, have ever made him the kindest of men.

CHAPTER II.

He resumes his trade — Determines to study law — Reflections upon
the importance of the step — Reads with Judge Wood — Sketch
of that gentleman — Goes to Buffalo — Lives within his means —
State of society — Political matters — Is admitted to the bar —
Goes to Aurora, and engages in practice — His first case — Teaches
school — Is married — Is regarded as a lawyer of ability — Nature
of his eloquence — Prospects brighten.

THE conclusion of the last chapter brings 's to the
nineteenth year of Mr. Fillmore's life. When we take
into consideration the difficulties under which he labored
in the prosecution of his undertakings, we must conclude
that much had been accomplished, and be impressed with
admiration for the energetic spirit displayed in all his
actions up to this time. In the spring of his nineteenth
year, he resumed for the last time the duties of his trade.
Notwithstanding he had been so very careful to acquaint
himself with the mysteries of his trade, with a view to
the assistance he expected to derive from it in the prosecution of his studies, he was so successful in his chosen
profession that its advantages were never called into
requisition. He had for some time conceived the idea of
reading law, a profession for which he seemed naturally
to have entertained a strong predilection. And, in fact,
a part of his leisure moments, during the latter portion of
his services in the clothier's establishment, was devoted
to the study of the law. During the spring and summer

of 1818, he prosecuted his business with his employer in his former double capacity of master workman and book-keeper. He performed his duties with the same spirit of prompt alacrity he had evinced in the preceding years, zealous to acquit himself to the entire satisfaction of every one connected with the business.

During that fall, so ardent had become his desire to engage in the study of the law, without the hindrance imposed by the duties of his trade, that he ventured to communicate them to his father. His father had for some time watched his zealous application to his books, and had often been very desirous of giving him increased facilities for the improvement of his mind. He was disposed, therefore, to view the wishes of his son in a light rather favorable than otherwise.

It was about this time he attracted the notice of Judge Wood, a lawyer of estimable worth, residing at no great distance from his father's, who persuaded him to devote his studies to the law.

Mr. Fillmore accordingly communicated his intentions to Cheney, his employer, and expressed a wish to purchase the remaining portion of the time for which he was obligated. So earnest had young Fillmore's endeavors been to promote the interest of his business from his earliest connection therewith, that he began to hope his services would be retained as a fixture to the establishment. He did not, therefore, at first, relish very well a proposition that was to deprive him of an apprentice whose services had become so important in the prosecution of his business. He at first rather dissuaded him from abandoning a business for which he had been so careful to prepare himself, and in the prosecution of which an independency, if not a fortune, was in store for him in the future. But young Fillmore was not to be dissuaded : he had familiarized himself with the examples of those who had gone before him; he had seen them embark in the study of the same profession, under circumstances equally discouraging to those with which he was surrounded ; he had seen their efforts crowned with triumphant success ; his young bosom had swelled with animation at the exhibitions of power and patriotism, displayed by Clay and others, who commenced the law under the same circumstances, with nothing for their reliance but their own determined will, and he longed to try his own powers.

His conference with his employer in reference to his contemplated engagement in the study of the law, resulted in obtaining his consent to allow him to purchase the residue of his time. This consent, however, was not procured without some reluctance. The position occupied by Mr. Fillmore in the establishment was one of no ordinary importance ; and he very well knew that, to get another incumbent, who would be equally careful in the discharge of its varied duties, would be exceedingly difficult. But he sacrificed all these considerations, and after young Fillmore had obligated himself to remunerate him for the loss he sustained by his withdrawing from his services before the expiration of the time specified in their original agreement, he quit forever the business to which he had applied himself with so much zeal and spirit.

Cheney was doubtless perfectly honest in his convictions, as regarding the impolicy of the step taken by his apprentice — throwing all considerations out of the question, but those for his own good. He was essentially a practical man, and much attached to Mr. Fillmore; and when he saw him sacrifice the certain profits of a trade, the entire mastery of which he had attained, to embark in the uncertainty of a profession, to qualify himself for the duties of which would require months and years of close application, he was no doubt honest in his misgiving, and in thinking the movement exceedingly unwise.

To represent, in its true light, the exact way, not only in which he looked upon this, as he thought, injudicious movement, on the part of Mr. Fillmore, but the exalted opinion which he had conceived for him during their intercourse, I give the following remark, which he is said to have made to a friend, a short time after he had left his employ. He and his friend were together in the yard, engaged in conversation, when young Fillmore passed along in sight, on some business in the neighborhood. "Do you see that young man, yonder?" said Cheney, pointing to young Fillmore. "Yes," was the reply. "Well," continued Cheney, "he is, for a sensible young man, pursuing a very foolish course; he has been engaged with me in business for some time; he was far the best apprentice I ever had, and the best workman I ever had; he understands the business perfectly, *yet he has abandoned his trade, and gone to reading law!*" Herein consisted the extreme folly of his course, in the conceptions of his employer. Time, however, dispelled the illusion, and demonstrated the course of Mr. Fillmore to have been most wise. Young Fillmore had not, however, come to the determination to embark in the study of the law without mature deliberation, in his own mind, as to the propriety of such a course. It was a step in which too much was at stake for him to take without reflecting well upon the weighty considerations it involved. On the success of such a step, he very well knew, depended, to an immeasurable extent, that of his eventual destiny. Before his embarkation, therefore, in a pursuit so pregnant with the fate of his most cherished hopes, he was particularly careful to weigh well the chances of success and defeat, to place them all in the balance, and see which stood the best chance for predominance. Subjected to this investigation, the chances of success, contrasted with those of defeat, would have been extremely diminutive, had not their proportions been greatly magnified by the weight of talent, zeal, and energy, on its side, that were more than sufficient to counteract all the discouraging circumstances penury and adversity could array against him. There are few steps so pregnant with the fate of a young man's destiny, and the decision of his happiness or his misery, as the choice he makes of his vocation. It is certainly one of life's most important events. Young men who are compelled to rely upon their own judgment, in a selection so replete with the fate of their eventual destinies, cannot be too cautious against an inappropriate investiture of their talents and capabilities. Such investments have resulted disastrously to the prospects, success, and happiness of hundreds, who, had their efforts been directed in a proper channel, more congenial with their talents and qualifications, would have been useful, good citizens. If, in a hasty preference for a profession, based mainly upon the dignity and *eclat* attached to it in the minds of many, an individual embarks in it without possessing the requisite qualifications for the discharge of its duties, he not only subjects himself to infinite mortifications, by a misapplication of his time, but often takes the first step that eventuates in his ruin. By such misapplication of time, they are prostrating their talents, and rendering them entirely useless for the performance of duties in a sphere for which they are naturally adapted, while they are certainly making no progress whatever in a sphere wholly uncongenial to their entire capacities.

It is not unfrequently the case, we see young men of the finest mechanical minds, possessing a peculiar constructive aptitude, put into some profession to which their energy, capacity, and feelings are entirely uncongenial, where they scarcely succeed in attaining a position of mediocrity, who, had they chosen a vocation for which they possessed a natural turn, would have been eminently useful to the country. Again, we find abstract, metaphysical minds, whose powers of language are scarcely sufficient to elucidate their smallest ideas, engaged in the study of the law — a profession wherein a fluency of speech, a retentive memory, and perceptive, analytical powers of mind, are essentially necessary to success. To this cause is attributable the larger portion of failures

3*

of young men in the outset of their career. Having no
natural taste for their profession, they embark in its duties
as though it was an arduous task imposed upon them, and
devote their leisure to something for which they have a
taste, until they are outstripped by those who are adapted
by nature to their profession. Nothing is more ruinous
in its influence upon a young man in the outset of his
career, than for failure to become associated with his
undertakings. Not that young men should expect entire
success in their early efforts in their vocation, as an invariable consequence of energy; it takes time, study, and
patience to overcome the inexperience and incapacities of
youth; and in combating these difficulties, they should
not be too easily discouraged by an unsuccessful effort, or
a defeat in an undertaking — they are occurrences incident
to the careers of the greatest. But the kind of failure to
which I have reference, as being peculiarly disastrous in
its results to their aspirations, is their entire failure in a
profession to which they are by nature wholly inadapted.

Before, therefore, young men embark in a vocation, the
discharge of whose duties is to receive the attention of a
lifetime, and which is to form the source of their enjoyment in every condition, and upon the prosecution of
which depends all their hopes of influence and prosperity,
they should have a very just appreciation of the importance of the event, and be well assured, by unmistakable
indications, that they have some natural adaptation to its
pursuit. Then, with energy and perseverance, in using
the appliances thrown in their way, their chosen vocation
being the focus where centre both effort and natural

inclination, triumphant success will follow as an invariable result.

From considerations, therefore, of the vast importance resulting from his choice of a profession, he felt it a responsible duty to arrive at safe and correct conclusions. He knew that the step about to be taken was a decisive one, and though, with spirit and industry, he hoped for the best, he felt many misgivings in regard to future success. He viewed the difficulties with which he knew he would be surrounded, carefully counted the costs, and summed up the strength of the opposition against him, then, like an experienced mariner, setting his compass to the pole, spreading his sails to the breeze, he launched upon the uncertain voyage of professional life — willing, with patient industry, to buffet the turbulent sea, and to combat the adverse storm, could he but reach the haven of success in the future.

Nobly triumphant has been the success of the voyager. Proudly did his craft emerge from the mist that enshrouded it, and speed onward in a course of unsurpassed success, till she anchored in the proudest harbor of fame. Gallantly, now, with sails full-spread to the breeze, the stars and stripes floating from her mast, the constitution of his country engraven on her sails, "America" written across her prow, and religious liberty for her propulsion, she glides onward in triumph, a life-boat of the Union, carrying more than "Cæsar and his fortunes."

The considerations connected with his profession being well weighed, and their importance thoroughly appreciated, Mr. Fillmore entered the office of Judge Wood.

Judge Wood was a man of considerable eminence in the legal profession, and very correct and accurate in the transaction of all business entrusted to his care. He was one of the early settlers of that part of the country, and was proverbial for his integrity and high toned moral worth. He had amassed immense wealth in the pursuit of his profession, and been exceedingly judicious in his investments. There was, at that time, a considerable amount of litigation in that section of the state of New York; but Judge Wood, though of acknowledged preëminence as a lawyer, did no great amount of practice. He was successful, however, in establishing himself in a lucrative business.

The nature of this litigation consisted principally in the contests between different claimants for lands in their occupancy. The settlers coming into the county would purchase government claims and open their farms, and often were permitted to enjoy their labors but a very short time, when prior claims to the same parcels of land would be presented, and the subsequent settlers had to abandon the premises. Of this nature was the principal amount of Judge Wood's legal practice; and, by taking parts of land thus gained from his clients as remuneration for his services, he became a very extensive landholder. But aside from his legal acumen and sound judgment in whatever pertained to his profession, Judge Wood was possessed of all those nobler qualities of heart that endeared him to his fellow men. In business, he was punctual and regular, manifesting a spirit of the exactest order, in the minutest details. The association of Mr. Fillmore with a gentleman of these commendable traits of character could not fail to result most happily. The office of the Judge was situated several miles from his father's residence. He boarded at home, however, during the first months of his studies.

The ready facility with which he comprehended the principles of law surpassed the progress, rapid as it had been, he had made in other departments of his studies. This was owing, doubtless, in a great measure to the maturer development of his mental powers, and partly to the peculiar congeniality of this branch of knowledge to his feelings, and the great importance he felt in the necessity of progressing as fast as possible.

He felt that this was his life experiment, and upon its successful demonstration depended the hopes he had formed and fostered from boyhood.

For rapid advancement in this peculiar sphere, he was not very well prepared by attainments previously made ; but he possessed a mind of natural vigor and comprehension that supplied all deficiencies. For the successful prosecution of the law, Mr. Fillmore, by nature, possessed the happiest endowments. He hoped to be able, through the medium of this profession, to make an adequate support, and attain, at last, a position of respectability as a professional man, but had no idea that it was to be the medium through which he was to be the recipient of undying fame. Yet, his aspirations were contracted by no limited sphere ; he was anxious to be of service to a country he had learned to love, and had he known then he was to fill the highest offices, he could have applied himself to the mastery of legal principles with no more assiduity than marked his eager efforts as it was. The great profound reasoning powers of his mind, enlarged and strengthened by their recent subjection to the solution of mathematical problems, ranged almost with intellectual rapacity through the mystic pages of the legal commentators, and comprehended their technical abstrusities as by the power of instinct; while the quick analytical acuteness of his perception, in a thorough comprehension of each principle, was ready at a glance to apply the theory to the practice.

Then, withal, by a close course of reading which he had been careful to observe for a great while preceding his commencement of the law, he had become an excellent historian, and as a basis of reflection upon the subjects of law and legal systems, he was somewhat familiar with the ancient laws of the Grecian and Roman republics. His spirits were vigorous and buoyant, the glow of youthful health bloomed upon his cheek, unimpaired by the vicious excesses too often incident to youth, and with determined animation he bent himself to the prosecution of his studies with an ardent zeal that no difficulty could resist. But, notwithstanding his anxiety to make rapid progress, and in that desire all else seemed entirely swallowed up, he was not forgetful of the kind courtesies due from him to those, especially Judge Wood, connected with the office. He was careful in discharging all these little courtesies, and to pursue a course calculated to win the esteem of all. These manifestations of kindness were, and still are, natural to Mr. Fillmore. He was, at that early day, as far from entertaining a feeling of selfishness as though self was a secondary consideration. With him the elements of happiness have consisted essentially in seeing those happy around him, and prosperity and general happiness pervading the common country. Acting in accordance with the dictates of this generous nature, it was impossible for him to be inattentive to any duty due those with whom he mingled. Such a course as pursued by Mr. Fillmore could not fail to be perceived by Judge Wood. His modest, unassuming deportment, his kind and generous disposition, and the ready eagerness with which he sought to perform every duty, were well calculated to make a man of the Judge's temperament look on his young pupil in a very favorable light. One thing that had much to do in superinducing this favorable opinion to young Fillmore, was the fact that he saw the incipient displays of a lofty soul at work in the Herculean task of mental labor he performed. The proficiency and ease with which he had comprehended those intricate parts of the law, the thorough understanding of which had, for most students, been the work of years, surprised Judge Wood not a little, and made him regard his pupil as one of no ordinary intellectual capacities. So favorable, indeed, was the light in which he now regarded Mr. Fillmore, and such an influence did his energy and love of study have upon his mind, that he proposed to him to come to his house and remain, and what writing he did for the office should pay his board. Than this proposition, nothing could have been more congenial to the feelings of Mr. Fillmore. He embraced it gladly.

He was now in a position he had much desired for a long while. The writing in which he was engaged was of a particular nature, and quite considerable in amount. He did not mind the imposition of this writing, however, inasmuch as he was defraying the expense of his studies and board. Judge Wood being a very careful man, the exact precision in which he had everything done about him, doubtless, had a very happy effect in conforming Mr. Fillmore so happily to the strictest principles of order, that characterize all his actions. The vast amount of writing he did, while in the office of the Judge, contributed much to the acquisition of neatness, regularity and dispatch of penmanship displayed in all Mr. Fillmore's compositions.

Few men have ever taken more interest in a pupil than did Judge Wood in Mr. Fillmore. Few ever felt more solicitude in the advancement and proper cultivation of the mind of a pupil than did he. Few pupils, too, have ever appreciated a solicitude in their behalf more highly than did Mr. Fillmore the interest Judge Wood manifested in his young aspirations; and certainly none ever more sucessfully demonstrated the utility of the instructions he thus early received. What Chancellor Wythe was to Henry Clay, Judge Wood was to Millard Fillmore From the examples of Wythe and Wood, let those possessed of the means to do so learn to extend encouragement to struggling worth — the ragged newsboys and apple-venders of our streets may contain "some mute, inglorious Milton" in their ranks, whose genius, if properly developed, would shed a halo of lustre upon the land of his birth. Had it not been for Chancellor Wythe, Clay would not, perhaps, have been able to construct upon the broad pillars of the constitution that pyramid of patriotism — the Compromise; — and had it not been for Judge Wood, we might not now, perhaps, have a Fillmore to protect that noble piece of architecture. Judge Wood not only extended to him the free use of his office and his books, and gave him all the encouragement he was able, but expressed a willingness to advance him means, and wait until, from the successful results of his professional labors, he should be enabled to liquidate them. This kind offer was accepted with feelings of profound gratitude. But gladly as he embraced this magnanimous proposition, he was unwilling to incur a debt to his benefactor beyond the prospects of liquidation in the pursuit of his profession. As a means of sustaining himself, and of preventing too great an indebtedness towards Judge Wood, he again resorted to school teaching. The same happy results attended his efforts in conducting this school he met with in the town of Scott, and resulted in the acquisition of sufficient means to render material assistance in supporting himself.

Mr. Fillmore learned very early to rely exclusively upon the results of his own exertions, as the only facilities to his advancement; and though gratefully delighted at the bestowal of all encouragement, he expected material assistance from no one ; hence, he was never disappointed when not its recipient. By teaching school, surveying, etc., during a portion of each year, he was enabled, from the profits accruing from these vocations, to defray all expenses attendant upon his studies the remaining portion. By this means, he contracted no debts; and what was still better, he contracted no evil habits. If bad habits are, as has been said, the offspring of idleness, their infection of Mr. Fillmore would have been illegitimate, for with him idleness was the parent of nothing.

He continued the study of law with Judge Wood nearly two years; and, by dividing his time somewhat between his studies and teaching, kept himself clear of all obligations. He was, in every sense of the word, of his own formation. But let not too much merit be claimed or ascribed to Mr. Fillmore; because, in early youth, he had all these difficulties to combat, and triumphantly succeeded in winning the proudest laurels of statesmanship. For so universally has it been the case, that the great men of the nation, through the happy facilities offered by the institutions of our country, have arisen from the humblest circumstances, that we begin to feel it is the source from whence they must come. So remarkable, indeed, does the fact strike the student of history, that an isolated case, who, from the lap of affluent wealth, and all the other advantages it could purchase, should rise to distinction and eminence, would be such a rarity, that his biographer, in the delineation of his early career, would have to say his prospects were gloomy enough, for he had to " combat all the disadvantages that wealth and ease could bestow."

We should be proud of a country whose peculiar boast is thus to open all the avenues of her rich resources, and **cherish the remembrance** of those who avail themselves

of them.   The associations of young Fillmore with Judge
Wood had not only resulted in the attainment of a vast
amount of legal and other important information, but had
been eminently agreeable in every particular. The Judge
had several sons, with whom he become quite familiar,
and to whom he became considerably attached.   The
disparity of circumstances created no barrier to their
social intercourse, and the attachment became mutual.

After enjoying the legal advantages placed in his way
by the kindness of Judge Wood, for a period of near
two years, he resolved on removing to Erie county. The
wisdom of this course was obviously manifest.   In the
sparsely inhabited portion of Cayuga county, where the
entire business of a legal nature was in the hands of two
or three, and none of those advantages arising from
social intercourse, the chances of familiarizing himself
with the practical part of his profession were very ordinary indeed.   Then, beside, he had reached that age of
maturity that made him desire a more extensive knowledge of his fellow men than the limited associations
of Cayuga county afforded.   It was time, too, he had
 bestowed some thought upon the people amid whom his
lot would be cast, and identified his interests with theirs.
Then, too, he was anxiously desirous of being so situated as to be enabled to avail himself of the practical
wisdom of those who were engaged as members of a
talented bar daily in the elucidation of legal principles.
Having once embarked in the law, he did it with a view
of making it his lifetime business; there was then no
time for halting or vacillating between different consid-

erations as to the wisest course for him to pursue in the regulation of his future career. The Rubicon was crossed—the die was cast. The considerations of his mind were directed upon the methods and appliances best calculated to advance him in the profession he had chosen, instead of looking round for an outlet by means of which he could effect an escape, and embark in a vocation that promised to be more lucrative, if not more honorable. For this steady determination to devote every energy to the prosecution of an enterprise, after he had once embarked in it, Mr. Fillmore had and still has a very happy faculty. Those unstable desires of individuals to bring themselves into notoriety, having neither the patience nor the capacity to achieve anything honorable to themselves or their country, that induce them to shift sails continually, hoping thereby to catch a favorable breeze to be wafted into the coveted port of fortune and success, were altogether foreign to those entertained by Mr. Fillmore, and wholly repugnant to his feelings.

His sails were already spread; his desires were to sustain them, until sufficiently strong and appreciated, to catch not only a favorable but a merited breeze, that would bear him and his fortunes successfully over the ocean of his adversity. In this, instead of being disappointed in his expectations, his anxious application has been rewarded in a manner that has far surpassed the realization of his brightest dreams as to the result when he first embarked in the profession.

His father and family had, for some time, been residing in Erie county, and, aside from the dictates of his own inclinations, he was urged by them to go there and continue the prosecutions of his studies. Accordingly, in the fall of 1827, he left Cayuga county, and, like the star of empire, took his way westward. He experienced many regrets in leaving those places endeared to him by the tenderest associations. There he had first felt the kindling glow of young ambition swell his bosom; there he had first learned the rudiments of an education that he has endeavored so successfully to honor; there he had, by vigilant application to the requirements of his employer, learned the entire intricacies of a trade which, from the extraordinary powers of his own intellect, he was destined never to follow; and there he had first received encouragement that bid his aspirations unfetter themselves, and, through the "thick gloom of the present, look forward to a glorious future, bright as the sun in heaven." So ardent had become the attachment of Judge Wood to his young student that it was a source of real pain to part with him; but seeing the wisdom, and the almost necessity of the course, he was more than willing to forego all personal considerations, if the sacrifice was to result in the promotion of his young friend's prospects.

The influence this gentleman exerted over young Fillmore was certainly very favorable in every essential feature. So kind had he been, so deep the solicitude he felt, and so disinterested the friendship he extended to him, that his affectionate regard was almost equivalent to that of a parent. How lastingly treasured on the tablets of memory is every kindness extended to youths under such circumstances as those that surrounded

Mr. Fillmore, when he first elicited the consideration of Judge Wood. What an influence such encouragements not unfrequently, too, have exerted in shaping the destinies of those who were their recipients. When Socrates was first discovered with his chisel in the rude sculptor's shop, who would for a moment have conceived he possessed the almost sacred sparks of Divinity itself, and was reserved to demonstrate the soul's immortality. Yet, through the kind intercession of a friend in his behalf, his mind expanded itself to so lofty a height, that the world became filled with the blaze of his intellectual philosophy. When Henry Clay, in the marshy swamps of Hanover county, Virginia, was benumbed with the blast from which his tattered garments afforded scarce a perceivable protection, toiled to feed a helpless mother, who would have thought that, a second father of his country, he was to preside over her Senate, and, like a demi-god, reign king in the proud realm of mind ? Yet, through the friendly intercession of a philanthropist, he was made aware of that genius that blazed like a star of the first magnitude, while others seemed but its satelites. When Millard Fillmore, embosomed amid the wilderness of the Hampshire Grants, in Cayuga county, was toiling to render his father assistance in the duties of their wild wood home, who would have thought that to him the eyes of a grateful nation would turn, as the pilot of their ship of state, the defender of her institutions ? Yet, aided by the counsels of a friend, and the examples of a friendly experience, he was enabled to guide her safely to port through the darkest political storms that have lowered over the horizon since the days of the Revolution.

Here, again, allow me to insist upon the minds of those who are so situated that they can do so entirely consistent with their own interests, the importance of extending encouragements and aid to aspiring merit, be it presented to view in whatsoever garb it may. It is not necessarily inferable, because a Clay, a Cass, and a Fillmore, have succeeded in combating the adverse storms that surrounded their boyhood, and wreathed their temples with chaplets of fame, that every one of genius and capacity will accomplish the same results. Those are among the immortal few of the illustrious names who, from the very fact that they have been thus successful, will be handed down to distant posterity, as affording useful and instructive lessons to the young aspirant after fame. But what is to become of the Clays, the Fillmores, the Marshalls, the Websters, and a host others in the bright array of natural talent who slumber in the undisturbed repose of oblivion — lost to their country, and to their God ? Of such, no record can be kept. Unseen of men, their aspirations must remain undeveloped, locked in the precincts of their own hearts, until they burn and blast the seat of its vital throb. Unfelt by the responsive thrills of another's breast, they prey in the bosom until the life-blood of pulsation is gone, and bury the victim in the ruin of his blasted hopes. The trumphs of life are noticed and recorded — they should be. The failures are not — they cannot be. Men's talents are not always commensurate with their success, neither is their success always commensurate with their talents. Success and prosperity are, therefore, not unfrequently very unsafe criteria whereby to form conceptions of individual capacity. Having then no correct indication from exterior appearances of the intrinsic value of mental treasure concealed within, we cannot be too careful to give every possible encouragement to all who are thus situated.

> " The words we speak, the smiles we wear ;
> A heart may heal — a heart may break."

It was in the fall of 1821 when Mr. Fillmore reached Erie county ; during that winter, in connection with the pursuit of his legal studies, he rendered assistance to his father in the comfortable arrangement of his domestic affairs. His father was then residing in the vicinity of Buffalo, devoting himself to the duties of his vocation, as a farmer. The application of Mr. Fillmore to his studies during that winter was distinguished by a restless activity unsurpassed. Before the completion of intellectual tasks assigned himself, minds possessed of less vigor would have sunk in exhaustion. Having concluded to go to the city of Buffalo the ensuing spring for the purpose of prosecuting his studies, he was anxious to exhibit as great a degree of advancement as possible, and applied himself with all the energy he could command. In the spring of 1822 he went to Buffalo, and entered the office of gentleman of considerable reputation as a lawyer. He was to test the result of his energetic application in a new and untried field. The situation in which he was now placed, however, favored him with more available facilities than he had previously enjoyed, and he made the best use of them with eager dispatch. Buffalo then

bore strong indications of becoming enventually a great
city. Though the hum of business that now resounds
through the streets, thronged with her population of
eighty-five thousand, had not then swelled into such a
din of prosperous activity, she bore unmistakable marks
of ultimate greatness as a city. Situated in a very fertile
country, her streets terminating in the very waves of
Lake Erie, she could not fail to become the commercial
emporium of western New York. Between Lakes Erie
and Ontario, she possessed fair anticipations of an excellent railroad communication. Such were some of the
advantages arising from her local position, whose tendencies were the full development of her resources. At the
time of Mr. Fillmore's arrival in that city, society was
established upon a correct basis, cemented by the strongest
of social compacts, resulting from a complete harmony
of feeling and concert of action, in a cause of common
defence. It had been but a few years since hostile fleets
floated over her beautiful lakes, and hostile troops were
quartered in her streets. The fame of Perry was fresh
in the minds of all, while the fields of Chippewa and
Lundy's Lane still bore marks of the hero blood of her
defenders. Thus, emerging from the smouldering embers,
where the incendiary torch of a rapacious soldiery had
left her, the city of Buffalo smiled with prospects of social
happiness as when first she doned the robes of her
independence.

Society, too, had reached a degree of refinement that
was excelled by few cities in the Union. Much attention
had been manifested on the part of the citizens in regard

4

to the successful operation of a regular system of instruction; consequently, there was pervading all classes a very happy diffusion of general intelligence. The establishment of libraries, etc., had been undertaken and to a great degree successfully accomplished; a large amount of healthy, high-toned literature was circulated among the entire population. The business men of the place manifested great public spirit and national pride, by decorating their city with public buildings, etc., and every department of business evinced indications of the most animated industry. Taking society in the aggregate, it was refined, moral and high-toned.

Such were the people with whom Millard Fillmore first cast his lot, thirty-four years ago. Such were the people with whose fortunes and interests he came, an entire stranger and mere stripling, to identify those of his own in the union of permanent citizenship. Yet, this unpretending stripling, who could then look over the entire city and meet no friendly glance of recognition — who entered the city, as thousands have done, unseen and unknown, is the same who, on his recent return from the old world, in the erective majesty of true nobility, entered the same city amid the thunders of cannon, the streaming of banners, the pealing of bells, and the deafening acclamations of welcome from thirty thousand freemen, in whose hearts he reigns an idol.

I was tempted into this contrast by the reflections I had, during the reception extended to Mr. Fillmore by his fellow citizens, on his arrival home from his recent visit to Europe. For any digression it may have caused me to make, I crave the reader's indulgence.

In Buffalo, he prosecuted his legal studies with char acteristic energy and perseverance, and continued to make the same rapid progress he had formerly done. The expenses attendant upon his studies he had to defray himself. These, too, were increased by heavier and more frequent drafts upon his means than he had formerly experienced in the country. He was frequently aroused from the enjoyment of his legal and literary studies, by the voice of a necessity that submitted to no procrastination. It was a voice, however, with which he had become perfectly familiar and was accustomed to obey from his earliest boyhood. They were companions of old acquaintanceship, but entire success was soon to dissolve the copartnership, with a "mutual consent" that caused no lingering look or parting sigh.

To sustain himself in his studies, and liquidate the expenses thereby entailed, he again taught school. Through this medium he sustained himself, during the entire time of prosecuting the study of his profession, in Buffalo. From the increased facilities thrown in his way to improvement, in the shape of books, young men's societies, and an uninterrupted intercourse with men of proverbial talents and attainments, with all the advantages of an enlightened, refined society, he began to derive very great benefit. By the course of zeal and industry he pursued, and the kind generosity of his nature, he could not fail to be universally esteemed by the citizens of the place. It was no uncommon remark among the young students in the city at that time, at the exhibition of unusual application on the part of a fellow student, that he was as studious as Fillmore.

Mr. Fillmore always made it a point, in his early life, to live entirely within his means; and those similarly situated cannot be too careful in emulating his example in this respect.

It was about this time he gave an emphatic endorsement to the conservative principles of the great whig party. At the time he adopted those principles, it will not be amiss to take a casual glance at the state of political affairs in the country. The nation had just been convulsed with the wildest excitement, by the agitation growing out of the Missouri question of 1821. In the whole political history of the United States, there has never been a period of more momentous importance to our vitality than the time of the excitement incident to the adjustment of those troubles, by the Compromise of 1821. So intense was the excitement in the councils of the nation, that we seemed verging upon the evils of anarchy.

Mr. Clay took his seat in Congress on the 14th day of January, 1821, amid flames of passion rarely seen in the deliberations of any legislative body, and a spirit of bitter party denunciation, pregnant with the worst results. Principally through his agency, these difficulties were peaceably adjusted, and quiet restored to the country.

The old conservative principles of the whig party were those regarded as the safe weapons wherewith to combat the pet bank systems, and other elements of the progressive democracy; and Mr. Clay, from the wise, conservative course he pursued in the Missouri and other questions of vital interest, was rapidly rising into that popular favor that was to result in his eventually assuming the leadership of his party. At the time when Mr. Fillmore came to Erie county, his great exemplar had just succeeded in establishing the measures of the Missouri Compromise. He endorsed the principles of the whig party, as embodied in the sentiments of Henry Clay, and to these principles he adhered with unwavering fidelity; an ardent supporter of Clay through all his fortunes, until the ultimate decay and disruption of that party. In the adoption of his political creed, it can not be asserted that he was actuated by motives other than those of the purest patriotism, for, in the state of New York, the whig party was, at that time, in a fearful minority, and the democrats held sway in both branches of her legislature. His father had ever been sternly identified with the whigs, and uniform in his support to the champions of his party. Mr. Fillmore was, at that early day, an ardent admirer of Henry Clay; nor was it in subsequent life in the slightest degree diminished. The similarity of circumstances under which they each commenced a career in which they were to be the acknowledged champions of conservative patriotism in their respective times was well calculated to produce a congeniality of feeling in his breast. The principles entertained by Mr. Clay, and the lofty patriotism he displayed, were not in confliction with his own. Side by side with Clay, he afterward fought most gallantly in their defence. And were Mr. Clay now living, and engaged in the din of political strife, there is no doubt but the views he would entertain upon the different subjects that agitate the country would be precisely identical with those entertained by Mr. Fillmore upon the same subjects — essentially patriotic and conservative.

In 1823, Mr. Fillmore was admitted to the court of common pleas in the city of Buffalo. The Buffalo bar was a very able one, presenting in its members an array of talent and legal research rarely excelled in any city of the Union. There were many old lawyers of acknowledged ability, who, from a long connection with the practice, had become familiar with all its details. There were, as practitioners at the bar, many young aspirants to success, who, from an intimate association with the best legal advisers in the city, and the assistance of every facility to success they could desire, possessed advantages superior to those of Mr. Fillmore. It is not surprising, then, that a man of Mr. Fillmore's unpretending temperament and natural modesty should feel exceedingly diffident in embarking in a profession for the discharge of whose duties his capacities were wholly untried, among competitors who had been its successful followers for years. Not having sufficient confidence in his own ability to make his first effort in the profession among such learned men as thronged the Buffalo bar, he removed to Aurora, a village some eighteen miles from the city. Here, to use his own words, he "labored as hard as Jacob did for Rachel," for the glimmerings of a successful result in his profession. The wisdom of this course is perfectly clear. The village of Aurora was a quiet little place, with a well cultivated, refined society, and afforded an opportunity for him to commence his profession without incurring that array of

talented competition which would have been the result
had he remained in the city. Here he could practice in
the courts, without contending with the overawing weight
of age and experience, until divested of that timidity incident to young lawyers, and peculiarly so to himself, he
could take his position at the bar with a degree of experience requisite to success. He could not expect at
first to get a practice, the profits accruing from which
would be adequate to defray the expenses he was necessarily compelled to incur at the commencement of his
duties. For a considerable time after his location in
Aurora, he sustained himself by teaching, and devoted his
leisure moments to study. He soon, by pursuing a
course of honor and steady qualities, developed such
traits of character that he became endeared to the inhabitants of the place, and won the entire confidence and
good will of the whole village. The first case in which
Mr. Fillmore was ever engaged as counsel was one of
larceny. An individual had been arrested for stealing
some articles from a neighbor, and was awaiting his trial.
From the circumstances of the case and the position of
the parties, the cause elicited very general interest, and
was much talked of and discussed by those acquainted
with the facts. The services of Mr. Fillmore were engaged in the prosecution. This was his first case. What
young attorney has not looked with interest, and attached
a fictitious importance to the issue of his first case ? He
was extremely careful in the preparation of his case, and
in looking up all the law of any relevancy thereto. In
these preparations he could not have been more careful,

had he believed his entire destiny dependent upon the successful issue of his effort.

On the day of trial, the court room was densely thronged with those whom the interest of the occasion had attracted, as much to witness the debut of young Fillmore as anything else. The prisoner was arraigned under the indictment, and the case was opened by the examination of witnesses by Mr. Fillmore on the part of the commonwealth. He conducted the examination with great judgment, and convinced the attornies of the opposition that they had more to contend with than they had expected. After they were through with the witnesses Mr. Fillmore opened the case in a happy display of facts and law, that proved a great readiness in applying them to each particular feature of the case.

With such clearness and force did he pile fact upon fact, and quote the particular law by which they were to be governed, and so perfectly unanswerable were the arguments he advanced, that before he took his seat, it began to be whispered in the crowd that " The man will be found guilty !" while the attornies for the defence, dispairing of success, began to say to each other, " We shall lose our case !"

The arguments in the defence, though advanced by men of much greater experience than Mr. Fillmore possessed, were far from removing the wall of facts showing their client's guilt, in which the prosecution had enclosed him. The result was, after the submission of the case, the prisoner was found guilty of the charge, and sentenced to the penalty of his offence. Thus he had gotten a case and gained it.

It is a significant fact that his first services in a career where he was to win such distinction was on the side of the people, and he was successful. The successful manner, and the marked ability he displayed in conducting this case attracted considerable attention. The fact of his having discomfited the older attornies in a somewhat closely contested case, by his superior knowledge of law and facts more than from any aspect of the case favorable to his side, was a theme of considerable talk in the community, and had a very favorable effect upon Mr. Fillmore.

He continued the practice of his profession at Aurora with increase of practice and an assiduous application, until 1830. In 1825, his prospects becoming somewhat brighter, and his vocation as a lawyer a permanently settled point, he began to contemplate the idea of a permanent location. In the succeeding year, he was married to Abigail Powers, the youngest daughter of Rev. Lemuel Powers, of Erie county. Mr. Powers was a gentleman of elevated moral worth, and of the strictest religious principles, and proverbial for the zeal and earnestness he displayed in his ministry throughout the limits of his entire acquaintance. His daughter had received all the advantages of a liberal education, and been schooled in the lessons of pure morality. She was possessed of a mild amiability, that was manifest in her entire social intercourse. A modest deportment that obtruded itself upon the notice of no one, and a love of virtue that could suffer no abatement, with a desire to promote the happiness of those around her commensurate with that for the promo-

4*

tion of her own. The kind gentleness of her manners, and her daily exemplification of so many virtues, endeared her to the hearts of her entire acquaintance.

Such was the happy choice made by Millard Fillmore. The gentleness of her manners, and the tenderness of her devotion were admirably adapted to the placidity of Mr. Fillmore's quiet disposition. The fruits of this marriage were two children, a son and a daughter. The daughter died at Aurora of cholera, in the summer of 1853. The son is now a practicing lawyer in the city of Buffalo. In 1827, Mr. Fillmore was regularly admitted as an attorney. He continued the practice of his profession with uninterrupted progress, until he occupied an elevated position in the conceptions of those of much more experience than himself. During his stay at Aurora, he studied well, and laid deep the fundamental principles of the legal profession. So thorough was his comprehension of the principles of law, and so accurate was his judgment in their application to his cases, that, limited as his practice had formerly been, he began now to be regarded as a lawyer of weight and ability, and, in addressing a jury, he seldom failed to carry conviction by the force of reason and fact. These qualities have constituted a large portion of Mr. Fillmore's strength as a lawyer. The eloquence of his addresses to a jury did not consist in the lightening-like impetuosity of Patrick Henry's, that darted upon the springs of the different natures of which his jury was composed, and tempered them at will; nor was like Clay's, flowing on smoothly, yet broad and deep like a vast river, bearing his hearers almost insensibly along with it, until they reached the point at which he aimed to bring them. Nor yet, was it like that of Prentiss', that gliding with graceful beauty into the fairy realms of poesy, would blind the vision of his jury with tropes and figures, and so lull the sense with the rich exotics of fancy that they lost sight of facts and law altogether. The eloquence of Mr. Fillmore consisted in its convincing powers.   In prosecution, systematic and methodical, he would pile fact upon fact, with such accurate compactness, and sustain them with such an unbroken chain of law and evidence, that between the individual and the chance of escape from conviction, he would establish a barrier no judge or jury could overleap, without a manifest disregard of official duty. In cases of defence, perceptive and analytic, he would discover the main cord of hope whereon the prosecution depended for the conviction of his client, and with ease he would untwist it, and separating it fibre from fibre, would leave his client free from its meshes. In the practice of his profession, Mr. Fillmore has never resorted to the artful chicanery practiced by many, who regard a talent for that as being an essential prerequisite to its successful prosecution, and which is, generally, about the only talent such possess. He looked upon the law as a noble profession, and embarked in it with a view of making himself useful — he has honored the one, and succeeded in the other. The gloom that had enshrouded the prospects of Mr. Fillmore from his earlist boyhood now began, gradually, to disappear, amid the dawning light of a more prosperous future. He hailed the first rays of his rising star with emotions of delight. To appreciate the happiness produced in the breast by these first beams of success, we must place ourselves in the same position. He had overcome obstructions of ponderous magnitude, at every step of his career. With his own young arm, he had pulled down barriers that had opposed his every effort. Unaided, by his own stout heart, he had repelled every thought that bid it throb to notes of despair. He had traversed, without a guide, save the footprints of those who had gone before him, a wilderness of terrific gloom, and now, approaching the vales of prosperity, he hailed their light as a Bethlehem star, that spoke peace to the soul. As we have endeavored to follow him through the thick gloom of the past, we now propose entering with him those fields of fame, until he plants himself in their midst, a pillar of colossal dimensions.

CHAPTER III.

At the head of his profession — Is offered an excellent connection in
Buffalo — Admitted to the supreme court — Individual sketches —
Legal profundity — Is elected to the Assembly — Sketch of that
body — Evinces legislative capacities — Party politics — Adherence
to his principles — His nature as a debater — Adjournment of the
Assembly — His devotion to his profession — Re-elected to that
body — On the committee on Public Defence — The law of imprisonment for debt — Governor Throop — Mr. Fillmore's active
endeavors for the repeal of the imprisonment law — His success —
Important measures of the Assembly — Close of the session —
Sketch of Mr. Fillmore in that body — Remarks thereon.

THE success of Mr. Fillmore in his legal pursuits very
justly placed him at the head of his profession. He
had applied himself to its labors with such assiduity that
he had become an advocate of distinguished ability; and,
though he was loved as a man and admired as a lawyer,
these were not the only inducements for clients to seek
to avail themselves of his services. They were afraid of
having him against them. From the high position which
he had attained, and the great reputation he had acquired
as a lawyer of depth and profundity and of apt perception, he had monopolized pretty much the entire practice
of the village and vicinity. The success of his efforts
could not fail to attract the notice of the members of the
bar, at all contiguous points, and his name became especially familiar in the city of Buffalo, and his ingenious
management of cases a theme of comment among the

ablest of the profession in that city. He had taken several cases, the importance of which had elicited general interest, and been more successful than he had anticipated. The success that crowned his efforts had placed him above the appeals of want, and enabled him to sustain himself without turning aside from the duties of his profession. He had already realized sufficient means through that medium to support himself and pay up the old note with interest, which he had given Judge Wood for means advanced to him by that gentleman in the outset of his career. From these unmistakable indications of prosperity and eventual success, he acquired confidence in himself, and became divested of that natural timidity under which he labored when first admitted to the bar. By the even, consistent course he had pursued, he had won the good will of his acquaintances, and established himself firmly in the affections of the people, a position which he has ever since maintained. He had wooed the law as a lover, and pursued the study of its abstruse principles with patient investigation, knowing that it took time to become a proficient in a science of which the learned and the great of the world were devotees.

The rewards of success now began to heap themselves upon him, as remuneration for the privations he had undergone in his endeavors to master the profession. He had not been an inattentive observer to the history of his country and the signs of the times while thus engaged. But though he made everything subordinate to success in the law from his earliest connections therewith, when not required in its duties, he was careful to acquaint himself familiarly with the leading political events of the day, and the characters figuring most conspicuously therein. So that in the discussion of the political affairs of the country, so well acquainted he had become, if a dispute occurred among the villagers in regard to a matter of importance, the confident disputant would say : "Go and ask Fillmore, if I am not right." His decision when thus appealed to as umpire was as conclusive with the parties as though it came from the lips of Jefferson himself.

To become familiar with the history of the country and the wise administration of the government by the early patriots in the purest days of the Republic, Mr. Fillmore, as a young man, thought it his imperative duty. He made the constitution the basis of his investigations, and the scales in which he weighed the actions of those in whose hands the management of the country had been entrusted Patriotism, the prompter of all his actions, in the outset of his career, he made the constitution the alphabet of his political creed, and the Mecca at whose shrine he would immolate his talents. Firm and unflinching has always been his adherence to that sacred instrument. In the investigation of his country's history, Washington, Adams, and other patriots at the helm of state, on whose brow the majesty of justice sat enthroned in the immaculate purity of heaven, made lasting impressions upon his mind ; and though he has ever been an exemplar rather than a copyist, the patriotism of their course in the administration of our government he determined should be the criteria by which he would shape his own actions Luminous have been the exemplifications of this patriotism in all the relations he has sustained toward our institutions. And as an embodiment of this pure elevation of soul, whose love of country towers a sightless distance above the bitterness of party faction, he stands by the Union and the constitution, almost the last of the Romans, the Aristides of the times.

Possessing, then, the experience of a considerable practice in the law, and occupying an elevated position commensurate with that of his professional brethren, and a knowledge of his country and of constitutional law far surpassing the attainments many of them had made, in 1829 he was admitted a counsellor in the supreme court of the state of New York. Than this supreme court, there were few places in the United States that displayed a brighter array of talent, or an exhibition of more profound legal research.

At the time of Mr. Fillmore's admission into this court, Mr. Savage was chief justice. He was one of those men who, by devoting the energies of a lifetime to the study of the profession, with such application that the very brain becomes a legal portfolio, impressed with the reprints of learned commentators. So perfect was his knowledge of the law, and so acute his judgment, that, from the very nature of a case, he was enabled to arrive at safe conclusions, with the instantaneous alertness and mathematical precision of a Newton, who could demonstrate a geometrical problem, on the mere statement of the proposition. He had been a lawyer of an extensive practice and acknowledged ability, before he was elevated to the bench, a position which he had occupied for a con-

siderable length of time. Being a man of quick perceptive faculties as well as profound research, he was
remarkable for the facility with which he dispatched the
business of the docket. The nature of some of the cases
tried in his hearing, as the highest tribunal of appeal in
the state, involved not unfrequently considerations of the
weightiest moment, and elicited as well as a general interest
on the part of the citizens concerned, a display of powers
from antagonistic advocates that would not have disgraced the Roman forum.

From the chief justice's long connection with the law
and occupancy of the bench, he was admirably calculated
to hear these important cases with dignity, and exhibit
entire and impartial justice in the rendition of his decisions. The first conceptions of Mr. Fillmore in regard
to the chief justice were very favorable. On the countenance of the man he saw delineated those qualities that
never failed to win his warmest admiration — justice and
virtue; in his actions and dispatch of transacting business,
he perceived those traits of character he never failed to
patronize — industry and regularity; in his eye he saw
the beams of true nobility, that never failed to kindle his
own bosom — a benevolent, liberal nature toward his fellow men, yet of the sternest justice, which Sheridan des-
cribes as being "lovely in her darkest frown." Jacob
Sutherland and Samuel Nelson, the two subordinate justices, were men of the highest legal attainments, and
were essentially qualified to "don the ermine robes" of
the supreme court. This high tribunal was, in that day,
regarded as an august body, and men of undoubted

capacity, as well as unsullied reputations, were invariably elevated to a position where they were to exercise superior guardianship over the people.

Those were purer days of the Republic, before the hosts of political vermin had crawled into the temple of justice and polluted the majesty of her sanctuary with the effects of selfish ambition. Sutherland and Nelson, in discharging the duties of their official capacity, evinced a thorough knowledge of legal principles, and an impartial administration of the laws, that proved they were true embodiments of that justice which it was their peculiar province to promote.

The attorney general was Greene C. Robinson, a gentleman whose talents as a lawyer were acknowledged to be of the first order, and whose legal successes in a career of some distinction admirably befitted him for the responsible position of state prosecutor.

Such was the supreme court of the Empire State, when Mr. Fillmore was admitted a counsellor, twenty-seven years ago. The counsellors who practiced at this court for the most part were lawyers of old experience and distinguished ability, whose services were solicited on account of the very great importance of the cases and their ultimate issue. Among the lawyers of notoriety for their extensive acquaintance with the principles of law and the success of their professional career, who figured somewhat a conspicuous part before the supreme court, at that time, was J. C. Spencer. This gentleman was exceedingly popular, and deservedly so, among his professional brethren, for his talents and ingenuity. He was a practical lawyer of the first quality, and in the preparation of his cases to come before the supreme court he had few superiors. Bacon and Kirkland were attorneys of eminence, to compete successfully with whom required a large amount of legal information as well as natural argumentative talents. The peculiar strength of these gentlemen consisted in a happy combination of reason and argument, with considerable eloquence in enforcing conviction upon the minds of their hearers. During Mr. Fillmore's practice before the supreme court, it was often his fortune to come in conflict with these and other gentlemen of no less distinction for their legal lore. Mr. Fillmore was much younger than a large portion of the practitioners before the supreme court, when he was first admitted to practice there. Yet, from the first, he occupied a position of prominence among the other counsellors, and frequently succeeded in discomfiting them in the argument of cases of great importance. His first appearance in that court was marked with courteous dignity toward the attorneys, and a respectful deference to the judges due their official station, which exhibited a refinement of feelings of the highest order. It has always been the desire of Mr. Fillmore, both in public and in private, not only to do his whole duty, but to do it in such a manner as to make himself beloved. The hold he has upon the affections of the American people show to the extent this desire has been gratified. On his admission into the supreme court he soon gave displays of those powers of mind he had used so efficiently elsewhere. So profound were the powers of his mind in comprehending the fundamental doctrines of the common law, and in grasping the whole range of learned disquisitions upon its most intricate and difficult parts, that he commanded the respect of the entire bench. Yet the unassuming modesty of his deportment, was as clearly manifest as though he were entirely ignorant of his powers. In the establishment of his positions, he ranged the wide fields of legal research with the restless activity of thought, culled a casket of facts, and fitted them to his case with the precise solidity of a marble pyramid. In demolishing the fortress reared by counsel on the opposite side, with the perceptive analyses of chemical process, he would tear it piece from piece, and expose the very foundation as being fallacious and untenable.

But, before following him through his career in the supreme court, where he won such glorious laurels and established a character of civic ability almost unsurpassed in the annals of judicial renown, it is necessary to notice the results of his labors in a capacity where the country was, more generally, the recipient.

The fame of his legal success became the theme of universal remark. He had reached a position far above young advocates of no more experience than he had enjoyed. His character, in fact, was essentially established, and the people began to regard him as one from whom they might expect services ameliorative of their condition, and in whose hands their interests might with safety be reposed. And he himself, from the success of the past, had began to feel and hope that, through the appliance of the same energy, he might attain a position, of usefulness. Already had the village in which he lived, and surrounding country, ceased to be the limits of his professional labors. He had frequently been solicited to engage as counsel in different places. Surrounded with these flattering prospects, he was offered a connection with the most successful law-office in the city of Buffalo. This connection promised great and very decided advantages, inasmuch as the counsel of the firm, from a position of eminence in the law, were doing about the heaviest practice in the city. Possessed of the capabilities he was, with the increased facilities afforded by the proposed connection, he was no longer necessitated to indulge apprehensions of expenditures not being met through the medium of his profession. The " Rachel " of success for which he had " labored, Jacob-like," so earnestly, was in his embrace, and with this trophy of his triumphs he could return to the city he had left through timidity and a want of confidence, to assume his position as a lawyer with the most respectable at the bar. He accepted a proposition that promised to result so advantageously to the development of his faculties. He closed his business in Aurora, and left the scenes of his first triumphs, and cast his lot a second time among the citizens of Buffalo, where he has ever since resided, except when engaged in official duties at Albany or Washington City.

Immediately after his arrival in Buffalo, he was thrown into practice of a lucrative nature. The fame of his ability having preceded him to the city, he found no difficulty in the acquisition of clients, or cause to complain of inactivity. The members of the Buffalo bar soon perceived that, during the comparative hermitage of his Aurora seclusion, like Demosthenes in the cave, he had developed intellectual powers of a giant nature. Like that ancient orator who left the city, where he would have remained to overcome the defects of his speech, and returned again to make her rostrums resound with his matchless eloquence, he left the city where he studied, to overcome the defects of his timidity, and returned again to make her streets resound with the anthems of his fame. His success at the bar was now excelled by no one of his age; business flowed in upon him from all sides, he had no superior at the bar. In his early practice, for days he attended courts of uninterrupted business from morning until night, and was counsel one side or the other in every case. Like Clay, he was a man of the people, and manifested, what he felt, a deep solicitude in having their rights protected and their wrongs redressed.

Being himself one of the people, their rights he regarded as a part of his own, and any infringement thereupon as an injury to himself, as a member of a great social compact, formed for mutual protection and defence. This manifest solicitude and regard, on his part, toward the people, could but result in a mutual reciprocity of interest, and excite in their bosoms feelings of the same regard and esteem, on their part, toward him. This love of Mr. Fillmore's for his fellow men has always been wholly divested of selfish motives and considerations. It is the dictate of a generous heart, whose happiness is commensurate with that of the people's. His great life idea has been to ascertain by what efforts of his the prosperity of the common country and the happiness of all classes would be best promoted; then, with incessant energy, he has directed them in that channel. In both public and private capacities the appeals of humanity have never been silenced by any sordid considerations of his bosom, but have always met a response of active benevolence. Liberal and generous, both in his views of policy and the feelings of his heart, nothing affords him so much gratification as to be enabled to render assistance in conciliating the elements of discord in his country, or to alleviate the sorrows of a fellow creature.

The Athenian* when dying with peace was blest,
   Because he had raised no mourner's sad voice ;
But nobler content can beam in his breast,
   For HE hath in kindness made many rejoice.

Possessing this generous nature, ever watchful for opportunities to promote the interests of the people and the prosperity of the common country, it is not surprising that he should become the most popular man of his county. So endeared had he become to the hearts of the people, and so implicit was their reliance in his virtue, patriotism, and capacities, that with great unanimity he was selected to represent them in the assembly of the state. This unexpected selection, except as a proof that he was appreciated by his fellow citizens, afforded no great gratification to Mr. Fillmore. He was not insensible to the esteem for him, on the part of the people, conveyed in the selection and their disposition to place

*Pericles.

him in office. He felt these manifestations of regard with emotional gratitude.

He had no sordid ambition to gratify. Considerations of self-elevation have never found an asylum in his bosom. Though a great portion of his life has been spent in public service, devoted to the duties of official station, he has never sought office. When he has turned aside from the discharge of his duties as a citizen and as a professional man to accept office, it has invariably been in compliance with the strongest solicitations of his fellow citizens. These solicitations, too, have always been made with such earnest and unquestionable indications of preference, and urgent appeals in behalf of their interests, that with his non-compliance would have been associated a manifest disregard of duty.

As Mr. Fillmore has never sought the honors and emoluments of office, so has he been equally careful never to shrink from the performance of any duty incumbent upon him to discharge. Setting out in his career with an ardent desire to render himself useful, he reposed unlimited confidence in the judgment and capacities of his countrymen, as being sufficient to select their own public servants.

Ever ready and anxious to be of service to his country, he was willing for his country to decide in what way his services would be most acceptable. In common with every good citizen, with no aspirations whatever for the elevation of himself, he gave himself to his country; and, though he has frequently occupied office, when obedience to his personal preferences would have kept him in the walks of private life, he has done so under the strongest convictions of duty. In this respect his whole career has evinced an exemplification of Henry Clay's noble sentiment: "I had rather be right than be president."

In compliance with the urgent request of the people and his convictions of duty as to the course he should pursue, he commenced his political career. He was elected to the assembly from Erie county in 1828, and took his seat in that body in the early part of the ensuing January. At the period Mr. Fillmore became a member of the New York assembly, the whig party, to which he belonged, was in a fearful minority in both branches of the state legislature. The progressive democracy had just commenced preparations for a combined onslaught that would eventuate in the entire annihilation of old conservative whig principles. Mr. Fillmore was then just twenty-nine years of age, and the inexperienced representative of a minority party, he had rather indifferent opportunities of exhibiting his powers. The democratic representation had become so accustomed to exert dominant sway, having monopolized the seats of both houses for several years previous, with arrogant assumption presumed to consummate what measures they deemed proper, regardless of the views and indifferent to the opposition of a respectable minority. It was during the time when, through the hands of Jackson, the regal or executive powers of the constitution were taking their defiant march into the legislative halls, to the almost entire exclusion of its democratical features, and usurping the people's

platform with their royal insignia. It was at the commencement of that political reign of terror that resulted
in the removal of the deposits, and the introduction of a
fiery partisan spirit in all classes of the country, that for
a number of years changed the bonds of union to the
clanking links of a rivalrous antagonism. This spirit of
radical, partisan fanaticism seemed to infuse itself into all
parts of the country, and wherever it took hold, the influences were as uncongenial to the prevalence of a patriotic
national feeling favorable to the protection of conservative principles as darkness to a sunbeam. So infectious
were these incipient effusions of young democracy from
the Jacksonian administration, that almost every department of the government became ulcerated with their corruptive virulence. So fierce was their prevalence in the
halls of congress, and so intense became the excitement
where the wildest passions flashed in the heat of mad-
dened rivalry, that they ultimately bid fair to consume the
very walls of the capitol. The administration, in the
assumption of almost kingly prerogative, under the much
abused name of democracy, impressed the irrevocable
signet of the veto upon measures embracing the true
import of the word, and placed the approving signature
to those with which it was at direct variance. Incumbents of office were led to the block of decapitation, by
an inquisitorial cabinet, with the merciless cruelty of
a Sejanus, and patriotism labeled with the imfamous
stamp of intrigue.

Such were some of the ultimate results of the almost
usurptional power and innovations that began to be

developed about this time. They were not confined, however, to the royal head-quarters of their emanation at Washington City, but infected the legislative assemblies throughout the country. Indications of their whereabouts were beginning to be manifest in the New York assembly, at the time Mr. Fillmore took his seat in that body, in 1829. The active members of that assembly were mostly of age and experience, and entertaining principles opposite to those of the " young member from Erie," they expected little opposition from that quarter. But merit and ability is not to be concealed by the excitement of party feeling, or the overawing influence of numbers. Mr. Fillmore took occasion upon some measure of vital interest to let them know the " young member from Erie " had not come there for nothing. Immediately after he took his seat, we find his name in the assembly journal of that session placed on a very important committee ; and by reference to the same journal we find he was the most active member of the house. When measures of a political nature came before the house, he was so capacitated as to exert no influence by his vote, but the small minority with which he was indentified never kept him from a bold and fearless avowal of his principles. Often did veterans of the " Hickory School" shrink in discomfiture from the discussion of their principles with the " Erie member." Though in political questions his vote was of no significance, on all measures he gave the " aye " or " nay," according to his principles, even though he met no response but the echo of his own voice. He was among the youngest members of the house, but was

determined not only to avow the principles of his party, but
to contest every inch of ground over which measures were
obliged to pass that were antagonistic with his views.
The boldness of his stand and the unwavering fidelity
with which he maintained it, filled the members of the
house with admiration for his firmness and intrepidity
Even those most bitterly opposed to his principles, who
differed most widely with him upon questions of national
policy, respected him most highly for the unbending de
votion with which he stood by his party, and the tireless
zeal with which he studied the interests of his constituency. The zeal which Mr. Fillmore manifested in the
advocacy of his principles was not, however, the blind
infatuation of party spirit that sometimes glories in being
in a minority, for the boast of contending against numbers,
and prides itself upon the honors of fighting " alone in its
glory," with none to respond amen. His zeal was the
offspring of patriotism, exhibited in the defence of principles, whose establishment he was firmly convinced
would promote the interests of the country. Nor did he
ever in their advocacy manifest the least peevishness
or impatience toward those who thought proper to differ
with him on the subjects of state and national politics.
He entertained opinions cherished from boyhood and endorsed in maturer manhood ; he was there the representative of a great party entertaining the same ; he wanted
the privilege of entertaining them, and was willing to
accord to every member on the floor the same liberty.
From the entertainment of different political principles in
regard to the various questions pertaining to national

politics, he saw no necessity for the existence of personal
bickering and animosities. This is a commendable trait
of Mr. Fillmore's character, impersonated to the same
degree, perhaps, in no other man, so much of whose life
has been devoted to politics and political pursuits as his
has been. Regarding the people in their aggregate capacity as being honest in their convictions in regard to
party issues, he concedes to all the privileges of their
birthrights, nor thinks any less of a man for entertaining
views contrary to his own. Politics and the social circle
he regards as separate and distinct spheres, and though
with intelligent, high-toned men, he could engage in a
political contest for the defence of his principles, at the
threshold of the social circle all antagonism must be
buried for the friendly intercourse of mutual good will.
No man can say Mr. Fillmore ever thought more or less of
him in consequence of the *mere* political opinion he entertained. Hence the fact of his universal popularity,
irrespective of parties or party influences. Those entertaining opinions directly opposite to his, concede that he
is a patriot of valued worth, and a man whom to know
is to love.

Among those with whom he has lived for a period of
thirty years, there is not *one* who can say he does not
admire Mr. Fillmore. His neighbors and acquaintances
in the city of Buffalo, irrespective of party distinctions,
love him, and love to do him honor. Throughout the
entire Union, men of all parties agree that he is a man
of the purest virtue and the wisest abilities of statesmanship. There is no intelligent man, be he blinded as he

may by sectionalism or party faction, be his judgment
warped as it may by the prejudice of years, who can say
Mr. Fillmore is no patriot.   All parties in all sections of
the Union agree in saying that, in his love of country and
his desires to promote her interests, he " knows no North,
no South, no East, no West."

There has not, since the days of Washington, been an
individual who, *as a man*, has taken such a hold upon the
great mass of the people as Mr. Fillmore.   He had
guarded well the interests reposed in his keeping during
the entire session of 1829.   In his intercourse with the
members of the house, he evinced all the marked courtesy and unassuming demeanor characteristic of his
nature.   In debate, though he displayed great powers of
intellect and a thorough acquaintance with the principles
of international law, he was uniformly kind, courteous,
and dignified.   His replications to members in debate
were characterized with no sarcastic repartees or witty
inuendos calculated to leave a sting of mortification.
He was aware that such sallies, though they might irri-
tate and annoy, instead of producing conciliation, and be
attended with convincing powers, would only engender a
spirit of retaliation and animosity of feeling in the end.
In discharging his duties as a member of the assembly,
he displayed great capacities for legislative usefulness,
and exhibited a judgment on which might be placed the
most implicit reliance.   Of all measures whose objects
were the promotion of benevolent institutions, the
increase of educational facilities, the development of the
country's resources, or to advance the interest of the

country in any particular feature, by reference to the journals of the house, I find he was a zealous advocate. Owing to the minority of his party in the house, the efficiency of his labors on the final issues of questions were restricted in fact entirely to measures of a general nature, with no political bearing. In regard to measures of this character, he was the most influential member in the house; and when such a bill was presented, the reception of his endorsement was almost equivalent to its adoption; for, so proverbial among the members was his correct judgment, that if one of them was in doubt as to the propriety of sustaining any such measure, he would say to those around him: " Fillmore says this bill is RIGHT, and I shall vote for it ! "   Or, on the other hand, if it did not receive his endorsement, its doom was sealed ; the doubting member would say: " Fillmore says this measure is WRONG, and I shall vote against it ! "   This unlimited confidence they had in his judgment to discriminate between right and wrong, when unbiased by political prejudices, shows the exalted opinion of his great worth entertained by that body. Alas, that men should be so blinded by partisan spirit as to sacrifice virtuous worth to the caprice of faction !   He closed his services in that session of the legislative assembly in a manner highly creditable to his constituency, and that reflected great credit upon himself. He won the esteem of every member of the house, whether he entertained the same political opinions or not, and displayed powers of legislative usefulness and capacities for political spheres surpassed by no member on the floor—not even the most prominent. The labors of the session were completed; over the interests of those whom he was deputed to represent he had exercised a faithful guardianship and he was now ready to embosom himself again in the midst of his friends and enjoy the quietude of his home.

On the adjournment of the assembly, he returned to Buffalo and resumed the practice of the law. To become a proficient in his profession was his most ardent desire, and he had not thought of devoting any less energy to its duties in consequence of his having participated in the political measures of the day. Mr. Fillmore has always pursued this course. His being an incumbent of office has never interfered with his professional labors in the slightest degree, longer than he was actually engaged in the discharge of official duty.

At the expiration of his term of office and the close of his labors connected therewith, he has always entered upon the duties of his profession with as much zeal and earnestness as though he had never been an official incumbent, and never expected to be again. This course, to which he has strictly adhered from the time he became a practitioner at the bar until he retired from the practice altogether, shows conclusively that he has never been a political or partisan aspirant, ready, as many are, to make everything subordinate to their own elevation, and to resort to any means, fair or foul, for the subservation of personal aggrandizement.

When the incumbent of office, he was profoundly impressed with the responsibilities of the station, and made every consideration subservient to the faithful discharge of duty. Careful to ascertain its requirements, which, by the assistance of a wise and patriotic judgment, he seldom failed to do, he was prompt and efficient in coming up to them. In the capacity of a public servant he has known no little duties, whose minor importance he could view in the light of insignificance. If they were duties at all, within the limits of his official jurisdiction, he regarded his acceptance of the position as a virtual obligation to those whose interests he was there to protect, to discharge them faithfully.

As a public servant, no man has ever been more solicitous to promote the interests of his constituency, or endeavored more earnestly, and, I might add, more successfully, to ascertain by what means their interests would be best protected, than has Mr. Fillmore. But when he ceased to be an official incumbent, he felt, as a public servant, he had discharged the obligation into which he entered with the people, and embarked in his profession as a private citizen, as though he had never labored in any other sphere.

Here I beg of the reader the indulgence of a short digression. The wisdom of this course on the part of Mr. Fillmore cannot fail to elicit the approval and admiration of all thinking men, especially young lawyers of correct judgment, in the outset of a professional career. How many young attornies, immediately after embarking in their profession, have yielded to the wishes of friends, and the impulse of feeling, and become the incumbents of some political station, to the entire destruction of their

5*

legal prospects! Their elevation to the office, in itself, is fraught with no injurious consequences. But, once an office incumbent, and a participant in the excitements incident to the station, they become lured and fascinated with the charms of political life, and lose all relish for the quiet course, and the monotonous studies of the attorney's office.

On the expiration of their terms of office, instead of devoting themselves to the duties of their profession with alacrity, they study and devise means and schemes through which they may be reëlected, or elevated to still higher positions. A sordid passion for self-elevation usurps the mind, to the entire exclusion of all nobler aspirations, until, while scheming and developing plans, such an one is outstripped by the more studious devotee to his profession, and his prospects, that were so bright in the outset, disappear forever.

To young lawyers, this desire to put themselves forward too fast, especially if they have once been honored, is certainly one of the most dangerous reefs they encounter on the voyage of professional life. The course pursued by Mr. Fillmore was certainly a very wise one, and those similarly situated cannot become too vividly impressed with his example in this respect.

On Mr. Fillmore's resumption of his practice in Buffalo, after the adjournment of the session of the assembly, he became the leading member of the bar, and the most actively engaged practitioner in the city. He became firmly established in a business at once honorable and lucrative. So untiring had been the application he

had made, and so admirably adapted was his mental
organism to the deep legal investigations, that he had
arisen to a prominent position, and took the lead of his
professional brethren. But the quiet pursuits of his profession, and the domestic happiness of home, he was not
destined to enjoy uninterruptedly, though it was his
desire to have done so. Contrary to his expectations
and wishes, he was again placed forward as their representative for the county of Erie to the state assembly of
1830. So zealous was the activity with which he guarded
their interests and protected their rights the preceding
session, that the people of his county were determined
to avail themselves of his talents and legislative capacities the ensuing session, and made their requisition upon
his services in such a manner as to admit of no repulsion.
Accordingly, in the early part of January, 1830, he for
a second time took his seat in the state assembly as a
member from Erie county. On the 5th of January, an
organization of the house was effected by the election of
Erastus Root to the speakership, and Francis Seger to
the clerkship. Among the members who composed this
legislature were many shrewd and experienced politicians. Mr. Savage, Mr. Granger, and Spencer, I find by
reference to the assembly journal, were very active members of that body. The democratic party, as they had
done for years, still exerted dominant sway in the house.
The minority party, of which Mr. Fillmore was a representative, had undergone no perceptible increase or
diminution, and when he took his seat, the political complexion of parties retained about the same hue it had the

preceding year. But he occupied a position more favorable to the exhibition of his natural powers of intellect
and display of his mental wealth than he had done the
previous session. He had in that very house political
antecedents to which he could appeal as testimonials of
extraordinary legislative capacities. His name was
stamped conspicuously upon the journals of the precedent legislature, and wise and important measures were
upon their pages, marked with legislative enactment, the
data of whose passage were the elicitation of his endorsement. Aided by experience, in the possession of the
unlimited confidence of every member of the assembly,
with a fine practical intellect, he took his seat in the legislature of 1830 under circumstances well calculated to
perform services for his state the intrinsic value of which
would be felt by all classes and in every department of
business.

Divested of the timidity incident to the inexperience of
his first efforts in a legislative capacity; with a heart
whose every beat was for the amelioration of his country's
condition, the identification of his affections, and his
interests with those of the common people being strong
as those of Jonathan and David, and a love of country,
and a patriotism of soul that towered above the fanatical
spirit of party feeling, he took his seat in the assembly,
resolved, with the constitution for his guide, to render
efficient service to his state. On page thirty-eight of the
assembly journal, in conjunction with the names of some of
the most prominent members of the house, I find that
Mr. Fillmore was placed upon the committee on "the

subject of the public defence." The position assigned
him in the appointments of committees was exactly in
common with his feelings. The public defence has always
been the main desire of his nature. The prophetic
sentinel on Horeb's height in the sacred hills of Idumea,
when he thundered forth through the still darkness the
interrogatory of watchman, what of the night? felt no
greater solicitude for the interests of Israel's host and
the ten commandments than has Mr. Fillmore in the public
defence of his country, and the unsullied preservation of
her constitution. In exact keeping, then, with his feelings
was the position he occupied as a committee-man of the
legislature. A sentinel upon the watch-tower of liberty,
he has ever stood hugging to his heart the laws of his
country, and grasping in his hand the sword of justice to
defend them from the rude attacks of fanatical assailants.

At the head of the committee on the " subject of the
public defence," he looked around him to see if there
were no assumptions of power that conflicted with their
interests, and against whose encroachments they needed
defence. His active mind, ever on the alert to be useful,
was not long in seeing where it could exercise its powers
so as to be a benefactor to his state. There had, from her
earliest history, been upon the statutes of New-York a
law whose requisitions were imprisonment for debt.
Than this law no greater species of barbarism ever prevailed in any country that made pretensions to a spirit
of progressive civilization. The infliction of its penalties
was at direct variance with the genius of any institutions
whose purport was the dissemination of republican princi

ples. Its tendencies were evidently to chill with the
dampness of death the springs of all social organization,
and to cast a withering blight, dark as despair itself,
around the fireside of home. I would have to go too far
back into the musty records of legislative enactment to
lay before my readers the original law, whose tendencies
did so much to retard the progress of the state of New
York for a number of years; but in order that they may
have just conceptions of its cruelty, and some idea of the
humane nature of the man, principally through whose
efforts it was repealed, I insert the following modification
it underwent for the relief of debtors, in 1813. On page
three hundred and forty-eight, chapter seventy-one, of the
old laws of the state of New-York, I find the following :

*"Act for the Relief of Debtors with Respect to the Impris-
onment of their Persons, passed April 1, 1813.*

" Be it enacted by the people of the state of New
York, represented in the general assembly, That every
person not a freeholder, who shall be confined in goal
upon any execution or other process, or by virtue of any
judgment or order of any court of justice, or by warrant from any judge or justice, for any debt, sum of
money, fine or forfeiture, not exceeding twenty-five dollars, exclusive of costs, and shall have remained in goal
for thirty days, if not detained for any other cause, shall
be discharged from such imprisonment by the keeper of
the goal on application to him by the person so confined;
Provided, always, that nothing herein contained shall
extend to cases of imprisonment under the act entitled

An act for the speedy recovery of debts to the value
of twenty-five dollars.' "

With this modification for the relief of debtors the law
of imprisonment for debt remained upon the statutes of
the Empire State, and preyed upon the vitality of social
happiness from 1813 until it was wiped from the books
through the instrumentality of Millard Fillmore in 1830.
It seems strange that a people proverbial for their progressive refinement as are those of New York, should
have suffered such an enactment to pollute the records of
their judiciary for such a length of time.   But a spirit
of radical partisanship pervading all classes of society,
patriotism, and the good of the people, were made secondary considerations by politicians, who, through the factions of a dominant party, exercised especial guardianship over the laws of the state, and under that law the
people were obliged to groan until the elevation to power
of some one who thought more of them than of his own
aggrandizement.

Immediately after the convention of the assembly, Mr.
Fillmore began to devote his talented energy to the
repeal of that odious law.   His anxiety for its repeal
was original with himself — the dictates both of his
nature and his duty as a committee-man for the public defence, were to plant himself the champion of the
people, to prevent the further operation of a law that
incarcerated the only support and head of a family in a
prison for a debt, no part of which was liquidated by
the cruel process.   His strong desire for its repeal orig-

inated from the humanity of his nature, as well as the
impolicy of the enactment.

I have examined carefully the message of Gov. Throop
to the assembly immediately after that body had convened, and though it is replete with wise suggestions upon
matters of state policy coming legitimately under cog-
nizance of that legislature, I find nothing in relation to
that odious law. Though he showed with mathematical
precision the condition of the state finances, and very
properly called the attention of the members to the condition of the hospitals, asylums, and state prisons, he
made no allusion relevant to the law by whose enforcement the prisons were filled — a law that manacled
instead of protecting the laboring classes, and while it
hand-cuffed the debtor was of no utility to the creditor.

At an early day after the organization of the house,
Mr. Fillmore opened his intentions to the members, concerning the repeal of that law. Much as they admired
his sagacity and firmness, and well as they were convinced of his intellectual powers, they were not prepared
for this bold stand against a law that had been venerated
by their ancestry, and sacredized by long usage. Though
the stand he took against it was sustained by arguments,
whose justness and logical force were unanswerable, it
met with fierce and instantaneous opposition.

Immediately after the disclosure of his intentions concerning that law his sentiments were endorsed by some
of the leading and most talented members on the floor,
who coöperated with him until it was repealed. Among
these were Thurlow Weed and Francis Granger, men of

acknowledged ability as legislators. On the 13th day of February, 1830, a memorial was presented to the assembly, signed by a large number of inhabitants of the city of New York, styling themselves the "general executive committee of mechanics, working men, and their friends, praying for the abolishment of imprisonment for debt." I have inserted this in the precise language in which it is couched on the records of the assembly, to show to what classes of population the operation of such a law was most injurious — "mechanics, working men, and their friends." This memorial was followed by others of a like nature, that poured in from all parts of the state, after the agitation of the measure, until they were piled, a voluminous mass, into the assembly. Such appeals as these, from mechanics, working men, and their friends, could not be made in vain to an assembly where Mr. Fillmore was a prominent member. In all three of these positions he had been himself. He had been a laborer from boyhood. He was a mechanic by trade, and though his talents and energy had placed him at the head of an honorable profession, and in the assemblies of his country, he was a friend to the laboring man. To their appeals for the abolition of a law that fettered their energies and threw them into prison for every unexpected or unfavorable turn of fortune, he responded with his efforts in their behalf.

For the "mechanics, the laboring men and their friends," as styled in the language of the memorial, Mr. Fillmore has always entertained the highest respect, and been solicitous to promote their interests. He evinced it not only in his efforts in the assembly, that resulted in the repeal of a law subversive of their happiness and detrimental to their best interests, but his whole career has been an exhibition of solicitude to protect their interests. Cradled in a wilderness, the tillage of whose soil was his early means of support, he was himself a laborer, and has always regarded "laboring men and their friends" as the true nobility of the country. Schooled in the lessons of adversity, as a young tradesman, in a wool carder's shop, he learned the morality of labor, and became a sympathizer with the mechanic. Such an appeal as couched in the language of the memorial, aided by his own ulterior convictions as regarded the enormity of the law, induced him to put his whole soul into the work of its abolition.

Bitter and fierce was the opposition he had to encounter. Reason and right were on his side as efficient weapons to contend with an assumptive arrogance and a dictatorial superiority of feeling on the opposition. In his advocacy of this measure, Mr. Fillmore was acting in compliance with a loftier virtue than even patriotism itself. It was the dictates of philanthropy, whose broad principles embrace not only a love of country, but whose divine attributes are a love for the human race, and a desire to relieve the oppressed. In vindication of his position against that law, he advanced arguments so unanswerable, and so calculated to impress conviction, the general interest created in regard to it became the one absorbing question of the assembly. Even party politics were for once forgotten in a democratic legislature, and the discordant elements of rivalrous creeds seemed to harmonize for the purpose of centrality around this important focus of general attraction.

The principles he entertained in regard to the repeal of the law he embodied in a bill, with a view to their ultimate passage, and incorporation into the laws of the state. The discussion of this bill of Mr. Fillmore's moncopolized a large portion of the time and talents of the entire body throughout the session of 1830. Mr. Fillmore was anxious for its passage. The petitions that flooded the house from all parts of the state, praying relief, filled his bosom with the warmest sympathies. Imprisonment for debt was practised by the old Romans, and other countries of ancient times, and had been handed down to more civilized ages, till in most of the European countries, great as was their boasted refinement at that time, under the sanction of law, the free citizen was dragged to prison for the non-payment of a debt which he was wholly unable to discharge. And to see the same barbarous relic upon the statutes of the greatest state of the only Republic in the world was to him a source of great mortification, to say nothing of the immediate suffering and misery it occasioned in the infliction of its penalties. Bold and fearless was the stand he took, and earnest were the denunciations he poured against its odious features. In his appeals to the members of the house upon the expediency of adopting his bill for its abolition, he gave expositions of its deformities that were calculated to fill the mind with disgust, when contemplating it divested of its drapery. With sympathetic pathos he portrayed the wretchedness it entailed upon the domestic circle, by tearing the parent from the embrace of his offspring, and fettering him in a dungeon. Then, with indignant warmth, he poured his denunciations against the cruelty of a law, that gave one individual the right to deprive another of his liberty, by placing him in a jail. Then again, he showed the absurd inutility of a legal enactment that gave to an individual the right to punish another as remuneration for something of value. He showed the extreme folly of a measure, the infliction of whose cruel penalties upon one individual was the only redress it afforded another; whose evident tendencies were to foster a spirit of revengeful cruelty on the part of those disposed to avail themselves of its power. Then, turning to the prayerful petitions piled upon their daily deliberations in behalf of suffering humanity, he appealed to the better feelings of the members of the house, in order to elicit their support of a measure he deemed so fraught with blessings to the whole state.

By an industrious application of his energies and talents to this his favorite measure, he fondly hoped to witness its passage before the expiration of the session. When we view the *modification* of that law, and see the pernicious influences its enforcement was bound to have upon society, it seems a matter of surprise that intelligent legislators would oppose a bill the object of which was its repeal. Yet such was the case. A large number of the members of that legislature arrayed themselves against the measure, and fiercely contested every inch of ground over which it had to pass, until its final adoption.

Their arguments were based certainly upon no considerations consistent with the advancement of the people's interest or upon the dictates of a patriotic desire to ameliorate the condition of the country whose interests it was their peculiar province to promote.

The idea of a law, prevailing in the most refined state of a republican government, whose penalty was the imprisonment of a freeman for the commission of no crime, for the perpetration of no heinous offence revolting to the feelings of humanity, no further back than twenty-six years ago, is strange enough. But to find men of talent identified with members opposed to the enactment of a bill whose object was to repeal a law containing such revolting penalties is still more strange. The only merit such a law could have was its similarity to some of those in operation in European and monarchical governments, and the predication of its principles upon custom and long usage. Singular enough it seems that the members of the democratic legislature, so progressive in everything else, should array themselves in such deadly hostility against the removal of this barbarous relic from the statutes of the state, and regard Mr. Fillmore's bill in the light of a dangerous innovation.

Mr. Fillmore, in discussing the principles of his bill, took the correct view in regard to the utility of measures calculated to promote the happiness of the people, and to preserve the dignity of the commonwealth. Imprisonment or the deprivation of liberty he regarded as a penalty whose infliction should only be enforced for the commission of a crime repugnant alike to the laws of

God and man. As a crime of this nature he was not disposed to view the indebtedness of one man to another. There are many causes of which such indebtedness may be the legitimate result. Through the treachery or incapacity of an endorsee, through an unexpected occurrence of an accidental nature, through an unseen and an unfavorable interposition of Providence, and many other causes, an individual in affluent circumstances to-day, to-morrow may be hurled into the abyss of bankruptcy. Then, under the operation of such a law, though to-day he is honored and respected, to-morrow, amid the rage and invectives of importunate creditors, a culpable wretch, he is torn from his family and thrown into prison. With such considerations as these, through the deliberations of the entire session of 1830, did Mr. Fillmore urge upon the house with zeal and warmth the necessity that existed for the adoption of his bill. But they remained unmoved. Though his arguments they could not answer, and saw, because they were compelled to see, the intrinsic excellencies of the bill, they would not endorse it. They commenced a violent opposition to its conditions on its first agitation in the house, and were determined at least to prove they were consistent in their hostility.

In the preservation of their consistency they created such obstacles to the passage of the bill, that the energies of its friends were constantly devoted to it through the labors of the whole session.

From the introduction of the bill into the house, it had been the leading general measure, and had encountered the fiercest opposition from some of the most talated members on the floor. The labors of the session were drawing to a close, a considerable amount of business remained to be transacted, and the friends of the bill began to despair of its success during that session. Mr. Fillmore had guarded the interests of his county with the same fidelity he had the previous year, and in his advocacy of his bill for the abolishment of imprisonment for debt had displayed marked ability and great legislative zeal. He had proposed and had been chiefly instrumental in the passage of many local measures, subservative of his constituency's interests, and occupied an elevated position among the members of the house. So zealous was he in behalf of his county, that by reference to the assembly journal of 1830, I find that the city of Buffalo and Erie county were the recipients of more legislative action upon measures of a local nature than was any other locality in the state, except Rochester. Earnest as had been his efforts in behalf of his bill, the session closed without being able to effect its passage.

On the close of the session he returned to Buffalo and again resumed the practice of law, hoping no further services of a public nature would be required at his hands by his fellow citizens. In this, however, he was mistaken. Too well were they convinced of the safe repository of their interests in his hands to allow him to surrender them to others. His earnest endeavors to be of service to his county, and the active stand he had taken against the imprisonment for debt law, had endeared him to the people, and especially to the mechanics, laboring men

and their friends, who had flooded the halls of the legislature with their prayers for relief.

From the philanthropic manner in which he had responded to their appeals, they regarded him as the champion of the laboring man's rights — the protector of the
people's interest. He was reëlected to the assembly of
1831, and took his seat on the fourth of January, firmly
resolved to devote himself to the passage of the bill
which had elicited such general interest the previous session. This session of the legislature was to be one of
unusual interest; the people looked to its labors for the
fulfillment of their hopes, in regard to the adoption of
some measure doing away with imprisonment for debt.
The whole state, in fact, manifested great interest in reference to that measure from the first agitation on the
floor of the assembly.

From the message of Governor Throop, delivered to
the assembly on the fourth of January, 1831, I make the
following extracts, showing that Mr. Fillmore's measure
of the precedent legislature elicited executive interest
favorable to its adoption: "Our laws relative to imprisonment for debt should be carefully examined for the
purpose of amendment. The notion of imprisonment, in
the nature of punishment for debt, is repugnant to humanity, and condemned by wisdom.

"Imprisonment for debt should be tolerated so far,
only, as it is necessary to enable the creditor to secure
the property of his debtor."

These wise and patriotic sentiments were the same as

embodied in the bill, for whose passage Mr. Fillmore labored so earnestly the session before.

Among men of prominence in the assembly who endorsed the principles of the bill and came to its rescue were J. C. Spencer and John Van Buren, who advocated its passage until it became a law. In the appointment of committees, Mr. Fillmore was placed at the head of the committee on bills coming under the requisitions of the constitution in accordance with the rules of the house, a position of considerable importance. Immediately after organization, the assembly halls were reflooded with petitions in regard to measures embraced in the repeal bill. It was discussed in the house with all the zeal its friends could command, and contested with fierceness by its enemies. On the thirty-first of March the house resolved itself into a committee of the whole upon the bill, and its merits were discussed in all their bearings. The special committee to whom it had been referred reported some amendments to it, and it was submitted to the house. This bill of which Mr. Fillmore was the principal drafter, covers several pages in the assembly journal, and is one of the ablest legislative enactments upon the statutes of the state of New York. That portion of it relating to justices' and other subordinate courts, is particularly able, and evinces a thorough understanding of the whole legal complexity of the times. No one can look over that bill without becoming convinced, that its drafter was not only a legislator of consummate ability and a lawyer of unsurpassed attainments, but that he understood well the principles of good government, and the nature of laws best adapted to the

6

necessities of the times. The requisitions of that bill, while they are sufficiently inductious of a spirit of prompt punctuality on the part of the debtor, embrace facilities of vindicatory redress, for the creditor, of a far more efficient nature than were afforded by the old law. While the humane provisions it embodied protected the creditor from the infliction of penalties due only the votaries of crime, they extended to the debtor the safest means for the recovery of his dues. While they preserved the liberties that God had given the creditor from subjection to the rigors of imprisonment, they gave to the debtor the legalized right to the proceeds of his labor. Thus, by giving the creditor no means for the collection of his debts but the chattels of his creditors, the inducements to permit the contraction of a heavy indebtedness were curtailed, and, by making the goods of the debtor liable for his debts, a desire to live within his means was created. By its operation, mutual protection was guaranteed to all, and the interests of the country promoted. Subjected to some amendments of no very material nature, it was submitted to the house on the thirty-first of March 1831, and was passed by a considerable majority; Mr. Fillmore, J. C. Spencer, and John Van Buren, voting in the affirmative. This was followed by its immediate passage in the senate, and, on the twenty-first of April, Mr. Fillmore and the friends of his measure had the pleasure of seeing it stamped with executive sanction, by the following message to the house:

" To the Assembly :

"*Gentlemen:* I have this day approved and signed the bill entitled an 'Act to abolish imprisonment for debt,' etc.

" E. T. Throop."

Thus the bill for whose passage he was so desirous had passed both houses, received the executive signature, and was incorporated into the laws of his state. At the result he was highly gratified. Thus the odious law was wiped forever from the statutes of the state. To Mr. Fillmore, more than any one else, are the people of that state indebted for the removal from their books of a law whose every feature is repugnant to the genius of a Christianized country and revolting to humanity itself. In the passage of many measures of great public utility, Mr. Fillmore took an active part ; among other laws, the establishment of a " Mechanics benefit society," and several measures for the promotion of educational facilities and the protection of industry. For three consecutive sessions he represented his country in the state assembly. He did it faithfully ; the happy results of his labors were felt not only over his own county, but over the entire state. For the repeal of the law of imprisonment for debt, he labored with zeal until the last day of the session, and was rewarded by the passage of his bill introduced for that purpose. The assembly of 1831, adjourned April 26th, and Mr. Fillmore returned again to Buffalo. These were his last services in that body : he was never again a member of the assembly. He resumed the duties of his profession, and the enjoyments of private life, with the esteem of his fellow citizens, and the plaudits of conscience.

The following, among the legislative portraits of the most prominent members of the assembly of 1831, was written by an excellent judge of human character, for one of the leading New York journals of that day, and shows the elevated position occupied by Mr. Fillmore in that body:

"Millard Fillmore, of Erie county, is of the middle stature, five feet nine inches in height. He appears to be about thirty-five years of age, but it is said he is no more than thirty, of light complexion, regular features, and of a mild and benign countenance.

"His ancestors were among the hardy sons of the north, and during the revolution were whigs, inhabiting the Green Mountains of Vermont. Mr. Fillmore, from the commencement of his political career, has been a republican. He is, in the strictest sense of the term, a self-made man. He was educated and reared in the western district of our state. At an early period of life he went to the fulling business; but naturally of an inquiring mind, and anxious to increase his limited stock of knowledge, his leisure hours were occupied in reading. When about twenty years of age, he retired from his former pursuits, and after having studied the law as a profession, he was licensed to practice. He was a member of the last legislature.

"Although the age of Mr. Fillmore does not exceed thirty years, he has all the prudence, discretion, and judgment of an experienced man. He is modest, retiring

and unassuming. He appears to be perfectly insensible
of the rare and happy qualities of the mind for which he
is so distinguished. He exhibits, on every occasion, when
called into action, a mildness and benignity of temper,
mingled with firmness of purpose, that is seldom concen-
trated in the same individual. His intercourse with the
bustling world is very limited. His books, and occasionally the rational conversation of intelligent friends, seem
to constitute his happiness. He is never to be found in
the giddy mazes of fashionable life, and yet there is in his
manner an indescribable something which creates a strong
impression in his favor, and which seems to characterize
him as a well-bred gentleman. He possesses a logical
mind, and there is not a member of the house who presents
his views on any subject which he attempts to discuss in
a more precise and luminous manner. He seldom speaks,
unless there appears to be an absolute necessity for the
arguments or explanations which he offers. Nor does he
ever rise without attracting the attention of all who are
within the sound of his voice — a tribute of respect paid
to his youthful modesty and great good sense.

"As a legislator, Mr. Fillmore appears to act with perfect
fairness and impartiality. He examines every subject
distinctly for himself, and decides upon its merits according to the best lights of his own judgment or understanding. He is now at an age when his character is to be
irrevocably fixed. As a politician, he is not formed to be
great. He has none of the qualities requisite for a political chieftain. He wants that self-confidence and assurance
without which a partizan leader can never hope for fol

lowers. Mr. Fillmore's love of books and habits of thinking will ultimately conduct him to a more tranquil but
higher destiny, if the one is not broken open and the
other diverted from its natural course to the too often
polluted and always turbulent if not mortifying results
of faction. If he has not sufficient courage to resist
the allurements which legislation presents to young and
ambitious men, then ought his friends to act for him, and
refuse him a renomination. It is a life which not only
casts to the winds of heaven all employment as a professional man, but it uproots sooner or later the germs of
industry and the delights of study. These are the admon-
itions of age and experience. As a debater in the house,
his manner is good, his voice agreeable. Toward his
opponents he never fails to evince a most studied delicacy.
He is mild and persuasive, sometimes animated. His
speeches are pithy and sententious ; always free from idle
and vapid declamation. His arguments are logically
arranged, and presented to the house without embarrassment or confusion."

The writer of the foregoing judged rightly of the evil
consequences of having once been engaged in politics as
regards the generality of young professional men, but
was wide off the mark if he supposed Mr. Fillmore
would be contaminated by political influences. The sound
judgment and the unambitious feelings of Mr. Fillmore
placed him beyond the necessity of his friends acting for
him. He was well aware of the fascination of political
strife, so far as the average of young men in the outset of
their political careers were concerned ; and to avoid the

consequences of falling into the same error himself, he was always careful, as before stated, to commence the duties of his profession as soon as his labors in a public capacity had ceased. As much sagacity, therefore, as the writer of the foregoing article displayed, and as much insight as he evinced, he was much mistaken as to Mr. Fillmore's capacity to assume the leadership of his party, or as to his incurring any danger from the contaminating influences of political station. Yet, as an article showing not only the high stand occupied by Mr. Fillmore among the members of the assembly, but the impression he made upon the spectators, newspaper correspondents, etc., the above sketch is worthy of note.

It must be borne in mind, that the writer, in his delineations of the various members of that body, confined himself to the prominent ones; hence the portraiture of Mr. Fillmore is a complimentary classification with those coming under that head. The confidence and self-assurance wherein he regards Mr. Fillmore so essentially deficient that he could never be a successful political leader, were then, in Mr. Fillmore's character, developments marked and conspicuous. The association of modesty with that of genuine merit, as an invariable accompaniment, is universally conceded by the truly refined in feeling, and those best calculated to form just conceptions of an individual's mental capacity. Luminous exemplifications of extreme modesty, on the part of those who have justly figured most conspicuously in the world's moral progress and developments, generally blaze upon the pages of their early biography. Washington, when he appeared in the house of burgesses, blushed with manifest confusion that in no way abated on being told by a prominent member of the house "his modesty alone was equal to his merit. Chief-justice Kenyon, than whom no greater was ever arrayed in the august robes of the judiciary, was overwhelmed by an inherent modesty, time and again, in his early legal attempts, that he could not suppress, until rising on an occasion in the court room, with his usual timidity and apprehensions of failure, he felt his wife and child pulling at his coat skirts for means of sustenance. By a sudden impulse, he launched into the loftiest sphere of oratory, and produced a masterpiece of forensic eloquence. Modesty is an attendant of true greatness. Men may be, and often are possessed of giant intellects, who exhibit no modest propensities ; but they are invariably men of no great moral calibre. The man who combines the essential elements of true greatness, and personifies them in his daily intercourse, until worn away and supplanted by experience or dignity of soul, will be possessed of a modest nature. Some men have by extraordinary talents constellated in the galaxy of the world's great, unadorned with the mild light of modesty, but their greatness consisted exclusively in their talents ; the purer fountain, the wellspring of the soul, from whence flow the better actions and feelings of human nature, have given no exuberant overflowings of benevolence and love, indicative of true worth. A young man who commences the battle of life with talents, but with no modesty, is but half armed—he has the sword of offence, but not the shield of protection. Mr. Fillmore, as inferable from the foregoing article, had both. He has established with one, and demolished with the other. Though his successful career has placed him among the distinguished of the earth, he is still modest and un-assuming.

6*

CHAPTER IV.

Mr. Fillmore as a lawyer — Brief review of his legal career — His view
   of the law as a science — Advantages of his connection — Spurns
   all artifice and chicanery— Responsibilities of the law — His views
   of its morality — His capacities as a lawyer — His ardent desire
   to promote justice — His weight of character — His faithfulness to
   his clients — In speaking, not a Patrick Henry— Examples of his
   success in civil cases — The Cattaraugus Reservation — The great
   importance of that case — The remarkable Ontario Bank case —
   His argument before the Supreme Court — His success in both.

IT will be remembered that Judge Wood, who first
perceived latent sparks of greatness in Mr. Fillmore
during his early boyhood, was principally instrumental
in directing his mind to the study of the law, and in
inciting it to continual and vigorous prosecution of its
principles. It will also be borne in mind that the difficulties under which Mr. Fillmore labored were of no
ordinary nature, and that in overcoming them he devoted
his energies with unwearied application. The incentives,
as we have seen, for him to assume the mastery of the
profession were of the strongest nature, inasmuch as he
possessed no means to fall back upon in case of failure.
The strong desires of his own bosom were so great to
make rapid proficiency, that he needed no more powerful
incentive. It was then he laid the foundation of his
legal studies, and fixed in his mind the fundamental principles of law. His school of preparation was a rigid one.
Those who are in the pursuit of mental acquisition, under

the tuition of a relentless necessity, have to submit to the most uncompromising of all task-masters. But the efficiency of this preparatory school was, perhaps, much increased by its own rigidity. Thus, bound and circumscribed by the entire control of its mandates, no avenue was open for an indiscriminate range of thought or action; hence a constant concentration of every energy, both mental and physical, was necessarily secured, and astonishing progress followed as an inevitable result. It is doubtless owing in a great degree to these very circumstances of his being thus situated, that he succeeded in laying the basis of his legal pursuits upon so correct a foundation, and impressing his mind so firmly with the groundwork of the law, that have made him a jurist of such consummate ability, and an advocate of such convincing powers and acknowledged worth. In fact, on his first commencement of legal studies, either from his natural reasoning faculties, or from a profound conviction of its importance — perhaps both qualities had an influence— he was particularly careful to acquaint himself thoroughly with the first principles, and to have a complete comprehension of one principle before proceeding to another. The ground he went over was reviewed, if necessary, until its maxims were understood with accurate precision.

After his removal to Buffalo, we have seen that the ardor and anxiety to master his profession suffered no abatement; but, with the increased facilities thrown in his way, burned if possible with increased warmth. In Buffalo, we have seen that he ranked among the most steady young men of the city, and was proverbial for his studious habits. Unallured by the fascinations of city life, he pursued his studies with the quiet, determined spirit to succeed he had manifested on former occasions, and was triumphantly successful in attaining a reputation for sobriety above the generality of young men in the city.

To this unwavering adherence to virtuous principles on the part of Mr. Fillmore, and the continual enforcement of his good resolutions to refrain entirely from all actions not in strict accordance with the dictates of moral principle how much of his success is attributable, it is impossible to imagine. Certain it is that it was the correct course, and the early means of establishing a character for morality and high-toned feelings, the weight of which he has ever since maintained. On his admission to the court of common pleas, which was granted as much through courtesy as otherwise, we have seen that through his extreme diffidence he went to a village which was more the central point of a rural agricultural community than otherwise. Here, in the pursuit of his profession, the great importance attached to his first case proves that he was entirely unconscious of his own great powers. Here, when the first signs of prosperity began to indicate themselves, he resolves to return to Buffalo. In that city we find him soon at the head of his profession, in a connection that was very advantageous to the development of his legal capacities, and to ameliorate his pecuniary condition. Here, attended with the greatest success, we find him engaged in an honorable and lucrative business, employed as counsel on one side or the other of every case for whole days together. We see him preëminently successful in all the courts, much more so than most lawyers of no more experience than he possessed. We find him loved for his good qualities and respected for his talents by the entire population of the city, and rapidly winning his way to the foremost position in the esteem and regard of his fellow citizens. We find him studiously endeavoring to promote the general interests of the people in a manner rendered efficient from the influential elevation assigned him by his fellow citizens. We find him, too, wending his way into the supreme court, and competing successfully with, and eliciting the esteem of Chief-justice Savage, the other associate judges, and the attorneys who practiced at that higher court. Careers of young attorneys may have been more brilliant and meteoric, but none have ever been more staple and sure than the one summed up in the above brief review. Young lawyers may have advanced a reputation a little faster than the progress indicated above, but none have ever established it upon a more solid basis, or attached to it more force and enduring qualities.

The meteoric flash of a precocious genius is frequently mistaken for reputation, and regarded by some as sufficient means for the effectual establishment of a character. There is a fascinating lure about these evanescent blazes of genius that dart their spiral flame above mediocrity and dazzle the eye for the moment, but while looking on it at its brightest period, it flickers into obscurity, and leaves us in darkness. These geniuses

spring up in a moment, and dart right ahead with impet-
uous velocity, and sometimes win our admiration by the
rapidity of their progress. But their careers are usually brief ones. A greater luminary, rising slowly but
surely, that was gathering light while the meteor was
flashing past him, soon overtakes it, and it dies out in
the full blaze of his power. Taking the foundation of
his studies, the vast amount of his legal knowledge, the
compact solidity of his attainments, the accuracy of his
judgment, the weight of his character, and all the essential prerequisites to success, and the career of Mr.
Fillmore as a lawyer is surpassed by no one up to the
time embraced in the foregoing review.

The law, Mr. Fillmore knew, was a difficult science —
an important one, and, in an eager haste to advance,
anxious as he was to do so, he was determined not to go
over it hastily — hence the solidity of his character as a
lawyer.

As this chapter will contain all we expect to say of
Mr. Fillmore's legal career, an enumeration of some of
the advantages derived from his connection with a law-
firm of eminence and celebrity, in the city of Buffalo, it
is presumed, will not be inappropriate. This connection
was, in the first place, the result of a justly high appreciation for his capacities as a lawyer, and his industrious
assiduity in devoting himself to the interests of his clients, and the great influence he threw into a case, by the
weight of his character. From the successful results
of his practice in the village where he had comparatively secluded himself, it was plainly inferable on the

part of the firm by whom the proposition for a connection was made, that, in the prosecution of a very lucrative and widely extended practice, his services would be a valuable appendant.

These, however, were not the only motives by which they were actuated in proposing a connection whose advantages to all parties concerned would be equally manifest. From a desire to promote the interest and extend facilities to deserving merit, which they saw impersonated in Mr. Fillmore, and which they very properly conceived would, with the extension of some advantages, develop itself, to the honor of the profession and the country, at no distant day — the equally advantageous results of such connection was, in making the proposal, doubtless the principal actuation.

With the formation of this connection, already in a very heavy business, from Mr. Fillmore's well known abilities as a practical lawyer of untiring zeal and great success, the business of the firm increased, until it became the foremost in the city. One very essential advantage of this arrangement to Mr. Fillmore, was the removal of an obstacle which, in the outset of their careers, all young, professional men are compelled to combat — the influences of old, established practitioners who, by a successful practice of years, monopolize the entire business of that nature, and leave little room for young aspirants to judicial fame to exert their powers. The business of a legal nature, at the time of this connection, as is usually the case in cities of any importance, was in the hands of **those who had been practicing their profession with suc-**

cess, and the firm with which it was made being a resident one, of course got a liberal share. His connection, therefore, threw him into immediate practice of a lucrative and an honorable nature without having to combat the obstacles alluded to, and, by his successful management of cases intrusted into his hands, and the position of universal popularity he attained among the people, contributed much to increase the business of the office. Of this, and all such advantages thrown in his way during the commencement of his professional life, than Mr. Fillmore, no one was more sure to avail himself to the fullest extent. By no one were such advantages more thoroughly understood, or their bestowal more highly appreciated. From this connection, to Mr. Fillmore the results were most gratifying, and most happy in facilitating his progress.

Another advantage, and a very decided one, was the daily association with men eminent for their legal acumen, and familiarly conversant with the details of the practice of a very efficient and talented bar, and immediate connection with an extensive business. The opportunities were good, under these advantages, for him to become familiarized with the difficulties of office practice, and to understand the application of the theoretical to the practical part of the profession. On Mr. Fillmore's return to Buffalo, those of a practical nature were the only parts of the law wherein he was in the least deficient, and only so in them from want of that experimental exercise necessary to insure, in all cases, a correct application of principles to a particular case. The theory of the law few understood better ; by the strict devotion of his time and talents to its principles from the time he commenced reading, he had assumed their complete mastery.   In the admirable school for its consummation, he now found him-self—with the same zeal that he formerly evinced in understanding the theoretical, he applied himself to the practical.   The incentive was no greater than formerly, but less diffident in his nature, and from previous indica-tions more sanguine of success, his efforts were charac-terized with a buoyancy of spirit and a vigor of feeling incident to a consciousness of an appropriate investiture of talents that did not attend his labors to the same extent through the wearisome hours of his studentship. So well had he become aquainted with the theory of law, and so correct was he in the formation of the basis of his legal investigations, by a thorough comprehension of its fundamental principles, that the practice, after he was once thrown into it, was readily understood.

Mr. Fillmore, in the early part of this connection, was the practical lawyer of the firm in most cases, and de-veloped capacities of a truly practical attorney.   Mr. Fillmore is essentially a matter-of-fact practical man.   In discharging the duties of a heavy office practice, mani-festing no desire for display, or to create an impression by any extraordinary rhetorical flourishes, he confined himself exclusively to the points at issue, and said no more than was necessary to explain the law and the facts. In doing this, making no attempts at eloquence, indulg-ing in no witticisms or sarcastic hits, he was plain, ear-nest, and pointed.   He was a business young attorney,

and consumed no more time than was absolutely necessary in the disposition of cases. Heavy business
pressing upon his hands, the transaction of which demanded his constant attention, he killed no precious hours
by indulging in long speeches. Quick and forcible, carrying conviction along with delivery, his addresses to a
jury or a court were only excelled in efficiency by their
brevity. The various courts of the city were excellent
schools wherein he could train his mind to a perfect state
of legal discipline, in the investigation of the various
causes there brought for trial. In the justices' and other
courts, before which for judicial investigation thronged
large numbers of litigants and offenders indicted for such
misdemeanors as are incident to a densely populated city,
he had ample opportunities for the development and cultivation of his legal capacities. Mr. Fillmore derived
great advantages from this connection, from the fact that
he was brought on terms of familiarity, and came daily
in intercourse, both legally and socially, with the numerous friends and acquaintances of the older resident members of the firm. In the contraction of acquaintances,
and the social intercourse of the citizens, and keeping
pace with the affairs of the city, this was a medium of
infinite advantage. The natural adaptation of Mr. Fillmore's character to the formation of friendships, and to
make pleasant those with whom he comes in contact,
made this avenue of social intercourse peculiarly pleasing,
to say nothing of the advantages accruing to a professional
man, from a medium through which he can become

acquainted with the citizens of a place, with whose interests he anticipates a permanent identification of his own.

As an instance of the high-toned nature of Mr. Fillmore in the practice of the law, and to show that duty and a high appreciation for his fellow-citizens' rights were his guide, it may be observed that, notwithstanding a long career of unexampled success as a lawyer, the friends and associations he formed at that early day are his friends still. Even those with whom he most frequently came in contact, in the various courts of their practice, both counsels and clients, against whom, in the discharge of his duty as an attorney, he labored, are, and have always been, his friends. This is indicative of the very exalted course he has pursued in his practice. Mr. Fillmore, in the practice of his profession, has taken the rights of his fellow men for his study, the constitution of his country for the basis of his actions, and the ten commandments for his guide. Those contained in Lord Brougham's celebrated eulogium are the views of Mr. Fillmore in regard to the law and its duties. His is the history of a career in the profession of eminent brilliancy, untarnished by a resort to that chicanery and artifice with which it is invested in the minds of many persons. Mr. Fillmore regards the law as a moral superstructure, round which the rights of the people gather for protection, and regards it the duty of the attorney to guard those rights with watchful anxiety. Law he regards as the noblest of sciences, the leading science as the protector of all others. The laws of his country he looks upon as the guarantee of those popular rights belonging to the

people, in their aggregate capacity, and secondary in point
of morals only to the divine code. Far from the views
expressed by Anacharsis, in regard to the law, are those
entertained by Mr. Fillmore. It has no entangling meshes
of such a peculiar construction that, while the poor man
is warped in its fibres, the wealthy one breaks through
with impunity, and defies with his lucre the violated law.
Based upon that of the divinity itself, though far from
immaculate purity, the law is the palladium of the
people — the bulwark of freedom.

Entertaining exalted conceptions of the laws of his
country second only to those of his God, when he embarked in the profession, in vindicating the one he felt his
actions were in obedience to the other. Looking upon
the law as the basis of the people's rights, and the great
umpire to whose decisions their grievances are to be submitted, he resolved if he impressed it at all, it should be
with the signet of virtue. Esteeming it as the highest
privilege to live the unfettered sovereign of a free soil,
under a system of laws whose principles are equal rights,
in the mazy labyrinths of legal investigation, he resolved
that justice should lead the van. Feeling with the genuine sensibility of nature's nobleman, the responsibilities
resting upon one whose duties are in the very sanctuary
of justice, he determined to make honor the expounder
of his theory, and in practice to be her amanuensis. Erect
in the majesty of his own moral purity, he regarded his
fellow men as his brothers, and resolved to devote his
talents to the promotion of their interests. Regarding
the laws of the land as belonging to the people, as a

sacred legacy secured by their ancestral blood, he determined to uphold them by the power of moral force, unsullied by any act of his. With these high opinions and resolves in regard to the laws of his country, he commenced their vindication, as a professional practitioner of their principles. He has maintained their honor and exemplified his good resolutions.

Being thus duly impressed with high and elevated sentiments of the law, and having embraced it as his profession, his next investigation was to ascertain the duties it involved. High and responsible were his conclusions in regard to their nature. The lawyer is the defender of justice — that great potent arbiter of man's destiny — the blind goddess who weighs our transactions, and hovers over human destiny with a retributive sword. In *her* august presence must the lawyer bring his client, to have his rights protected and his wrongs redressed. Impartial to all, blind as she is to all save the equitable rendition of her own decrees, he must stand in her presence, her own advocate, or the advocate of a fellow man. The advocate — the defender of justice, the immaculate attribute of a God. In what vocation are the responsibilities so great as in this? As a defender of justice, Mr. Fillmore, in the practice of the law has been blind as she, save in the attainment of her ends. Justice has been his maxim, and in the practice of the law he conceived it his duty to make everything subordinate to its attainment. Instead of making principle subservient to policy, he always made policy subservient to principle, and success subservient to right. Away with the Jesuitical notion of ends sanctify-

ing the means, when you expect its demonstration by his
resorting to any artifice, not strictly embraced in the true
code of honor, to gain a cause, or to consummate any
other undertaking !

As a follower of a profession whose objects are the
protection of the people's rights and the redress of their
wrongs, to their fullest extent, he has appreciated his
duties as a conservator of the general wellfare. In discharging his duties as a lawyer, he never overlooked
those of a relative nature, but regarding the main object
of his profession the promotion of the general interests
of the country, he was faithful in the discharge of every
duty. Entertaining correct views as to the ennobling
nature of his profession and its objects, when not perverted
for the subservience of individual interests, he felt it his
duty to honor his vocation, and to exemplify that virtue
and justice its design is to promote. As a lawyer, he
was a repository of the people's aggregate interests, and
he felt the magnitude of the responsibility to its fullest
extent. Notwithstanding the chicanery that has become
attached to the law in the minds of many, he fully understood the influence exerted by the profession in moulding
opinion and giving tone to society, and he resolved in his
conduct to personify the virtues to whose protection his
profession was a constant guarantee. This was not
merely the suggestive dictate of the importance of exem-
plifying the virtues of his profession, but it was in obedience to the dictates of a heart ever alive to an active
moral principle. These duties, as pertaining to his profession, he endeavored to understand thoroughly and to

demonstrate in his daily practice. In both he has succeeded most admirably.

He also entered upon the law with full convictions as to its morality. He looked upon it as being a protector of public and private morals, and felt that, as such, there was an intrinsic morality attached to law itself. In an extensive practice of several years, from causes over which he had no control, he has often been counsel on the wrong side, but frequently on the right, as preference for the right side produced some attention on his part to be there, when not inconsistent with previous arrangements. This preference indicates his feelings as regards the morality of the law. He has often, from a nice sense of duty, declined the acceptance of a fee from individuals, the gaining of whose cause would be in violation of moral principle and subversive of public justice. In his office, while engaged in a heavy practice at the different courts in the city, he was frequently consulted by clients who were anxious to become acquainted with the law in regard to certain cases in which they were, or expected to be, litigant parties. It was his custom to answer them frankly, holding out no false hopes of success beyond those that really existed; and if, after an investigation, he perceived there was no chance for the client, he never deluded him with false hopes of success, for the sake of a fee. On such occasions, he would tell the applicant frankly there was no chance of his being successful. These things show that deep current of moral principle that ever flows in Mr. Fillmore's bosom. Looking upon the law as a noble profession, he wished to honor it, and manifest in his actions the importance he attached to an exemplary life as a lawyer.

Mr. Fillmore has always attached a high toned morality to the law, which he was anxious to see infused into the minds of his professional brethren, thereby giving tone to the vocation. This elevated idea was, at that time, considerably in advance of the day, and is yet, to a great extent. This high moral principle in connection with Mr. Fillmore's legal practice has been evinced on all occasions. He always refrained from taking advantage of any legal technicality, to gain his case at the defeat of public justice. In examining creditable witnesses, he never subjected them to the torture of a cross-examination, with a view of making them contradict themselves, by becoming so confused as to invalidate their own testimony. Nor did he ever twist and distort evidence elicited before courts for the purpose of gaining a cause. In no case has he entered into a cause merely for a triumph, at the sacrifice of justice.

Among the admirably adapted capacities of Mr. Fillmore for the successful prosecution of the law, may be classed his extreme coolness and entire self-possession. Be the cause important as it might, and though it elicited a general interest amounting to excitement, unmoved in the prevailing tumult, he has sustained his entire equanimity, and never lost sight of the important issues involved, or neglected any precautionary step necessary to secure success. Mr. Fillmore is wholly invulnerable to the influences of wild excitements and tumultuous exhibitions of feeling. He feels upon subjects of general interest, as well as those of a professional nature, the great importance involved in their different bearings, as keenly as any one ; but the feeling is essentially inside, and while, with a clear, vigorous perception, he scans the course for him to pursue, his self-control subdues all manifestations of excitement.

Thus, in the practice of his profession, he coolly, and by deliberate reflection, investigated his case, and thoroughly understood all its points, and the principles of law relevant thereto, so that, in presenting it to the court, in a calm, self-possessed manner, he laid it all systematically open, and by his logical reasoning seldom failed impressing conviction. This self-control which is of itself indicative of an elevated soul, threw great weight into his arguments, especially as it was accompanied by a forcible impressment of his views. It also gave a true cast to the natural dignity of his character, that was always sure to elicit the respect of the court and the entire members of the bar, who witnessed the management of his cases.

Instead of being excited himself, the preservation of his self-control and entire dignity enabled him to elucidate the complications of cases in such a manner as to impress the court with his superior legal attainments, and to convince it of the force of his reasoning. This coolness and self-possessed dignity are decided advantages in the practice of the law.

An individual rises before a court as counsel in a case without these qualities, be he eloquent as he may, though he succeed in eliciting the respect of the court and the

7

attention of the jury — though he may please with his fluency and attract with his gesticulation, his excitement lessens the potency of his arguments, and, notwithstanding the rivited attention he secures, he fails to produce conviction. He pleases, but does not convince; and, on being replied to by a cool, methodical attorney, who systematically brings up his facts, his law, and his evidence to the point at issue, and throws the weight of his dignity and self-possession into the case, he is lost sight of altogether.

There is a marked difference in the elements of an orator whose sphere is to touch the springs of feeling in mixed and popular assemblages by eloquent appeals, and those of the practical attorney, whose sphere is to investigate the different judicial decisions, and to analyze the actions of men when subjected to the test of legal enactment. Phillips was an orator — a very great one; but as a practical attorney, except in cases admissive of those mighty appeals and spontaneous outbursts of oratorical powers characteristic of him, he was not very extraordinary. Of the practical attorney's requisites to success, these analytical faculties of mind and clear reasoning powers may be classed among the most essential.

There is a potency in this dignity and self-possession, so consummate a blending of which we find in Mr. Fillmore, that is not fully understood by young attorneys, nor sufficiently sought after in the outset of their professional career. In an eager haste to drive forward and to take a prominent stand at the bar, they too frequently attach more importance to display than to the attainment of the more solid qualifications; hence, they follow their profession without the stability of a correct basis, or the weight of solid proportions. Mr. Fillmore, as a practitioner of superior and inferior courts, always manifested this trait of his character. He has never had any unimportant cases, upon which he conceived the bestowal of but little attention a sufficient discharge of duty. His high conceptions for the rights of his fellow man has always made him regard all cases where the adjudication of these rights were involved as a matter of great importance, ánd devoted his attention to the promotion of a little right—to use the expression—with the same promptness and fidelity that he would a large one.   In this respect he has known no small rights, and discriminated between no small wrongs. The enforcement of right, be it of whatsoever nature, and the redress of wrong is sufficient to secure his undivided attention. Hence, in all cases he maintained his dignity and self-control, careful not to overlook the performance of duty from any unimportant aspects of the case. From the circumstances that surrounded him from his commencement of his studies, in having to use inflexible perseverance, and in his school of preparation, this quality of self-control was most happily developed.

Among the attributes of his success, his weight of character may be ranked prominent and conspicuous. This, on the part of Mr. Fillmore, was not an attainment acquired by association or otherwise. In point of stability of character he was always in advance of his age.

In early childhood, his quiet, grave, and obedient deportment was superior to other children. In boyhood, an age when the frolicsome gaieties of youth first begin to develop themselves, he exhibited these traits of character. So, we perceive that, instead of its being the result of association or cultivation, it was an inherent part of his nature, and the more effective because entirely divested of all semblance of affectation. In the trial of causes wherein the talents of the most prominent members of the bar were secured, this array of reason, fact, logic, and weight of character, presented by Mr. Fillmore, was a formidable barrier, not easy to demolish or overleap. This is the most important and most difficult of construction of any part of a young professional man's qualifications.

The first thing to be sought after is the establishment of a character. This is, and must be, the basis on which he builds his profession. It is consequently the most important of all qualifications. No talents, be they transcendent as they may, can exert an influential potency, if deprived of the moral impetus of character. An individual who can throw no weight of character into an argument can have no great influence in producing conviction. One whose talents blaze most conspicuously in arguments to a court or jury loses more potency than he is aware of, if deprived of the weight attendant upon a moral calibre. A man who embarks in the law is presupposed to entertain desires vindicatory of justice, truth. and moralty. It is very manifest that in such vindication he loses much power by a continual violation of these precepts, in pursuing a course inconsistent with all moral principle. Such an one may be eloquent — attractively so, and please the attention, but, like the rainbow, it is based upon mist, and disappears with the ray that produced it. Not so with the man of moral calibre. He is a man of character, of weight — the very fact of his engaging in a cause, gives tone to the side on which his services are secured. And when it is brought forward for trial and elucidation, each argument he deduces with a view to promote justice possesses weight, and is regarded as such, because his whole past character has been its exemplification. Any principle he advances, any law he quotes, any idea he may produce, are favorable to the development of truth, because his whole character has displayed an undeviating adherence to its principles. All his actions and movements, instead of being watched like an artful trickster, are regarded as honorable, and receive implicit reliance, from the fact that his past character is an unsullied exhibit of virtuous principles. Such are some of the advantages possessed by men of moral weight in the pursuit of a profession. These advantages Mr. Fillmore has always possessed in an eminent degree. Looking to his example, let young professional men learn to "get knowledge," "get an understanding" of their vocation; "but with all their getting" let them first get that most desirable of all qualifications — *a character.*

Mr. Fillmore, as before indicated, owes no part of his brilliant success as a lawyer to any extraordinary endowments of forensic eloquence, that more than anything else builds a man up in the outset of his profession, because

the deficiency of experience is partially supplied with oratorical powers. Unlike Patrick Henry, of whom it has
been said, with six weeks' preparation and but little
knowledge of the law, he commenced a career of unexampled success, and was in the very outset called the " forest-
born Demosthenes." Mr. Fillmore possessed no such advantages. He is no orator — makes no pretensions to
oratorical powers, yet, with the other, and not less effective
mental endowments, he is a good speaker, and always says
something to the purpose, and that will be remembered.
For the bar, in judicial proceedings, his eloquence was
well adapted for its convincing and logical attributes.
The earnestness of his manner in addresses to courts and
juries gave great force to his arguments and reasoning, and
has had a very favorable influence to his success. His
zeal in the prosecution of a case, when he had once undertaken it, was surpassed by no one. On taking charge of
a case, he felt himself the repository of his client's rights,
and was as careful and zealous in a faithful discharge of
duty as if those rights had been his own.

The activity and zeal he always displayed in the protection of his client's interest, and the faithful guardianship he exercised over the rights reposed in his keeping,
added greatly in the attainment of that universal popularity for which Mr. Fillmore became proverbial, immediately after his embarkation in the practice.

This zeal, too, in the exact preparation of his cases,
and to be in possession of all the law needed in their
prosecution before they came into court, was the precursor
of many early successes, and contributed not a little to

the establishment of a reputation at once enviable, and commensurate with the most successful.   From this careful zeal in the complete arrangement of his business, before announced from the docket he was fully enabled to have his thoughts arranged, and prepared to avail himself of all honorable advantages arising from any deficiency in that respect, on the part of the opposing counsel. Combining, then, the advantages of these previous investigations with those derived from his superior insight of character before mentioned, he came to the case not only in the " whole armour of the law," but doubly fortified by extraneous facilities.   Mr. Fillmore's appearance before the court in the argument of cases, though he threw no enchanting charm about him by a terrific blaze of oratory that captivates hearers, was one of great dignity, and calculated to draw the attention of the most casual observer.

A desire to promote justice in all its impartial rigor, and to advance the rights of those who came to her temple for redress, was manifest in his actions.   Standing erect in his dignity, with an expression of feature sternly benevolent, self-possessed, and calm, exhibiting a superiority of which he seemed entirely ignorant, he forcibly, and with all the earnestness and weight of character belonging to his nature, presented his case, and piled facts and principles around it that would be difficult to remove, then gave it all into the hands of the jury, and took his seat with a complacent consciousness of having done his duty.   I use the past tense in this connection, as having reference to Mr. Fillmore's past legal career, before he became invested with the performance of higher duties that conflicted with those of his profession.

Among the many examples of Mr. Fillmore's success in the civil law which show the extent of his legal attainments I have selected the following, decided in the supreme court of New York. The nature of this case was well calculated to, and did, elicit very general interest throughout the country at that time.

The case was originally tried in the Erie circuit court, December, 1842. It was an action of trover for some timber that had been cut on, and taken from, a parcel of land known as the Cattaraugus Reservation, lying partly in the counties of Erie, Chautauque, and Cattaraugus.

The Cattaraugus Reservation had been subject to the government of Massachusetts, prior to 1786, when that state ceded to the state of New York her title to the government sovereignty and jurisdiction.

New York at the same time ceded to Massachusetts the right of preëmption of the soil from the native Indians, which she then held. It was stipulated, that Massachusetts should have the right to sell her right of preëmption to any one who had a right to purchase the claims of the Indians, who were the original occupants — such purchase to be confirmed by the state. Massachusetts afterwards conveyed by transfer her preëmption right to one Morris, who subsequently disposed of his preëmption right and other interests, to the plaintiffs of this suit, Ogden and Fellows. It must be borne in mind that a preëmption right was all that either party had acquired or disposed of by these several transfers. The Indians, themselves, having the right of occupancy in fee simple.

The preëmption right, therefore, was nothing more than
a right to the ultimate fee, if the Indian title should become extinct. The Reservation was then in the occupancy of the Seneca tribe of Indians — they being one
of six tribes of Indians, between whom and the United
States treaties had been entered into, whereby they held
by right of occupancy, their several parcels of land.
The Seneca tribe of Indians during the winters of 1833
and 1837, cut and sold saw-logs from the Cattaraugus
Reservation to the value of one thousand and forty-seven
dollars.   Ogden and Fellows who had purchased the
preëmption right of Robert Morris, assigned him by the
state of Massachusetts, in 1791, averred that this was an
infringement upon their rights. The defendants of the
suit were Lee and Ellsworth, who purchased the logs of
the Indians. The action then was Ogden and Fellows,
against Lee and Ellsworth, for the amount of money
paid by them to the Indians — the value of the logs.
The cause came up in the Erie circuit court before Judge
Dayton, in December, 1842. Mr. Fillmore was for the
defendants. The value involved in this suit was not very
great, so far as the damages claimed by the plaintiffs
were concerned; but it was not from the amount of
money involved, that the suit derived its importance.
The cause came up before the court in regular order, and
all the treaties between the states of New York and
Massachusetts, with the subsequent transfers to various
individuals, until the preëmption right came into the hands
of the plaintiffs, were introduced as evidence to establish
7*

the validity of their claims by purchase. The defendants moved a nonsuit, upon the grounds of the invalidity of the plaintiffs' claims to the land from whence the logs were taken, and consequently their right to any alleged damages they averred to have sustained. In their motion for a nonsuit they were unsuccessful, and Judge Dayton instructed the jury to render the verdict for the plaintiff. The defendants moved for a new trial on a bill of exceptions.

This was a somewhat complicated case, and required consummate ability in a lawyer to combat the opposition of the plaintiffs' counsel. The only right the plaintiffs possessed was that derived as the assignees of the Robert Morris preëmption right, ceded by the state of Massachusetts; while the defence hinged upon the validity of the Seneca Indians' claim, and their consequent right to sell to them the timber in question. In the management of this case there was a vast amount of labor devolving on the attornies, in having to look over old Indian treaties and colonial enactments, whereby the claims of Indians to the soil by occupancy until extinguished by purchase was guaranteed and their rights protected. The interest Mr. Fillmore felt in the issue of this case was very great, and the indefatigable industry with which he investigated the whole complexity of its bearings was unsurpassed. He was compelled to go back to the old decisions for precedents and to look deep into the intricacies of the law in regard to it. The decision of the court in favor of the plaintiffs would have been almost a gross outrage, and, as we shall presently see, replete with the worst conse-

quences to the Indian occupants of the reservation, of
whose interest the states of both New York and Massachusetts had been especially careful in all their transactions — so much so, that it was explicitly stipulated by
the convention of 1786, that Massachusetts could only
transfer the preëmption right of the reservation to those
who had the right " to extinguish by purchase the claims
of the Indians." So jealous, in fact, were they of the
rights of this oppressed race, it was stipulated that all
such purchases from the Indians should be invalid, unless witnessed by a superintendent appointed by the state.
Mr. Fillmore urged the claims of the defendant to a verdict with the greatest zeal and ability. For reasons which
will soon be made manifest, he had engaged in few cases
during his entire practice in a favorable issue of which to
his clients he was so much interested and felt so deep a
solicitude. This was one of those causes that have frequently fallen to the lot of Mr. Fillmore to defend where
he knew he was on the right side. He was not only on
the right side so far as pecuniary considerations were concerned, but he was on the right side of morality. Every
speech he made was an appeal in behalf of oppressed humanity, the very vitality of whose existence depended upon the issue of this cause. This was one of those cases,
in the management of which all personal considerations
and the emoluments derived from its successful issue were
thrown altogether out of the question, and swallowed up
in the weightier consideration of protecting humanity in
the homes of their fathers. This was a case exactly
adapted to his nature, to his feelings, and the philan

thropic promptings of his heart. New York had never, and to her honor be it spoken, has yet never procured a foot of land from the Indians only by purchase in the return of an equivalent, unless it became extinct by the desertion of its occupants; and he, in defending this suit, was not only discharging his professional duty to his client, but he was preserving his state from the stain of her people monopolizing the Cattaraugus Reservation, whose very name imports its design was the Indians' home until they became an extinct race. He was not only laboring for the untarnished preservation of his state from that usurptional stain, but he was laboring in the cause of a suffering, friendless people, the fragment wreck of a mighty nation, who once, round the shores of his own beautiful lakes, reigned lords of the soil, and filled the land with their wildwood joys. It was just the case for Mr. Fillmore to call up all the great energies of mind and body of which he was master. Either one of the incentives in this case was usually enough to make him act,.and act nobly. But here, in defending this suit, he was discharging his duty to his client, in endeavoring to procure a verdict favorable to his side, and in all the efforts he put forth he was promoting the interests and preserving the honor of his state; and by his masterly appeals in behalf of the remaining relics of a ruined race, he was pleading the cause of humanity. Here, then, was a blending of the three great virtues he has so happily exemplified — duty to his fellow man — patriotism to his country — philanthropy to the oppressed.

This case, after receiving the laborious attention of the

counsel on both sides, was finally carried to the supreme court of the state of New York. Few cases of a civil nature ever elicited more general interest, and few ever possessed a nature so complicated and perplexing. In many features it was a novel case — an extraordinary one. To give some idea of the nature of patient investigation, and of the legal authorities to which the counsel was subjected in its prosecution, I insert the following from the old reports of the supreme court of that day:

" Mr. Fillmore, counsel for the defendants, cited: 1 Bio. Laws of the U. S., 307, 309, 311, 377; Public Land Laws, part 2, p. 158; Opinions of Att'y Gen. of U. S., p. 344; Worcester *vs.* State of Georgia, (6 Peters, 544;) Mitchell *vs.* United States, (9 Peters, 745;) Georgia against Canatoo, a Cherokee Indian, (Nat. In. of 1842.) "

These are a few of the authorities cited in the prosecution of this cause, from its institution in the Erie circuit court until its final disposition in the supreme court of the state. From the time Mr. Fillmore first engaged in it as counsel, he had devoted himself to it when necessary with untiring earnestness. He fought every inch of ground over which it passed, from the subordinate court until it reached the supreme tribunal. Here, with the same characteristic activity, he prepared for a final struggle. He, with usual promptness, was well prepared to put forth a powerful effort, and the opposing counsel was equally so. So much general interest had the cause created, that the counsel on each side were exceedingly anxious to gain the case.

After a patient hearing and a fair investigation, the

decision of this case was given by Justice Bronson, in October, 1843, in favor of the defendants.

Thus ended a suit, when we take into consideration all its bearings, the rights it destroyed, and the injuries it inflicted, was replete with the most serious consequences to the state of New York. Few have been more so. The land from whence the logs were taken was a part of a large portion held by the Indians as a reservation for their homes. The whole tract embraced a considerable area of territory, over which they exercised as occupants exclusive jurisdiction. Here they had their domiciles and all their home fixtures — their families, agricultural implements, and everything necessary to secure comfort and happiness. The tribes, in their aggregate capacity, numbered hundreds. With their families they were pursuing their vocations in their own rustic simplicity, in the full enjoyment of quiet repose. The great consideration involved in this suit was the validity of the Indians' claim to the entire body of land they occupied. If the plaintiffs had gained the suit, and there had been no reversion of the verdict of the Erie county jury, then the point would have been definitely settled that Lee and Ellsworth, the defendants to the suit, who purchased the logs from the Indians, had made the purchase of those to whom they did not belong. It would then have been settled that the $1,047 paid to the Indians for the timber was due Ogden and Fellows, as the rightful owners of the soil; and by the rendition of a verdict requiring the repayment of that sum to the plaintiffs, the validity of their claim to the timber on that specific part of the

Indian Reservation would have been legally established. But it does not stop here in influences injuriously detrimental to the peace and prosperity of the Indian settlements. An establishment of Ogden and Fellows' right to the timber upon the basis of the Morris transfer to them of his preëmption right ceded by Massachusetts in 1786, would have been equivalent to a legal establishment of similar claims to the timber upon the ground of the entire Indian settlements, which we may readily believe the claimants, under such preëmptive right, would not have been slow to assert.

Nor does it yet stop here. Had the plaintiffs been successful in this action, their right to the timber on the land claimed by preëmptive purchase was established, and the right of all persons possessing similar claims would have been established, which would have included the entire timber on their settlements ; and if by the purchase of preëmption right the purchaser acquired a right to the *timber* on the land from the date of such purchase, then they acquired a legal right to the land also, and the Indians had no valid title to their own lands and their own homes.

Such would have been the result of Judge Dayton's decision and the Erie county jury, had it not been reversed in the supreme court. A casual analysis of the bearings of the case will convince the reader of the important considerations it involved, and how replete it was with the destinies of hundreds of helpless beings, who were the primal monarchs of the whole country. Let us look at it a moment as Judge Dayton left it, and see the results. Nearly all the land included in the Indian settlements was held in the same way as that was from which the timber in question was taken. Had the plaintiffs the right to one parcel, then those holding similar claims had the right to theirs. Then, under the seal and sanction of law, they would have taken possession of the entire settlements, timber and everything else, and drove the Indians from the country. Under this state of case, the solicitude of Massachusetts and New York to protect the rights of the Indians in the Cattaraugus Reservation would have amounted to nothing.

These, then, are the considerations involved in the investigation of this case. To those acquainted with Mr. Fillmore, it is no matter of surprise that he manifested so much anxiety for the success of a client, in an issue where not only his, but the fate of hundreds were involved. The parties against whom the action was brought, the honor of his state, and the reserved homes of the Indians, were all involved in the case, and regarded as his client's. It is questionable whether in the judicial annals of the state of New York, replete as they are with grave and important decisions, there is to be found another civil individual suit, in the investigation of which so much was involved. The interests attached to it were of a peculiar nature, as well as of great magnitude. The whole country was deeply interested in its decision, especially the counties of Erie, Chatauque, and Cattaraugus, in which the reservation was situated.

Another very important case, the novelty of which elicited a very general interest, and involved some very nice principles of law, was that of Lightbody against the Ontario Bank. The facts in the case were about as follows: The plaintiff had made a deposit of over two thousand dollars with the Ontario Bank, at their banking house in Utica. On the thirtieth day of May, 1828, he presented his check, and drew two thousand dollars. Five hundred dollars of the money thus drawn was on the Franklin Bank of the city of New York, which he sent to that city the same day. The next day it was returned to him as being worthless, the Franklin Bank having stopped payment the twenty-ninth day of May — only one day before he drew the money. He took the five hundred dollars to the Ontario Bank, and demanded the sum in good money. The bank, at the time they paid him the notes on the Franklin Bank, did it in good faith, not being aware of its failure, and refused to make good the five hundred dollars.

This case, then, was an action of assumpsit, to recover the amount of the notes received from the Ontario on the Franklin Bank. Mr. Fillmore was for the plaintiff. The question involved in this very singular case was, whether bills received in payment on a bank that has stopped payment — both the party paying and the party receiving being ignorant of such stoppage — should be made good by the party paying.

The features presented in this case were rather novel ones. Had the money been paid the day before, it would have been in the plaintiff's hands, at the time the Franklin Bank suspended payment; but, as it was, it was in the hands of the defendant. The question was, who should

sustain the loss of the five hundred dollars, it being paid
and received in good faith.

The following arguments urged by Mr. Fillmore, in the
supreme court, will convey some idea of his research and
discrimination :

" When the plaintiff drew his check, the Ontario Bank
was indebted to him in the sum of two thousand dollars,
which has not been paid.   One of the bills received by
the plaintiff was not what it purported to be on its face—
the representative value of money, to the amount of five
hundred dollars.   For nearly a year afterwards it was
without value, and, in reference to the rights of the parties, must be considered as entirely valueless, as the per-
centage paid by the receiver must be viewed as paid to
the plaintiff for the use of the defendant.   The bill was
no better towards satisfying the just claims of the plaintiff than had it been counterfeit.   The rule of the civil
law is, that if a creditor receive, by mistake, anything in
payment different from what is due, and upon supposition that it is the thing actually due, as if he receive
brass instead of gold, the debtor is not discharged ; and
the creditor, upon offering to return that which he
received, may demand that which is due by the contract.

" This rule was approved and adopted by this court in
Murkle against Hatfield, 2d Johns. Reports, page 455, in
which it was held, that a *counterfeit* bank bill received on
the sale of property is no payment, and that the vendor
may treat it as a nullity, and resort to the original contract.   The principle of that case controlls the present.
It is conceded the defendants acted in good **faith, and**

believed they gave good value, but their obligation to pay was not therefore discharged. A bill of sale of a horse or other animal, not present, believed to be alive, but dead at the time, does not discharge a contract; nor is the transfer of a bill of lading of a vessel at sea operative, if at the time the cargo is lost by the ship having foundered. In all these cases, the loss falls upon him who is the owner at the time of the happening of the event, when the property becomes of no value; and notwithstanding the attempted change of ownership, the parties are restored to their original rights. The bill in this case became of no value on the *twenty-ninth* of May, the day on which the bank stopped; and allowing that, until then, it was a representative of the currency of the country, and that the rule of law, as to the receiving of current bills, is the same as is applicable to the receiving of current coin, the defendants reap no benefit from it; for on the *thirtieth*, when the bill was paid to the plaintiff, it had ceased to be the currency of the country, it was no longer the representative of money, although the bills of the Franklin Bank were current at Utica on that day. Whether the bills of a bank represent the currency of the country is not to be tested by the value put upon such bills in one or another section of the state, but by the ability of the bank to meet its engagements. When the bank stops payments, its bills cease to be the representative of the currency of the country, and are no longer entitled to be treated as cash. This rule determines with certainty, uniformity and universality the time when the notes of a bank become worthless, and closes the door, against frauds upon the uninformed by those having superior facilities of early intelligence. But it is insisted that a bank note in this country is not money, except by conventional regulation, and the negotiation of the note of the Franklin Bank in this case is subject to the same rule which governs the transfer of the notes of individuals, according to which the transfer of a promissory note is no payment of a *pre-existing debt,* unless it be expressly agreed to be received as payment at the time of transfer. Chitty on Bills, Starkee's Evidence, etc. The cases in Strange show that a goldsmith's note or banker's check, taken for a precedent debt, is no payment if the drawer fail after the negotiation and before presentment. Here the bank had already failed, when the bill was passed to the plaintiff. The receipt of dividends from the receiver of the bank does not prejudice the plaintiff; 10 Vessay 206 ; 6 Wendell 369; its only effect is to reduce his claim."

The above extract shows the practical analysis of Mr. Fillmore's mind as a lawyer, and conveys some idea of its grasping and logical powers. We do not often see a specimen of more systematic reasoning than is displayed in the foregoing. The supposition of the existence of parallel cases in the extract evinces a perceptive aptitude in arguing cases of extreme nicety in principles of law.

To this argument the opposing attorneys replied in a very able and elaborate manner, displaying considerable ingenuity in the management of the case. But the force and clearness of Mr. Fillmore's reasoning had made the matter too plain to admit of effective argumentation from the opposite side. The decision was by Chief-justice

Savage, and given for the plaintiff.   Mr. Fillmore's legal career is replete with difficult complex civil cases, where the nicest points of law and great interests were involved. He has been in many criminal suits of great importance, that created considerable excitement at their respective times of adjudication ; but I presume quite sufficient has been said under this head.   Mr. Fillmore's life as a lawyer, though pregnant with no very great *events*, is impressed with true greatness.   Though there are connected with it no extraordinary exhibitions of eloquence, and no fitful blazes of excitement, it has been the consistent flow of a moral current, broad and deep, continually gathering strength in its progress.   Mr. Fillmore's compliance to the urgent appeals of his friends to engage in other duties has frequently exerted an influence to his practice injurious and detrimental.   As this is the last I expect to say of his legal career, I must be allowed to call the minds of young men commencing the law to the importance of building upon a moral basis, of acting from correct principles, emulative of those I have endeavored to set forth in the foregoing.

CHAPTER V.

State politics — Political Anti-masonry— The Morgan outrage — The
Clintonians and Bucktails — Anti-masonic convention — How the
action of the Anti-masons should be construed — National politics of 1832 — Leading measures of the Whig party — Mr. Fillmore is elected to Congress — Sketch of that body— Jacksonism
and its effects — Mr. Fillmore's view of the U. S. Bank, and the
removal of the deposits — Mr. Clay's Compromise Tariff of 1833 —
Excitements occasioned by the removal of the deposits — Internal
improvements — Mr. Filimore's efforts to reduce high salaries —
Mr. Fillmore and Mr. Polk — Mr. Fillmore's qualities as a legislator — Other measures of Congress — Its adjournment.

BEFORE giving a record of Mr. Fillmore's congressional
career, it is necessary, perhaps, to take a casual glance
at the aspect of state and national politics.   The politics
of New York had assumed a somewhat singular feature,
growing out of a most outrageous affair connected with
the respected and ancient order of Free Masons.   As Mr.
Fillmore commenced his political career as an Anti-mason,
it would have been more proper, perhaps, to have adverted
to it at his outset.   But the excitement growing out of
the affair that originated eventually in the formation of
Masonic and Anti-masonic political parties did not assume
so serious an aspect until August, 1830, two years previous
to Mr. Fillmore's election to Congress.   To infer from the
fact of his being an Anti-mason that Mr. Fillmore enter-
tains principles opposed to those embodied in Masonry
would be doing him very great injustice.   The affair
that threw him into the ranks of the anti-masons,

placed him with some of the ablest statesmen and wisest patriots in the state of New York. The excitement and the formation of parties by blending Masonry and politics, resulted from the Morgan outrage. I do not expect to enter into the details of that affair in this connection, nor would I advert to it at all were I not aware that misconceptions exist in the minds of some in regard to Mr. Fillmore's early Anti-masonic principles.

Morgan was a resident of Batavia, Genesee county, in the state of New York, and belonged to the fraternity of Masons. From some source it became known to the order that he was preparing a book for publication, containing a full exposition of the mysteries of Free Masonry. On the eleventh of September, Morgan was seized upon a charge of larceny, and carried as a prisoner to Canandaigua county, to be tried for the offence. The investigation of the case resulted in his acquittal, but he was rearrested upon a process for debt. Judgment was obtained, and on the issue of the execution Morgan was thrown into prison. The day after his imprisonment, he was released for a still greater outrage. He was gagged, and carried with the utmost secrecy and dispatch to Fort Niagara, and with merciless cruelty concealed in the magazine of the fort.

But secret as had been this movement, the vigilance of an excited populace was not long in finding a clue to the perpetrators. The Masons in the neighborhood of Batavia being apprized of Morgan's intentions of exposing their mysteries, and resolved on the suppression of his forthcoming book, had made several violent and unwar-

rantable attempts in view of accomplishing that purpose.
So great had been the violence of the Masons toward
Morgan from the time they became apprized of his intentions concerning their order, and such vindictive manifestations had been seen on the part of the citizens in the
vicinity of Batavia, that they were immediately settled
upon as the offenders, and openly associated with Morgan's abduction.   After Morgan's seizure the feelings of
the community became wrought into a blaze of excitement, and a vigilant search was instituted for the purpose
of discovering his whereabouts, and to ferrit out the
perpetrators.   This search was fruitless.   Although they
knew it was accomplished through the agency of the
Masons, they could not ascertain on whom to fix the
blame of so outrageous an act.   A public meeting was
held at Batavia, and committees appointed for the purpose of making discoveries in regard to the transaction.
These committees succeeded in tracing Morgan to Rochester, but could not learn anything further.   Subsequent
developments brought to light the fact above stated, that
he was carried secretly in the night by relays of horses,
and deposited in the magazine of Fort Niagara, where he
was doubtless murdered in cold blood.   The excitement
spread like wild fire over western New York, and a spontaneous outburst of indignation issued from the mass of
the people, not identified with the Masonic order, rarely
witnessed.   Meetings, expressive of the people's feelings,
similar to the one held at Batavia, were called and held
in all parts of the country.   The secrecy which was
practiced in the abduction, and the great mystery that

enveloped the whole transaction seemed to indicate the existence of a premeditated design, and an efficiently organized conspiracy. The secrecy, the boldness and dispatch, and the mysterious vagueness connected with Masonry generally, affixed to this deed a peculiar kind of horror in the minds of the people, and it became invested with the drapery of the blackest of crimes — that of murder.

That the excitement of the people was but natural will be admitted, when we think of the intolerant attrocity of the deed. That a foul murder had been committed they felt well assured; that it had been done by the Masons or through their operative agency they felt equally sure. And, as strong confirmation of these suspicions, the Masons kept entirely cool during the entire excitement that, like a whirlwind of fire, was swallowing up every other feeling on the part of the people generally. In all the searches instituted for the discovery of Morgan, the Masons took no part; in all their investigation meetings, they did not seem to be the least indignant; in all the denunciations heaped upon the perpetrators, they did not denounce anybody, but kept cool and quiet, taking no part in the excitement, and manifesting no anxiety in regard to Morgan or his fate. All these indications tended to affix to them, in darker hues than ever, the malignity of the crime, and the people became more incensed than before. At these indications so confirmatory of their guilt, the people regarded them as a band who would not hesitate to murder a fellow man to pre-

8

serve their secrets, or to make the laws of their country subordinate to the requirements of their mystic rituals.

The circumstances connected with the whole transaction were of a very aggravated nature from first to last ; and in that day, before the principles of Masonry became so widely diffused as at the present, it is no matter of surprise that the fraternity, in its aggregate, was implicated in the murder of Morgan. The zeal manifested by the citizens, in their endeavors to unravel the whole, and through the mist in which it was enveloped, to see the true state of the case, was certainly commendable. The allegation of larceny, brought against Morgan in the first place, was but a pretext, to which they resorted to effect the suppression of his forthcoming exposition of their creed, as was already shown on the subsequent trial, where, for the want of the smallest evidence to establish his guilt, he was acquitted. The failure to produce any evidence showed the fabrication of the whole thing. When Morgan was released, they availed themselves of a law then operative, and had him thrown into prison for a small debt, and to complete the outrage, under pretext of relief, conveyed him in the night time to the seclusion of an old fort at the mouth of Niagara River, since which time he has never been seen ; and, from the mani festations of hostility toward him on the part of the Masons, it is plainly inferable he was cruelly murdered. These considerations, it will be readily admitted, were sufficient to arouse the indignation of any people not wholly insensible to the infliction of the grossest outrages upon the majesty of that justice to which they looked for the protection of their rights and the promotion of their interests.

It is no matter of surprise, either, that, after the transaction, from previous indications of the Masons towards Morgan, and their refusal to take part in their efforts to discover his whereabouts, that the guilt of the whole affair should be affixed to them. In the meantime, Morgan's famous book, which was the origin of the whole matter, was published despite the efforts of the Masons to suppress it.   The public mind being already agitated to a perfect state of furor at the startling nature of recent events, was badly prepared for the reception of the still more startling and exaggerated disclosures of Morgan's book.   So eager was the excitement to get hold of that celebrated effusion of the traitorous Morgan that, like a Pandora box, was to reveal the awful mysteries of a sect whom it had invested with the sable of crime, that they would almost have protected its issue at any risk.

The book, when it was at length issued, contained features of a more glaring nature than they even supposed, dark as had become their suspicions in regard to the secret order.   Among other things in that book of a startling nature, calculated to impress one with feelings of extreme horror for an order, who presumed to go by its ritual as their fraternal creed, was an oath imposed on all initiates, to espouse the cause of their brothers in distress, and devote their energies to secure their extrication, even though it were in direct violation of all law. Another oath enjoined the strictest secrecy in regard to all crimes or misconduct committed by the brotherhood, except murder or high treason. A third, and more terrible oath still, and one the meaning of which was more immediately connected with Morgan's abduction, bound the initiate to a revengeful retribution upon those who disclosed the secrets of the order. Such disclosures were sworn to be avenged with death to the offender!

Here was an oath contained in a book purporting to be a fair and correct expose of the whole Masonic fraternity, thrown upon the public in the heat of a great excitement, engendered by recent developments coinciding precisely with its requirements. The public very readily believed the contents of the book, and construed these dark oaths into a literal interpretation. In the heated state of the public mind, and surrounded by such coincident circumstances, this literal interpretation was nothing strange. There was the oath by which they were sworn to keep each others' secrets inviolate; there was the oath by which they were sworn to kill a brother who published their secrets. Morgan had published them — there was a violation of the rule, to which was affixed the severest penalty. Morgan, subsequent to such violation, disappeared; therefore, the penalty had been incurred. The Masons took no part in ferreting out the cause of his disappearance; therefore, it was in strict accordance with the oath to keep inviolate each others' secrets.

Morgan's book conveyed the idea of great and very exaggerated mysteries connected with the measures of the whole order; the disappearance of the author was all shrouded in the vaguest mystery, therefore the book was literally true.

That Morgan was murdered somewhere on Niagara River, not far from the old fort to which it was subsequently ascertained he was removed, there was and still is but little doubt. The disappearance and mystery connected therewith were so coincident with the requirements of the book, that they produced a belief that every word in it was true; while the oaths and mysteries of the book fitted the abduction so well, that it was supposed by the most incredulous before, that Morgan had been visited with its penalties. Such was the coincidence, that while the book established conclusively the guilt of the Masons in the murder of Morgan, his mysterious disappearance established the correctness of the book — one confirming the other. On the reception of the publication, the excitement of the people knew no bounds. To see such defiance of all law, both human and divine, as contained in Morgan's book, looked like treachery, and the sudden disappearance of its author like the fruits of it ; and they thought it was incumbent on them to seek the perpetrators and have redress, and when the individuals who perpetrated the deed could not be found, they laid the whole crime upon Masonry in the aggregate, as a compliance with their creed, a correct publication of which they honestly believed was in their possession. Such became the excitement to ascertain who were the real actors in this atrocious tragedy, that the towns and cities generally throughout the surrounding country participated in it, and expressed their feelings in the most indignant manner. Politics had not, however, entered as a feature into these measures, or actuated the committees in their investigations, in any

degree. The Clintonians and Bucktails were the names
by which the two parties in New York politics were
designated at that time, De Witt Clinton and William B.
Rochester being their respective leaders. These gentlemen in the fall of 1826 became candidates for governor
of the state. Though the Masons were, by a great many,
implicated in the outrage, both of the candidates being
members of that faternity, masonry did not become a
feature of discussion in the canvass. The excitement
engendered by the outrage was confined to neither
political party, but prevailed throughout the entire community, irrespective of opinions or party predilections.
The refusal of the Masonic fraternity to participate in
their public meetings, and to endeavor to relieve themselves of the odium attached to them by the outrage,
invitations to which were often extended to them, made the
prejudices against them much greater than it otherwise
would have been. " There were some who early implicated
the whole Masonic fraternity in the guilt of the transaction.

" This, however, was not at first the general public sentiment ; but when, as the investigation proceeded, it was
found all those implicated in the transaction were Masons ;
that, with scarce an exception, no Mason aided in the
investigation ; that the whole crime was made a matter
of ridicule by the Masons, and even justified by them
openly and publicly ; that the powers of the law were
defied by them, and the committee taunted with their ina-
bility to bring the criminals to punishment before tribunals where judges, sheriffs, jurors, and witnesses were
Masons ; that witnesses were mysteriously spirted away,
and the committees themselves personally vilified and

abused for acts which deserved commendation, the impression spread rapidly, and seized a strong hold upon the popular judgment that the Masonic institution was in fact responsible for this daring crime. Upon this particular point, the public at the west early began to divide into parties, and take sides not as a political question at first, upon the fact whether the Masonic institution and Masons generally were essentially and morally guilty of the crime which had been perpetrated."* From the above extract it will be readily perceived that a determination on the part of the citizens to assert the supremacy of the laws of the country over all creeds and rituals was the incipient origin of the Anti-masonic party. In January, 1827, Lawson and others of the alleged participants in the outrage were arraigned for trial, and plead guilty of the offence, thereby disappointing public expectation in regard to the developments which was supposed would be elicited in the prosecution of the case. Judge Throop, who was afterward governor of the state, in passing sentence upon them, used the following language, which shows the Anti-masonic party was actuated by patriotic principles, and was composed of the ablest men who figured in New York politics at that day:

" Your conduct has created in the people of this section of the country a strong feeling of virtuous indignation. The court rejoices to witness it — to be made certain that a citizen's person cannot be invaded by lawless violence, without its being felt by every individual in the commu nity. It is a blessed spirit, and we do hope that it will not

* Hammond's Political History.

subside, that it will be accompanied by a ceaseless vigilance and untiring activity, until every actor in this profligate conspiracy is hunted from his hiding place, and brought before the tribunals of his country, to receive the punishment merited by his crime. We think we see in this public sensation the spirit which brought us into existence as a nation, and a pledge that our rights and liberties are destined to endure."

The above language shows in what light the Anti-masonic feeling was viewed by the purest patriots of the land — "the spirit that brought us into existence as a nation" — Mr. Fillmore's identification with this party then, was an identification with the patriots, where he has ever since been found. Subsequent to Lawson's trial, a number of delegates from various committees met in convention at Lewiston, on Niagara River, and ascertained by their investigations the fate of Morgan. The details of their discoveries flew like lightening over the country, in a thousand exaggerated forms, and fanned the blaze of excitement into still greater intensity and magnitude. At the ensuing election, Clinton was elected governor, and the Bucktails got majorities in the legislature. The excitement incident to a political campaign having subsided, that engendered by Masonry increased, there being nothing else on which to exhaust itself. In 1827, the sentiment was embodied, in a resolution adopted by some of their meetings, that Free Masons endorsing the Morgan outrage, thereby making the law subsidiary to their rituals, were not proper persons to receive the suffrages of the people at the ballot-box. Masonry was first brought to this test in the counties of Genesee and Monroe, and originated as much in the efforts of the Masons to put down the committees as anything else. At all events, it was the starting-point of an organized political Anti-free-masonry. But it was some time after this, that, from the aspect assumed by both state and national politics, it became an efficiently organized political party. After Clinton's election as governor, and his avowal to support Jackson for the presidency, those of the Clintonian party who were Anti-masons and on the investigating committees, by appealing to the prejudices of an excited populace, successfully construed Clinton's support of Jackson as being the result of Masonic influence — both Clinton and Jackson being High Masons. Thus those Anti-masons who had supported Clinton denounced their leader, and with success appealed to those Bucktails who were Anti-masons, to give up Jackson upon the grounds of the alleged Masonic league existing between the two.

In this way, by the assistance of politicians, in no way chagrined at the turn things had taken — the Anti-masonic party was formed, composed of an amalgamation of Clintonian and Bucktail seceders.

From various causes, this new party gained strength with unprecedented rapidity. Though disavowing any feature of a political nature, the Anti-masons, irrespective of party politics, presented their nomination, against those of the Adams and Bucktail parties, and carried several counties at the election by very respectable majorities. This was the dawning of their success, and indicated pretty strongly, the eventual strength it attained.   **Many**

8*

Masons left the order after the publication of Morgan's disclosures, and were enrolled into the ranks of the Anti-masons. The party now began to be quite formidable — so much so that, early in the spring of 1828, a general convention was held at Le Roy, with a delegated representation from twelve counties. This was the first general Anti-masonic convention, where it assumed an avowed political aspect. This body recommended the holding of a state convention at Utica in the ensuing August, and appointed a number of their leading men, among whom was Thurlow Weed, as a central committee. Jackson was a Mason of a high degree, and Adams was not; consequently, there was a strong indication on the part of the Anti-masons to vote for Adams.

While occupying an independent position of hostility to both the political parties, manifesting no desire of affiliation whatever, Anti-masonry was somewhat petted by the friends of both presidential aspirants, with a view of conciliating them to their particular favorite. In the winter of 1829, the Anti-masons again assembled in convention at Albany, for the purpose of establishing their influence upon a consolidated basis, and to produce concert of action. At the election of 1829, they carried western New York by an overwhelming majority. They met in convention again at Albany, in February, 1830, and drew up a memorial which was subsequently presented to the legislature of the state, requesting the appointment of a committee to investigate the conduct of the Masons in regard to the Morgan outrage. This request was refused by a large majority of the members, and was construed by the petitioners into hostility against them, on the part of the legislature.

This conviction of legislative hostility was increased, by the reduction of John C. Spencer's salary, who, under a law passed in 1828, was acting as special counsel to investigate the Morgan outrage.

The fund appropriated for such services was two thousand dollars, but was reduced to one thousand. This was construed into a premeditated insult — Spencer resigned his seat, and the Anti-masons became firm and decided in their hostility to the Jacksonian dominant party.

An Anti-masonic convention was held again at Utica, in August, 1830, and for the first time openly avowed their sentiments upon the political measures of the country. They nominated Mr. Granger for governor, who, notwithstanding the most sanguine expectations, was beaten by a considerable majority. In 1833, the excitements connected with the outrage and the progress of the party subsided to a great extent, and the Anti-masonic became identified principally with the whig party. So much for political Anti-masonry. It had its origin in the murder of Morgan, and the disclosures connected with the book gained strength by some injudicious measure of the legislature, and was fanned into public sentiment through a desire to maintain the supremacy of the laws. Hammond, in his Political History of New York, says : " It must be believed that, from honest convictions of its propriety, most of those joined the party of Anti-masons." He further says, that such men as " Thomas C. Love, Millard Fillmore, Albert H. Tracy, of Buffalo ; William

H. Seward, of Cayuga; John C. Spencer, and John Birdsdale, could hardly have joined the Anti-masonic party from mere personal or selfish considerations." Among the best men of the country was of that party — men whose patriotism cannot be called in question. That it did much to establish the ascendancy of the whig party in that state no one will deny. In fact, the political historian, in speaking of the Anti-masons, says: " The whig ascendency in this state, (New York,) is mainly indebted for its permanence, if not for its first success, to the steady opposition of the Anti-masonic counties, and to the uniformly heavy majorities which those counties have constantly given at every contested election." It is evident that, through the unwavering hostility of that party to the Van Buren party, the aspect of state politics underwent an entire change.

Mr. Fillmore became identified with the Anti-masonic party, at the early stages of its development, from the wise and patriotic considerations above mentioned — to assert the supremacy of the law. Mr. Fillmore was a young man at the time it was first brought upon the tapis; and after the perpetration of such an outrage, and the taunting defiance manifested by some to the investigating committees; after the publication of Morgan's awful disclosures, oaths, etc.; after it had received the support and commendation of such men as Throop, Spencer, Birdsdale, and William Wirt himself, it is not strange that Mr. Fillmore should become an Anti-mason. It must be remembered too, that, at that time, Masonry was not so fully understood as at the present day, and the literal interpretation given to Morgan's book, immediately after the occurrence of such atrocious and coincident circumstances, was nothing unnatural.   To the causes, embraced in the foregoing, may be attributed Mr. Fillmore's identification with that party; the high position assigned him in it by Hammond, in his Political History, is attributable to the same causes that his high position in every other sphere is — his superior capacity and matchless industry.   More has been said on this subject than I had anticipated, but no more I trust than was necessary to its full elaboration.

As the conclusion of this synopsis of political Antimasonry brings us to the time of Mr. Fillmore's commencement of his congressional career, when his talents are to be exercised in the national councils, it may not be amiss to take a glance at the aspect of national, as we have of state politics.

Jackson had been elected to the presidency, and, in the exercise of the veto power, and by dismissing from office old incumbents, and the almost regal enforcement of many other measures hostile to what the people conceived to be their best interests, was filling the whole country with the wildest excitement.   On his reëlection to the presidency, the very fact of the vote he received was construed into an emphatic endorsement on the part of the people of all the measures of his previous administration; and, throwing off the mask of conciliation, in the assumption of executive power, he was piloting the ship of state to whatsoever port he thought proper, dismissing all officers of the old vessel who refused to render implicit obedience to his commands. Excitements engendered by his veto of the bill for the recharter of the United States Bank, were agitating the country from one end to the other. The commercial business that had been transacted with the cities and states of the south, south-west, and the Atlantic states, the people alleged was interfered with to a material extent. Checks which they received in the south for their produce and stock on the United States Bank, at a premium of one-half per centum, they averred would be exchanged for one of two and a half per centum, thereby producing an aggregate expenditure on the part of the producer that would be enormous.

Some of the western states, entirely deficient in specie-paying banks, had but little circulating medium, except the bills of the United States Bank and its branches. The thirty millions of dollars with which they were supplied through that institution, they alleged, was a great stimulant to industry and enterprise. Deprived of that facility in the liquidation of such a sum, inevitable ruin and general bankruptcy was predicted. The purchase of public lands, they said, was interfered with. The merchants and manufacturers of the Atlantic states complained that, in the destruction of the checks on the United States Bank, for which they had been supplying the merchants of the west, their business sustained a serious injury. The facilities of remittance they declared annihilated, and business essentially crippled in every department. A public distress, bankruptcy, and general business prostration was predicted, in various forms, as an inevitable result of the veto of the bill, and the consequent removal of the deposits.

The old United States Bank was incorporated in 1816, under a charter limited to twenty years, and so long had it been regarded as the protector of American finance, that the evils predicted to result from the veto of the bill for its recharter were greatly magnified, and have been subsequently proven to be pregnant with no such disastrous consequences as were anticipated. The excitement the veto created was very intense, and prevailed throughout the extremities of the Union. The charter, according to the twenty years limit, expired in 1836. A bill for its recharter had passed the senate by a majority of eight votes, and, after going into the house, and being discussed, and having produced crimination and recrimination, it passed that body by a majority of twenty-two votes. This was a leading, and the most engrossing of all the questions involved at that time in national politics. Both in the senate and in the house, it elicited the gravest considerations, and excited interest from all parties. The friends of the measure regarded it as of extreme vitality to the existence of a healthful currency, while its enemies were equally sure that it was a disadvantage to the country. That both the senate and house of representatives regarded it as of essential utility, is tested by the fact of the bill's passage through both. The recharter of the bank they regarded as sure, and the currency of the country safe ; but on the tenth of July, 1832, President Jackson returned it to the senate with his veto, and, for want of a concurrence of two-thirds of the members in favor of the bill, it was defeated.

Both branches of the national legislature were being flooded with petitions in regard to this, then considered, high-handed act of the president, praying for the enactment of measures avertive of the ruin they saw foreshadowed in the destruction of the United States Bank. Henry Clay was pouring forth his eloquent denunciations against the president, and portraying the sufferings he presumed would grow out of a refusal to recharter that institution. All parts of the country seemed to be startled by his alarms, and infected with his feelings, until Jackson, the veto, and the deposits formed a theme of discussion among all parties, and of excitement for all communities. Such was the condition of one of the leading measures of national politics, in 1832, when Mr. Fillmore was first thrown upon the arena, to take active part therein.

The old protective tariff that had been in operation for years met with bitter denunciation and the deadliest hostility from the southern states, especially South Carolina, headed by Mr. Hayne. The American system of protection was vigorously assailed, and the assailants as vigorously and promptly met, Clay figuring with his usual conspicuity among the defenders of protective industry. The existing system, by its assailants, was alleged to be unconstitutional and legally inoperative, and defended by its friends by enumerating the advantages of a protective tariff, and reference to the signature of George Washington for its constitutionality. Thus, the debates and excitements upon that subject were continued until numer ous propositions for the reduction of duties on various articles imported were brought before the house.   In July, 1832, John Quincy Adams presented a bill in Congress, modifying the existing protective system.   This measure was not satisfactory entirely to those who had assailed the old tariff; but, inasmuch as it was less obnoxious to their feelings than the old one, and reductive of former duties, they made a virtue of necessity, and the tariff of 1832, as it is called in the political history of the country, was adopted, and became the American protective system, until the subsequent measures embraced in Mr. Clay's compromise tariff of 1833 made the scale of duties on imported commodities still more diminutive.   This was a leading feature in the political controversies of the day for a number of years, and cuts a pretty conspicuous figure in the history of the country's politics.   With the reduction of duties embraced in the Adams' measures, it was still a measure of Congressional interest at the time of Mr. Fillmore's election to that body.

The public land question, also, had just received the polish of Mr. Clay's genius and statesmanship, by his devising his great plan for the distribution of their proceeds among all the states.   The large bodies of public lands, over the distribution of the sale of which there existed for a number of years such an incessant excitement, out of which was built so many hobbies of political preferment, consisted in parcels ceded to the government by the Atlantic states, in very extensive possessions in the western states and territories, and in immense parcels acquired by treaties and negotiations with the aborigines, and the purchase of Louisiana and Florida. At the time that part of the lands owned by cession came into the hands of the government, a large portion of the old Revolutionary war debt remained unliquidated, and these lands were designed to assist in its payment. During Jackson's administration there existed some indications of the entire liquidation of that old debt, and he recommended to Congress to convey the public lands to the several states wherein they were situated. Disputes in regard to the public lands were of very early origin. Jefferson, it will be remembered, as far back as 1806, recommended the adoption of such measures as would secure the proceeds of these lands to internal improvements and educational purposes.

During the presidential campaign of 1832, Clay and Jackson both being in nomination, the friends of Jackson required of the then acting committee on manufactures, information as to the most suitable appropriation of the public lands. Mr. Clay was chairman of that committee, and just at that particular time, the duty required at his hands was of a very delicate nature. For the presentation of such a report, without incurring the censure of either the old thirteen states, or those recently coming into the union, would have taken more than human wisdom and sagacity. Mr. Clay, however, by one of those masterly strokes of ability for which he was so justly celebrated, devised his plan for the *distribution of the proceeds* of the public lands. This was the first occasion on which that plan, as a famous article of the old whig creed, became incorporated into the party. It afterwards, however, cut no small figure in the history of its politics. Until then, this great plan for the distribution of the proceeds had not been devised. Thus, this new plank had just been hewn, and put into the whig platform, about the time Mr. Fillmore was ushered upon it in a national official capacity. The sub-treasury — another measure that afterwards figured pretty largely in the political discussions of the country—had not then assumed the importance, as a national question, it eventually acquired. Internal improvements and other measures were not themes of legislative discussion, to any great extent, everything being swallowed up in the more engrossing topics of banks and tariffs.

Such was the condition of the great leading political measures of the country in 1832. The bank veto and protective system were the most exciting questions of the day, and pretty much monopolized the talents of both houses of the national Congress. The blaze of nullification was being kindled into a perfect fury in South Carolina, and Mr. Clay was putting forth his greatest efforts to allay the excitement. Mr. Fillmore took his seat in Congress at a time of great political excitement — a time when some of the most talented statesmen of America were figuring in her national councils. In the senate, Mr. Clay, Mr. Calhoun, Mr. Benton, Webster, and many other statesmen of eminent distinction, figured in all their power of eloquence and wisdom. Among the members of Congress who distinguished themselves both there and in subsequent capacities, were Polk, Dickinson and others of no less note. The senate and house of representatives, in their combined capacity, presented an array of talent and patriotism rarely convened together at the capital of any nation. The names connected with the proceedings of the twenty-third Congress have had a powerful influence in shaping the destinies of this country, and in moulding public sentiment so as to make it accord with the dictates of patriotism. Of the greatness and worth of the men who composed that Congress, the institutions of our common country, in all their glorious majesty stand unmarred, as living authority.

The house was organized by the election of Andrew Stevenson of Virginia, speaker, and Mr. Franklin, clerk. On the third of March, 1833, President Jackson sent his annual message to Congress, from which I make the following extract, as having direct reference to the exciting questions of the day : " Since the last adjournment of Congress, the secretary of the treasury has directed the money of the United States to be deposited in certain state banks designated by him, and he will immediately lay before you his reasons for this direction. I concur with him entirely in the view he has taken of the subject ; and some months before the removal, I urged upon the department the propriety of taking that step. The near approach of the day on which the charter will expire, as well as the conduct of the bank, appeared to me to call for this measure, upon the high consideration of public interest and public duty. The extent of its misconduct, however, although known to be great, was not at that time fully developed by truth. It was not until late in the month of August that I received from the government directors an official report, establishing beyond question, that this great and powerful institution had been actually engaged in attempting to influence the election of the public officers, by means of its money; and that, in express violation of the provisions of its charter, it had, by a formal resolution, placed its funds at the disposition of the president, to be employed in sustaining the political power of the bank.   *   *   *   *   *   *

"In my own sphere of duty, I should feel myself called on by the facts disclosed, to order a *scire facias* against the bank, with a view to put an end to the chartered rights it has so palpably violated, were it not that the charter itself will expire as soon as a decision would probably be obtained from the court of last resort."

The language of the foregoing extracts was well calculated to produce in Congress the very results that were manifest. The United States Bank, and the removal of the deposits to which it had reference, were, from the first of the session, the leading topics of congressional discussion, and the causes of excitement throughout the entire country. Of those who were most fierce in their denunciations, and irreconcilable to what they regarded as an unjust exercise of executive power, Mr. Clay was the acknowledged leader in the deliberations of Congress. The position assigned Mr. Fillmore was on the committee on the District of Columbia, a position where he had no power particularly to display his talents and capacities for legislative usefulness, which he possessed to an eminent degree. In an assemblage of the ablest and most experienced legislators that America has ever produced, it could not reasonably be expected that a young man of Mr. Fillmore's modest, unassuming deportment, would evince any great exhibitions of talent and intellectual powers — especially in the midst of that kind of an assembly, the leading topic of whose discussion he could not feel interested to the same extent. Subsequent events have shown Mr. Fillmore's views on the leading questions exciting the deliberations of that day to have been most wise, and in advance of the times and his party. Keen and penetrating as was Mr. Clay's sagacity, he attached a fictitious magnitude to the evils resulting from the refusal to recharter the United States Bank, and the subsequent removal of the deposits. The disastrous consequences that seemed to him foreshadowed in the consummation of those measures have never befallen the country.

Mr. Fillmore never fully endorsed the denunciatory views entertained by a large number of his party, in regard to these measures and the evils apprehended therefrom. He never attached that importance to the usefulness of a United States bank, to feel that a financial crisis and a severe panic would be the inevitable consequences of its veto. Instead, therefore, of participating in the discussions of a subject definitely settled, and in regard to which, the president had already asserted that " the responsibility had been taken," — a measure whose pregnancy with such direful calamities to the country he could not discover; he studied the interests of his constituency, and the country generally, with reference to their promotion, and devoted himself to the discharge of his duties with characteristic energy and devotion.

Though, in the twenty-third Congress, he won no very great civic laurels, he made it an excellent school to learn the fundamental basis of government organization, and won the respect and esteem of the house. Unpretending as he was, no duty was neglected, and in all measures of interest, he was always at his post, and ready to promote the right. The support he gave his party was firm and unwavering. He made no long speeches, nor evinced the smallest desire of attaining notoriety. Throughout the entire deliberations of the twenty-third Congress, Mr. Fillmore, though a new member and the representative of a minority party, was vigilant in the discharge of every duty devolving upon him as a member of the house, and in studying the interest of those whom he was deputed to represent in that body.

Mr. Fillmore, in this and the subsequent sessions of Congress to which he was elected, exemplified the time-honored maxim of, in time of peace keep prepared for defence. As will be seen in his subsequent labors in Congress, he urged upon that body the necessity of fortifying the northern frontier, in a very masterly style. This principle of being prepared for emergencies he regarded as the safest means of preserving the dignity of the nation from insult and injury. The Canadian insurrection, and developments connected with that movement, that occurred no very great while after this, evinced the wisdom of the measure, and suggested the necessity of keeping the northern frontier in a state of defence sufficient to awe the invaders, and divert their rapacious intentions into another channel. On the twenty-third of

December, Mr. Fillmore introduced the following resolution into Congress, regulative of the military department.

" Resolved, that the committee on military affairs be instructed to inquire into the expediency of so modifying the existing law in relation to the militia of the several states as to permit each state, in time of peace, in the discretion of its legislature, to require no person to bear arms, under twenty-one or over forty years of age; and to permit the inspection of arms to be taken by companies instead of by regiments or battalions; and also, into the propriety of providing arms and accoutrements at the public expense, for those liable to bear arms; and that they be required to report to this house by bill, or otherwise."

This resolution was afterwards changed, with its reference to a select committee, whose duty it was to investigate measures of this character.

The objects embraced in the resolution are the relief from military service of all persons over the age of forty and under twenty-one, and the supervision, on the part of committees, over the condition of the militia, thereby insuring an efficiently organized corps brought under the immediate superintendence of the national legislature. Mr. Fillmore, though strictly a conservative man, and opposed to all dangerous innovations in his public services to the country, has always advanced the doctrince that to be well prepared with means of public defence was an essential prerequisite to the maintenance of public peace. In this, his views have been in uniform coincidence with the wisest patriots who have presided over the destinies of our country. Jefferson, and even Washington himself, embodied this principle in their respective administrations, as being the safest measures of insuring tranquility by presenting an appearance of being prepared for the attacks of the foes of freedom. The northern frontier was exposed to these attacks more than other portions of the country, and hence the solicitude in regard to her preparations of defence. Already had she been the theatre of a devastating invasion, and felt the heel of the foe upon the very vital seat of her existence. Her towns and cities had been burned by the incendiary torch of foreign troops, and the whole frontier thrown into the greatest consternation. To prevent a recurrence of these transactions, and the reënactment of such scenes as were committed through the want of means of public defence, it was certainly the duty of all the lovers of their country to take these preparations for defence into consideration, and to make them subjects of legislative action. This is a duty of paramount importance, on the legislation of which our government has, perhaps, always been too remiss. With those at the head of affairs who justly appreciate the measures of defence, and of being prepared for war in time of peace, the vast resources of America could soon be so developed, and put into such shape as to present giant military preparations that would be equaled by no power under heaven. More deficient than perhaps any other feature has been the government in regard to these preparations, and the keeping efficient operative means at command to combat the events of any unforeseen emergency, great soever as it may be.

9

Few legislators seem to have understood the very great importance of such measures. Mr. Fillmore, throughout his labors in Congress, manifested much solicitude in this particular. He wished to see his country, while conservative and patriotic, occupying a position of defence calculated to awe into respect the invidious monarchies who were watching with a jealous eye the development of her gigantic proportions.

As the celebrated compromise tariff of 1833 had just gone into operation when Mr. Fillmore took his seat in Congress, and produced a temporary settlement of some of the leading measures of political controversy, a brief history of that act, though not strictly pertaining to our narrative, is deemed necessary.

On the twelfth of February, 1833, Mr. Clay introduced his measures in the United States senate, with some able remarks, of which the following is an extract :

" In presenting the modification of the tariff laws which I am now about to submit, I have two great objects in view. My first object looks to the tariff. I am compelled to express the opinion, formed after the most deliberate reflection and on full survey of the whole country, that, whether rightfully or wrongfully, the tariff stands in imminent danger. If it should be preserved through this session, it must fall at the next session. By what causes, and through what causes has arisen the necessity of this change in the policy of our country, I will not pretend now to elucidate. Others there are who may differ from the impressions which my mind has received on this subject. Owing, however, to a variety of concurrent causes, the tariff as it now exists is in imminent danger ; and if the system can be preserved beyond the next session, it must be by some means not now in the reach of human sagacity. The fall of that policy would be productive of consequences calamitous indeed.

*   *   *   *   *   *   *   *   *

" History can produce no parallel to the extent of the mischief which would be produced by such a disaster. The repeal of the edict of Nantes itself was nothing in comparison to it.   That condemned to exile and brought to ruin a great number of persons.   But, in my opinion, sir, the sudden repeal of the tariff policy would bring ruin and destruction on the whole people of this country. There is no evil, in my opinion, equal to the consequences which would result from such a catastrophe."

This bill came into the deliberations of that body under the denomination of " An act to modify the act of the fourteenth of July, one thousand eight hundred and thirty-two, and all other acts imposing duties on imports." The act, of which it was designed to be a modification, was the Adams' act of the previous year, before referred to.   The provisions of the act were substantially as fol- lows.   That all *ad valorum* duties of more than twenty per cent. should, on the thirty-first of December, 1833, be reduced one-tenth, and such reduction to take place on the thirty-first of December, 1835, and so continue, once in two years, until 1841, one-half of the excess to be taken off; and from June, 1842, the other half.   In this bill were involved some very excellent and wise principles.   It was the effectual abolishment, from and after the thirty-first of June, 1833, of all credits for amounts due the government on foreign imports, thereby requiring payment before the goods exchanged hands. By its requirements, also, all value of goods had to be assessed in the ports at which they were landed ; thereby preventing any advantages by practicing fraudulent invoices, etc., on the part of foreign speculators.

Such were the provisions of the measures introduced into the legislative councils of the preceding Congress by Mr. Clay, since known in our political history by the " Compromise Act of 1833." This bill created great excitement both in the senate and in the house. The diminutive scale of reduction on duties on imports was firmly resisted. In the discussion and eventual enactment of this measure, difficulties of the greatest magnitude were to be overcome. Its way to final adoption was immediately under the hammer of the veto of President Jackson, and over the heads of South Carolina nullification. The fiery ordeal of the heated southerns passed. It was subjected to the president, who had no hesitancy in taking responsibilities. Nullification in the south was raging in a perfect blaze. Between Jackson and Clay, the greatest political, if not personal, enmity existed. He was in no way favorable to Mr. Clay, or any measures in whose origin and advocacy he took an active part. Old party lines were to be redrawn, and able advocates and warm friends were to become alienated and arrayed one against the other in all the heat of talented antagonism Friends were to change place with foes, and the aspect of things to undergo a political transmogrification.

Majorities were to be created for it by convincing proofs
of its utility to the country, and through the influence of
such majorities Jackson was to be conciliated and the
veto withheld. All these difficulties were to be overcome before the compromise tariff could be adopted by
Congress. The opposition to the measures of that compromise was led by some of the most talented men in the
senate and house, and was of the most relentless nature.
It was a complete and masterly change of the old system
of protective policy, and was regarded by some as a very
dangerous one. Mr. Forsyth, of Georgia, was among the
formidable of the opposition. So far did he carry his opposition, that he heaped ridicule upon some of the measures of the act, and contested the passage of others with
zeal and warmth. He met the arguments of its advocates
with sarcasms and inuendoes, and in every way manifested the deadliest hostility to the entire measure. Webster, of Massachusetts, was identified with the opposition to
the compromise. Other northern senators of no less distinction opposed it with all their talents and energies.
The position they took was, that the proposed diminution
was too great a surrender, and too great a sacrifice of protective principles. Webster took that view of the case,
that it was equivalent to an entire destruction of the
American policy of protection. He threw his mighty
talents into the opposition with all their force. That
great excitement should be engendered by the collision
of two such minds as his and Clay's, should be no matter of surprise when the resistless perseverance of both
is taken into consideration. Together they had been used

to laboring long and hard, and when they thus labored they overcame all opposition; but when one was arrayed against the other, it was the only opposition they could not overcome. Clay and Webster could rule a senate when combined, but when one came in contact with the other, one man was more than either could overcome.

The compromise tariff was finally, after being discussed in all its ramifications, submitted to the house of representatives on the twenty-sixth of February, and passed by a majority of twenty votes. Mr. Fillmore, as will be shown in the passage of the tariff in 1842, was always a friend to the American protective policy, and had a fair opportunity of giving evidences of that friendship in the various discussions upon that branch of American politics during the different sessions he served with such distinguished ability. This compromise act was among the most important measures adopted by the preceding Congress. From the discussions it had elicited, and the vote of Congress on the subject, all doubts in regard to its being a revenue bill, which was an objection urged against it by some of the opposition, were removed, and on the tenth of March it passed the senate by a majority of thirteen votes. Thus the measure, notwithstanding the fierce opposition it encountered at every step, and the great obstacles that impeded its progress from its incipient agitation, by the almost superhuman efforts of the friends of protective policy, passed both houses, and escaped the veto.

As the veto of the United States Bank by President Jackson, and his removal of the deposits which had just taken place prior to the convention of the present Congress, formed the principal grounds for discussion and excitement in that body; though in such discussion Mr. Fillmore participated to a very limited extent, to be enabled more thoroughly to understand and appreciate his views upon these measures, some remarks in regard to them are deemed indispensable.

On the second of March, 1833, from inferences drawn from the president's message in regard to the removal of the deposits, the following resolution was introduced into the house of representatives : " That the government deposits may, in the opinion of the house, be safely continued in the Bank of the United States." This resolution passed by a vote of a hundred and ten for, and forty-six against it. This resolution, however, was effective of no good or harm, so far as the deposits were concerned. Overlooking the fact entirely, that the secretary of the treasury, as the executive of Congress, was amenable to that body for his action in the discharge of his official duties, he was regarded by the president as rather *his* agent, for the execution of his requirements. On the third of June, the president communicated to Mr. Duane, the secretary of the treasury, his intentions concerning the deposits, informing him, that his cabinet was divided in opinion in regard to their removal, and desiring him to give his opinion in regard to that measure. On the twenty-second of July, he was asked whether his intention was to refuse to remove the deposits, to which Duane replied in substance, that he would resign his office, in case of a nonconcurrence with the views of the president in regard to the measure. This course of Mr. Duane was by no means satisfactory to the president, and a pretty lengthy correspondence, of no very amiable nature, ensued between the parties, until a positive refusal of the secretary to remove the deposits elicited the following quietus from the president :

The President of the United States to the Secretary of the Treasury:

SEPTEMBER 23, 1833.

SIR: Since I returned your first letter of September twenty-first, and since the receipt of your second letter of the same day, which I sent back to you at your own request, I have received your third and fourth letters of the same date. The last two as well as the first, contain statements that are inaccurate; and as I have already indicated in my last note to you that a correspondence of this description is inadmissible, your last two letters are herewith returned. But from all your recent communications, as well as your recent conduct, your feelings and sentiments appear to be of such a character that, after your letter of July last, in which you say, should your views not accord with mine, " I will, from respect to you and myself, afford you an opportunity to select a successor, whose views may accord with your own on the important matter in contemplation," and your determination now to disregard the pledge you then gave, I feel myself constrained to notify you that your further services as secretary of the treasury are no longer required.

I am, respectfully, your obedient servant,

ANDREW JACKSON.[*]

*Niles' Register.

This dismissal of the secretary of the treasury, who had accepted the post by solicitation, because he refused to indorse and assist in the removal of the deposits from the United States Bank, was regarded by Mr. Clay and others opposed to the Jackson administration as an unwarrantable exercise of executive power, and created very great excitement. The alarm was sounded from Dan to Beersheba, and awful results predicted from the catastrophe, which, however, never came to pass to the extent anticipated. Mr. Taney, who was afterwards chief-justice, was appointed secretary of the treasury, in the place of Duane, the former incumbent. On the first of October, 1833, Mr. Taney, in compliance with the president's command, removed the deposits from the United States Bank, and placed them in the different banks specified ; and on the convention of the twenty-third Congress, made to that body a full report of his proceedings as secretary of the treasury. On the reception of that report, the subjoined resolutions were presented by Mr. Clay :

"Resolved, that by dismissing the late secretary of the treasury, because he would not, contrary to his sense of his own duty, remove the money of the United States deposited with the bank of the United States and its branches, in conformity with the president's opinion, and by appointing his successor to effect such removal which has been done, the president assumed the exercise of a power over the United States treasury not granted to him by the constitution and laws, and dangerous to the liberties of the people."

"Resolved, that the reasons assigned by the secretary
9*

of the treasury for the removal of the money of the United States, deposited in the bank of the United States and its branches, communicated to Congress on the third of December, 1833, are unsatisfactory and insufficient."

The resolutions were adopted almost by acclamation ; so intense had the excitement become, that any resolution denunciatory of the movement would have been adopted, even though they transcended the bounds of moderation and propriety. During all the excitement and prediction of ruin to the country incident to these measures, Mr. Fillmore as a member of the twenty-third Congress examined the causes engendering it, with solicitous care. The United States Bank and the removal of the deposits, and their bearings upon the prosperity of the country, he studied, with an ardent desire to acquaint himself familiarly therewith. With that keen and penetrating sagacity which so eminently qualified him to foresee the result of important national measures, he acquainted himself thoroughly with the whole subject. With financial capacities of no ordinary nature, as will be shown when we come to investigate his duties as the incumbent of an office exclusively financial, he weighed well the circumstances likely to grow out of the measure.

Coolly and dispassionately he went to work, as though it was a great mathematical problem he had to solve, and in the solution paid great attention to all the points involved. The result of this investigation, notwithstanding the excitement of those about him, and the predictions of such ruinous consequences to the country, was his conviction that the calamitous consequences apprehended were not justified by the aspects of the case. He felt well assured that they were magnified, and were creating unnecessary alarms. Subsequent events have shown that these convictions were correct, and that his foresight upon the great question of the day was superior to the leading men of his party, and in advance of the times.

This is a very happy faculty of Mr. Fillmore's. Be questions exciting as they may, though the whole spirit of the country be fanned into a terriffic blaze, he stands unmoved, facing every danger, looking coolly on, and making safe and reliable calculations of escape. These calculations and conclusions are seldom incorrect, as is proven by his views on the great questions of which we have been speaking. Not being infected with the excitements that rage around him, he forms them by judgment and wisdom, and the subsidence of the excitement discloses their correctness, as in the case of the measures discussed in the foregoing. He never attached the importance to a United States Bank and the deposit operation that Mr. Clay and the leading men of that day did. Mr. Fillmore's views in regard to these measures were correct; time has demonstrated their genuineness and wisdom.

As a committee-man on the District of Columbia, the plan for the construction of the Potomac bridge devolving on that committee, Mr. Fillmore, with the aid of his associates, proposed a plan for the erection of the work by which it would not exceed in cost the sum of $130,000, while the president proposed a plan to the secretary of the treasury running up the cost to *three millions*. This

was a difference well worthy of eliciting the consideration and action of the house. The question being before
the house, comments were made by several members as
to what committee's jurisdiction it more properly belonged,
when " Mr. Fillmore advocated the claims of the committee of the district to have the subject referred to them,
and he considered that it was unreasonable to suppose
that this committee would not be as much disposed to
check extravagance as any other committee. Without,
therefore, wishing to detract from the intelligence, patriotism, and purity of conduct, which the chairman of the
committee on roads and canals, and the other members
of that committee, acted, it was only fair to suppose that,
if the subject was sent to the committee on the district,
they would act up to their economical views; and, having
an opportunity to examine witnesses, from their testimony
have new light thrown upon the subject." Here we
have a principle by which Mr. Fillmore has been guided
in all his relations, both public and private. He learned
in early boyhood to entertain economical views, and he
demonstrated them through the career of his studentship,
and practiced them in his profession. When he became
the public repository of the people's interests, he was
careful still to give them a strict adherence, by retrench-
ing, as much as possible. all expenditures of the public
funds. In this respect, in all the capacities in which he
has served as a public servant, he has been especially
careful. His disposition to check extravagance in the
outlay of the public fund has been manifested cn all
occasions in a happy degree. The careless manner of

transacting business and making appropriations for public works on the part of those to whose views of expediency and propriety the squandering of vast sums of public treasure is a matter of no moment, never failed to receive the proper censure of Mr. Fillmore.

In propositions before legislative assemblies of which it has been his fortune to be a member, to make appropriations for public improvements, his first object was to investigate the utility of the measure proposed, being thoroughly satisfied of which, with economical views he devoted his attention to the ascertainment of its cost, and opposed a heavier draft upon the treasury than was absolutely necessary to its completion. Being a man of great practical as well as theoretical talents, he was always, in proposing such plans and arrangements, happily constituted to see what was necessary, and to retrench useless expenditures. The public treasury he has always watched with a jealous eye.

During the entire deliberations of the twenty-third Congress, the interminable bank excitement raged incessantly, and the halls of legislation were continually flooded with petitions praying relief from the oppression weighing upon different sections of the country, in regard to the veto of the United States Bank, and for a recharter of that institution. On the seventeenth of March, a large number of petitions and remonstrances were presented, by the citizens of different states through their respective representatives, among others, was one from the city of Boston signed by several thousand citizens of that place ; one from Vermont, signed by a large number of

voters of that state; one from the city of Buffalo, presented through their representative, Mr. Fillmore, signed
by several hundred names, and accompanied by certain
resolutions, expressive of their views upon that exciting
measure, without reference to party or party feelings.
Mr. Fillmore presented the memorial and resolutions,
desiring to explain the hostility manifested by his constituents against a United States Bank on former occasions. After the memorial was read, setting forth their
grievances, and the disastrous consequences they saw
impending over them by the veto of the bank, and praying its recharter or some mode of relief, Mr. Fillmore
moved that it be laid on the table. This was the universal consignment of that species of document. So numerous had they become, the bestowal of more time than
was required for their reception was utterly impracticable.
This shows the extent to which these memorials were
sent into Congress, praying redress for the infliction of
what was conceived to be an incurable ulcer upon the
system of American currency.

This was a duty which Mr. Fillmore several times had
to perform during the sessions of Congress. No section
seemed to take greater interest, or manifest more concern,
in reference to the movements of the president, than did
the people of western New York. These petitions and
memorials, when they came to his hands from his constituents, invariably received the attention from him due
the people from their public servant. Faithfully devoted
to the preservation of the interests of those he was representing, whether he attached the importance to certain

measures they did was not a consideration to deter him from giving his attention to their views and wishes. Representative he construed into its proper interpretation, and felt that he was there for the people — standing in their place — and was faithful to their interests. He stood up to his party with the same unflinching zeal that characterized his labors in the state assembly, giving his influence and his vote to the advocacy of his principles upon all political measures, and in all matters of a general nature he was assiduous to promote the local interests of his constituents. There have been men in Congress who, during their first session, developed a more brilliant career than did Mr. Fillmore; but none were ever more faithful; none were ever the recipients of greater approbation, in both the plaudits of his constituents and his conscience. Some may have won brighter laurels, but none ever more enduring ones.

On the seventeenth of August, 1834, an amendment to the annual appropriation bill being before the house, and the exorbitance and inequality of many officers' salaries in government employ under discussion, Mr. Fillmore urged the reduction of certain high salaries, as follows:

" He insisted that, as the measures of the government had the effect of raising the value of money, whilst on the opposite side they depreciate the means of subsistence; it was only acting justly to the people, from whom these salaries were derived, to place them on a similar footing, in these points, with themselves; and he contended that, if three dollars could now purchase those articles which it formerly would have taken four to do, the salaries of their public officers, with the reduction now contemplated by the amendment, would be practically as high as they had been. The objection as to the time of making these reductions did not appear to him to be so essentially important, when the necessity of doing so was so generally conceded. He found there were propositions in the bill granting increased compensation. If it was proper, then, in the estimation of the committee, thus to alter the salaries of officers, fixed by law, he could not see the force of any objection to their reducing the amount. He referred to the salaries paid in the state of New York, as instances how much more economically the highest offices in that state were filled, in comparison with those under the general government; from which he inferred that, as these offices were all well filled, and the appointments not objected to, but sought for on the score of emolument by the most competent men in the state, one or the other of the rates of paying for public services might be unjust. He referred to the fact that the judges of the supreme court of New York received but two thousand dollars a year. He desired to have a reduction now, instead of waiting the result of an inquiry, for another reason. It would become the interest of those whose salaries are reduced, and which they would never do in any other case, to come forward and oppose the effects upon them, and in this way only could they expect that any inquiry could be promoted with any hope of a good result."

From the considerations embraced in the foregoing extract, he voted for the amendment to the appropriation bill, having for its object the curtailment of certain salaries, among others that of the commissioner of the land office, whose salary was as much as the judge's of the supreme court of the state of New York. The arguments in the foregoing are plain, practical, sound, and common-sense like, displaying the reasoning, penetrative qualities of his mind, characteristic of all his speeches. The sentiments embodied in the remarks are those which he has evinced in every public capacity, a disposition to effect a retrenchment of the expenditures of the public moneys, to give to the various public servants in government employ nothing more nor less than value received for such services, with a watchful care that all moneys expended were for services absolutely required by the government.

Among other improvements of a national character promoted by Congress, was the erection of a harbor at George's Island, the design of which was for fortification more than otherwise. Judicious investments for internal improvements, especially if their design was to increase the means of public defence, always found in Mr. Fillmore a zealous advocate. One of the leading men in the opposition to the construction of this harbor was Mr. Polk. He opposed the measure, and Mr. Fillmore advocated it. It is a little singular that Mr. Fillmore, the leading man for, and Mr. Polk, the leading man against, that measure, should have both been elevated to the chief magistracy of the United States. The circumstance of the harbor erection was an enterprise of no great magnitude; but it is illustrative of the spirit of the times, and shows in what attitude these two statesmen stood in relation to each other in the comparative outset of their political careers. Mr. Polk was in the majority party, and the warm friend of President Jackson; Mr. Fillmore was in the minority, and not identified with the Jackson party; consequently the former was at that time in the smoothest way to success. Subsequent developments threw them both into the presidential chair — both were incumbents of that high office during times of great excitement; both evinced great capacities as statesmen; both have left their names upon the pages of their country's history; and both were great men.

Many other very important measures came before the twenty-third Congress, both of a local and general nature, upon the action of which Mr. Fillmore participated with great credit to himself, and usefulness to his constituency and country. The proceedings of that Congress were marked by a spirit of excitement and party feelings, engendered by the course of the president in his veto of the bank bill and the removal of the deposits, rarely witnessed in a legislative body. But amid all the excitements of party and party animosity, he maintained his characteristic firmness, and guarded with special care the interests reposed in his keeping, throughout the entire session. The compromise tariff of Mr. Clay, as before stated, had effected a temporary settlement of some of the leading measures advocated by his party, and to the remaining ones he gave an undeviating adherence. Internal improvements found in him a warm and zealous advocate, who, on all proposed investments of a nature to develop the resources of the country, took favorable and decided ground. The local measures, in whose passage his constituency was immediately concerned, suffered not the least neglect. Modest, unassuming, courteous, and dignified, he elevated himself to a very enviable position, for a young member in his first session. He was always at his post rendering service in the various measures of the day, never exhibiting the least neglect of duty as a legislator.

He won the respect and esteem of the entire body, and established himself in the hearts of his constituency.

He was among the most industrious and vigilant members of the twenty-third Congress.

An enumeration of all the measures in which he participated, and proposed, during that session of Congress, would swell the pages of this chapter to too great a length. Suffice it to say, that every measure he advocated and every vote he cast met the entire approbation of those he represented, from the assemblage of Congress to its adjournment.

CHAPTER VI.

Reëlected to Congress —Van Burenism— Distinguished characters —
Polk elected speaker — Fourth installment of the Deposit Act —A
bill to postpone the payment of the installment — It passes the
senate — Mr. Fillmore's opposition — His able speech against the
bill — Mr. Fillmore gives his views of the U. S. Bank — The passage of the bill — Mr. Fillmore and Mr. Clay — Slavery in the
District of Columbia — The right of petition — Mr. Clay its champion in the senate, and Mr. Fillmore in the house — His views on
the subject of slavery at that time — The North and the South —
Mr. Fillmore's conciliatory nature as a statesman — His patriotism.

THE commencement of this chapter takes Mr. Fillmore
again from the retirement and pursuits of his professional
labors, so congenial to his feelings, in which he was
placed by the adjournment of the twenty-third Congress.
After the close of his labors in that body, he resumed the
practice of his profession in the city of Buffalo, which he
continued with marked success and distinguished ability
until 1836.   The high estimate placed upon him by his
fellow citizens, from the faithful manner in which he had
discharged his duties as a public servant, would not permit him long to enjoy the retiracy of private life.   In the
fall of 1836 he was again elected to Congress by the people of his district.   Since his last labors in that body, the
political elements had again been stirred with the thunders of party strife.   Jackson's star was not so brightly
in the ascendant, and the bank deposit excitement had, to

some extent, been supplanted by Van Burenism and the sub-treasury. Van Buren and Harrison were the presidential candidates during the campaign of 1836. The majority for Van Buren over the whig candidate, Harrison, was overwhelming, while White received the vote of a fragmental portion of the democratic party. Thus, the incoming administration bid fair to give its adherence to the Jacksonian principles of the previous one, with a strong progressive tendency opposed to the fostering of conservative measure. The democrats still held sway in the house by a pretty large majority. Among the members of the twenty-fifth Congress who have figured conspicuously in the politics of the nation and enrolled their names high in the book of fame, was Millard Fillmore, J. Q. Adams, J. R. Underwood, James K. Polk, and Henry A. Wise. To the great service these gentlemen have been to the country, her own great institutions bear the best attestation. Three of them filled the presidential chair. A fourth occupied an elevated position in the United States Senate, as the colleague of Henry Clay, second to none; and in the adjustment of the fearful difficulties of 1849 and 1850, rendered efficient and patriotic services that entitle him to the lasting gratitude of the country. A fifth is the acting governor of Virginia. All five of these gentlemen were colaborers in the twenty-fifth Congress.

Congress was organized by the election of James K. Polk to the speakership, and the message of President Van Buren was received on the fifth of September.

One of the first measures of importance proposed in

the first session of this Congress was from the committee
on finance. This committee, the day after its appointment, reported, through their chairman, the following

" *Bill to Postpone the Payment of the Fourth Installment
of Deposits with the States.*

" Be it enacted by the senate and house of representatives of the United States of America in congress assembled, that the transfer of the fourth installment of
deposits directed to be made with the states, under the
thirteenth section of the act of June 23, 1836, be, and
the same is, hereby postponed until further provision by
law."

This bill, having originated in the senate, elicited the
opposition of Calhoun, and the non-concurrence of
Webster, though he was of the finance committee, from
whence it was reported. These two gentlemen were the
leaders in the opposition to the bill, while Mr. Wright
was its warmest advocate. The bill was warmly discussed in the senate for several days, until it became the
leading subject. After being before the senate for two
or three weeks, it was, after some amendments, submitted to that body, and passed by a majority of eleven
votes — Mr. Clay voting against it.

The deposit act of 1836 made it the duty of the secretary of the treasury to ascertain the precise amount of
surplus that would be due each state on the first day of
the ensuing January. In compliance with that act, in
his report to Congress, he had specified exactly these several amounts, and three of the installments had been duly

paid over to those properly delegated to receive them. The bill introduced into the senate by the committee on finance was to postpone the payment of the fourth install- ment, upon the ground of the embarrassed condition of the government, without specifying any time when such payment should be made, leaving that entirely to the discretion of Congress.   Taking into consideration the fact of the secretary's having already made his report, and giving the amounts of these several installments, the opponents, with great justice, argued the inconsistency of the measure that would counteract their payment as promised.

This bill was introduced into the house on the eight- eenth of September ensuing its passage in the senate.

It became a subject of great interest, in the house of representatives, and on the twenty-fifth of September, it being the special business of the house, a very animated discussion was being carried on, in regard to it, by some of the most prominent members, when Mr. Fillmore, among others, delivered the following speech, which is inserted as showing the views he entertained at that time, on the great questions of national politics, and the style of his address in legislative bodies :

"I am now prepared, sir, notwithstanding the lateness of the hour, to offer what I have to say on this subject ; but if the committee prefer to rise, and continue the dis- cussion to-morrow, it will suit me quite as well.   For the purpose of testing the sense of the committeee on that point, I will cheerfully yield the floor for a motion to rise.

"What then, sir, is the history of this surplus revenue,

upon which the bill upon your table is to operate, and which has elicited such a warm discussion? It is this, sir — our revenue had been graduated upon a scale sufficiently large, for many years, to collect from the people, chiefly by duties, a sum, which, together with moneys received from the sale of public lands, not only defrayed all the expenses of government, but left annually a large surplus to be applied in payment of the national debt. This debt, sir, which, at the adoption of the federal constitution, was upwards of $75,000,000, had, by the operation of this system, been gradually reduced, so that, in 1812, before the commencement of the last war, it was only about $45,000,000. The expenses of that war, sir, again increased this debt, so that, in 1816, it was upwards of $127,000,000. A wise forecast had made ample provision for its payment, and year by year it was lessened, until 1834, when it was finally extinguished.

"It was apparent, sir, to all, before this debt was finally liquidated, that when that event did occur, the same system of indirect taxation, which could not suddenly be changed without injury to our manufactures, must throw a large amount of surplus revenue into the treasury. This money having been thus collected from the people, or being the avails of the public lands, it was thought no more than reasonable, as it was not wanted for government purposes, to return it again to the people, from whom it had been taken, and whose it was. I shall not now stop, sir, to inquire into the justice or constitutionality of the measure. It was clearly just. The government had this fund as the agent of the people. I hold, sir, that the government, in all cases, is but the agent and instrument of the people, constituted to execute their collective will.

"To restore this large amount of money to the use of those from whom it had been taken, with as little injury as possible to the country, Congress passed a law on the twenty-sixth day of June, 1836, by which it was declared that the secretary of the treasury should, on the first day of January, 1837, ascertain how much money there was in the treasury, and deduct from the whole sum thus found $5,000,000, and that the remainder should be deposited with the several states, or such of them as should consent to receive the same, one-fourth on each of the first days of January, April, July, and October, in 1837, upon the conditions prescribed in the act; which were, that the states should keep it safely, and return it again to the United States, in sums not exceeding $10,000 per month, from any one state, and so in the like proportion from other states, when wanted for the use of the government, and demanded by the secretary of the treasury. But the secretary was authorized to draw for $20,000 on giving thirty days' notice. I do not pretend, sir, to give the words of the act verbatim, as I have it not before me, and I only speak from recollection. But this is the substance of the act of Congress.

"This, sir, was the proposition on the part of the United States of the terms upon which they were willing to deposit this money with the states. This, too, was a proposition emanating from the highest — nay, from all the separate departments of this government. It was
10

pledging the national faith in the most solemn manner that it could be pledged, by a law which received the assent of both houses of Congress, and the approbation of the president.

" The state of New York, sir, by an act of its legislature, passed, I think, in January, 1837, agreed to accept this proposition made by the United States, and to receive the money, and safely keep and return the same when called for, according to the terms of said act of Congress ; and pledging the faith of the state for the faithful performance of these acts. This, then, constituted the contract or compact between the parties.

" The secretary of the treasury, as directed by the act of Congress, ascertained, on the 1st day of January last, the amount of money in the treasury, and after deducting, as he supposed, $5,000,000 from that sum, found there remained to be deposited with the states $37,468,859.97. I say, as he 'supposed,' sir ; for it now appears by his late report to this house, that there was $1,670,137.52 in the treasury, (that is, sir, in the pet banks,) on that day, of which he had received no account. So that, in reality, he reserved $6,670,137.52, instead of the $5,000,000, as directed by the act.

" Well, sir, the portion of this which belonged to the state of New York, by the terms of the compact, was $5,352,694. 28, three-fourths of which has been received by that state, and the bill now on your table proposes to postpone the payment of the remaining $1,338,173.57, to which that state will be entitled on the first day of October next, by the terms of the compact.

" Now, sir, let it be borne in mind that this is one entire contract, in reference to one entire sum of money, and that it has been partially performed. I say, sir, the sum is entire. Although it was to be paid at different times, yet the appropriation was of the entire sum that should be found in the treasury on a certain day. That sum, when ascertained in the manner prescribed in the act, was the money set apart for this specific purpose. It was, in legal intendment, as definite and fixed as though the money had been counted out at the several banks where it was deposited on that day, and laid aside for this object. True, it was to be paid out at different times; but this was to accommodate the banks, and prevent a derangement of the currency, and consequent distress of the community, by calling for too large sums at once.

" But, Mr. Chairman, I am opposed to the bill upon your table. I am opposed to it, first, sir, on the ground that it is hypocritical and false in its language. The title of the bill is an ' act to *postpone*' the payment of this fourth installment. This is a false label, sir, to the door through which we are to enter into the mysteries of this bill. But let us look at the bill itself. It declares that the payment of this installment ' shall be *postponed* until further *provision by law.*' What is this, then, sir, but a *repeal* of so much of the act of 1836 as authorizes the payment of this fourth installment? It does not merely postpone the payment to a definite time, then to be made without any further legislative action; but it postpones it until further ' provision by law,' that is, until by a *new law* Congress shall direct this payment to be made. If this bill pass, nothing short of a new law can ever give this money to the states. Then the effect of this bill is to repeal the law of 1836.

"Why not say so, then? Why profess to postpone when you absolutely revoke? Why not call things by their right names? Is there some iniquity in the transaction that it is necessary to conceal? Is it intended to excite expectations among the people that are never to be realized? Sir, I disdain such a course. I will never give my vote for a law that, on its face, bears evidence of fraudulent concealment and hypocritical designs.

"I am aware, sir, that an amendment has been offered by the gentleman from South Carolina, (Mr. Pickens,) that, if adopted, would obviate this objection. But as that amendment is undoubtedly intended to sugar over this nauseous pill, to make it a little more palatable to some who loathe it now, and as I should still be opposed to the bill if the amendment were adopted, for reasons which I shall hereafter give, I am inclined to let those who are prepared to swallow anything take the dose as it is, and vote against the amendment as well as the bill. If this money be not now paid, I have no idea that the states will ever receive it. Let us have it now, according to promise, or tell us at once we have nothing to expect. Do not tantalize us by exciting further hopes that are never to be realized.

"But, sir, I am also opposed to the bill for another reason, and that is, that this sudden change of the destiny of near ten millions of dollars is calculated still further to derange the currency and business operations of the country, and add to the accumulated distresses of the community under which they now labor. If there be one truth, above all others, well settled in political economy, it is this: that if you would make a nation prosperous and happy, give them a uniform and unchangeable currency. It is as essential as uniformity and stability in your weights and measures. This currency is the life-blood of the body politic. Its supply should be equal and uniform. Every throb of the heart is felt to the utmost extremities. If the regular flow and pulsation fail, languor and faintness follow; but ' overaction,' as the president calls it, often produces instantaneous paralysis and prostration. The political empyrics have administered dose upon dose, and tried experiment after experiment, until the patient is prostrate and hopeless, writhing in agony and imploring for relief. If ever there was a nation or an individual to whom that epitaph was peculiarly appropriate, it is this nation and this administration:

" I was well; I wished to be better ;
I took physic, and here I am."

" I am also opposed to this bill, sir, for another reason. Its object and intent is to violate the plighted faith of this nation. I shall not enter into an examination to see whether the offer on the part of the United States, which was acceded·to by the state of New York, in the manner that I have already stated, was or was not a pecuniary contract, according to the strict rules of the common law, which might be enforced in a court of justice. This point has been most fully and eloquently discussed by my colleague immediately in front of me, (Mr. Sibley.) I could add nothing to what he has said on that subject. It is said that the United States have received no consideration for the promise. But, sir, I am disposed to place this question on higher grounds. Does it become this nation or the American Congress to stand here paltering about the redemption of its plighted faith to one of the daughters of the Union, on the ground that it has received no consideration for the promise which it has made ? Has this nation, indeed, sunk so low that it takes shelter from its engagements, when it finds it inconvenient to perform them, behind the statute of frauds ? The reason why a consideration is required to enforce a contract between individuals does not apply to this case. That is a rule adopted by the courts to protect the inconsiderate and the unwary from the consequences of their own folly, in making hasty promises without consideration. But, sir, even as between individuals, if the manner in which the contract has been made evinces a due degree of deliberation, then the courts will enforce it. If, for instance, the contract be sealed, that is regarded as so solemn an act, and evidences such caution and deliberation that the courts, by the common law, preclude all inquiry into the consideration, and compel the obligor to perform his contract. This case shows the reason of the rule, and I submit that it has no applicability here. Will gentlemen say that Congress was surprised into the promise ? that there was not due deliberation had on the subject ? or that the congregated wisdom of this nation requires such a miserable subterfuge as this, to justify to its own conscience the violation of its plighted faith? Sir, was not the contract sufficiently solemn? It is among the sacred archives of your nation. It is of the same high and solemn character with your treaties with foreign nations. Nay, if possible, sir, it is still higher, and more obligatory upon the nation. A treaty is only sanctioned by the president and the senate. This, sir, has been sealed with the national honor, and attested by the national faith of both branches of Congress and the executive; and you may call it contract, compact, or treaty, it is clearly a *promise* by the nation, in the most solemn form that a promise can be made.

"Sir, have gentlemen who are in favor of this bill duly reflected upon its nature and consequences? Have they duly considered the value of the national honor? Would any one dare to make a proposition to break our national faith, if it had been pledged to a foreign power, as it has been to the several states of our Union? I trust not. Then, sir, is the obligation less sacred to the various states of this confederacy, especially when made for the benefit of the people themselves, in reference to their own money? I hope not. But, sir, if we violate our plighted faith here, may we not do it in other cases? Your pension laws, passed for the relief of the care-worn veteran and hardy mariner, promise to those individuals a mere gratuity. It is the bounty which a generous nation bestows upon its brave defenders. But it has no elements of a pecuniary contract. There is no such reciprocity in those cases, as in this, to continue a contract. No promise or service is required from the pensioner, as a *quid pro quo* for the bounty you bestow. But in this case you have required and received the plighted faith of the state of New York to receive the money, keep it safely, and repay it in certain proportions. Would any member of this house have the hardihood to propose a bill to withhold the payment of these pensions, and then assign as a reason that there is no valid contract for paying them ? I presume not. Sir, there is something of more value to a nation than money. It is untarnished honor — unbroken faith. They should be as spotless as female chastity.

> " One false step in vain we may deplore ;
>   We fall like stars that set to rise no more.

" The reason why every promise should be performed is, that it has raised expectations which, in justice, ought not to be disappointed. The whole business of life is an endless chain of confidence growing out of these promises, express or implied. And frequently the breaking of one link sunders a thousand.

> ——" Whatever link you strike,
>   Tenth, or ten-thousandth, breaks the chain alike.

" Look at its effects, in this case, upon the state of New York. That state, relying upon the plighted faith of this nation, has gone on and agreed to loan out all this money to citizens throughout the state, giving to each town and ward their ratable proportion. Bonds and mortgages have been taken for the whole amount ; and the three-fourths which has been received by the state from this government, has been paid over to the borrowers, and promises in the shape of certificates given to pay over the remaining fourth on the first of October. The state has relied upon the promises of this government for the money to pay these certificates. Now, sir, unless the money can be raised in some other way by the state, if these be withheld, all those numerous borrowers must be disappointed. Those who have struggled from day to day, and from week to week, to bear up against the pressure of the times, until they could obtain this pittance of relief, are to sink down in utter despair.

"But, sir, what is the difference between the promise on the part of the state to loan this money to individuals, and the promise on the part of this government to deposit this money with the states? A deposit is a loan; and the person with whom the deposit is made becomes the borrower, liable to pay the money according to the terms agreed. This government, then, has agreed to loan the money to the state of New York; and has taken the bond and mortgage of that state, in the shape of a solemn act of its legislature, to repay it on certain terms. The state has agreed to loan the same sum to individuals, and has taken their bonds and mortgages for the repayment of the same. Then, if this government can be justified in breaking this agreement, much more will the state of New York be justified in the breach of the agreement to the individual borrowers. The state may not only plead the high example of this nation in the breach of its promise, but may urge, with perfect justice, that the breach of faith by the United States, on which the state had unfortunately relied, had prevented the state from fulfilling its engagements. Will any of my colleagues who

now urge a breach of faith on the part of the United
States, in withholding this installment, say that they believe the state of New York will be guilty of a similar
breach to the borrowers of this money? I know they
will not stain her honor by such an insinuation. Then
how can they justify themselves to their God or their
country, in lending their votes or their voices to dishonor
this nation in such a manner as would be regarded a reproach and disgrace to the state in which we live? I
hope gentlemen will pause and reflect before they finally
act.   *   *   *   *   *   *   *   *

" Let me not be misunderstood in what I am about to
say. I have never been a particular friend of the United
States Bank. I regard it, as I do all other banks, as a
necessary evil. I have never been its advocate, and am
not now. It has gone down to 'the tomb of the Cap-
ulets;' let it rest in peace. And I should have great
doubts of the expediency of establishing a new United
States Bank at this time, for the relief of the community.
I fear that an attempt to put it in operation would rather
aggravate than mitigate our sufferings. But on this point
it is not necessary to express an opinion. I only allude
to it, to prevent any improper inference, and that the
committee may understand that all I have to say of the
United States Bank is as matter of history, and not of
opinion, as to its expediency or usefulness at this time.
Times have essentially changed; and what might have
been proper or useful then, may be wholly improper or
useless now. Then, such a bank, with the confidence of
the government and people, might be useful in regulating

the currency. Since the war upon that institution, banks have multiplied beyond all former example. To add another at this time, and collect together the requisite specie to put it in operation, would, I fear, add greatly to our present embarrassments. People must learn from actual suffering that it is much more easy to tear down than to build up, to destroy than to create, and to derange than to restore. Ignorance and folly may accomplish the one; wisdom, prudence, and time can alone perform the other.

" But, sir, I said I was opposed to these measures, because they promised no permanent relief to the country. Why has the president, after witnessing the sufferings of this community — after calling us together, as every one supposed, to propose some measure of relief— turned thus coldly away, without recommending anything to restore a uniform currency ? Are the prayers, and tears, and groans of a whole nation, suffering all the horrors of impending bankruptcy, not worthy of his consideration ? Are members of the administration prepared to return and look their constituents in the face without making one effort for the relief of the country ? We, of the minority can do nothing. We are powerless. But you have all power. Then why not exert it to bring back the days of prosperity and sunshine that existed before this fatal war upon the currency, and commerce, and business of our country.   *   *   *   *   *   *   *   *

" But, sir, this war against the United States Bank, got up for political effect, regardless of the peace of society or the interests of the country, was made to unite the extremes of society. The more intelligent of the middle class never engaged in it; or were drawn into it, from political associations, with reluctance. It was really a war of the state banks against the United States Bank, got up by artful politicians to elevate Mr. Van Buren to the presidency. They tempted the cupidity of the thousand officers and stockholders interested in these banks, with the bribe of the public deposits, and the prospect of destroying a hated rival that kept them in check, and loaned money at six per cent. It was a Shylock feeling of avarice and revenge. On the other hand, all the affiliated presses connected with state banks cried out against the monster, until the more ignorant part of the community thought their liberties in danger, and joined the strong bank party against the weaker, to put down the United States Bank. Having effected this and brought the country to the verge of ruin, and overwhelmed these state banks with infamy and disgrace, is it strange that the same unprincipled course should be pursued against them, that has been pursued against the United States Bank? It is what they had a right to expect. It is but ' commending the poisoned chalice to their own lips.' We may pity their folly; we may condemn the heartless perfidy that first seduced them from their duty, and prostituted them to the vilest purposes of partisan warfare, until their infamy has rendered them useless, and now casts them aside; but we cannot deny that the retributive hand of justice is seen in their sufferings.

"Sir, in corroboration of what I have said about this being a war of the state banks against the United States

Bank, got up by designing politicians, I will mention a
few facts connected with a little secret history on this
subject in my own state.

"It is known, sir, that we have a peculiar system of
banking in the state of New York, called the safety-fund
system. It had its origin with Mr. Van Buren, when
governor of the state in 1829. Although he did not claim
the merit of an original inventor, yet he adopted it as his
own, and recommended it to the legislature. This system, sir, establishing a community of interest between the
banks, and being under the immediate supervision of three
bank commissioners, is admirably well calculated for use
as a political engine. It was no sooner put in operation,
than it was brought to bear upon the legislature of that
state. In 1830 or 1831, while I was honored with a seat
in the legislature of that state, resolutions were introduced
into that body against a recharter of the United States
Bank. These resolutions, sir, originated with the banks
in that state. Not one solitary petition from the people
on that subject had been presented to the legislature.
The bank then had three branches in that state : one at
New York, one at Utica, and one at Buffalo ; and the people were contented with the currency which they furnished. No murmur, no complaint, was heard from the
people. But, sir, day by day, as those resolutions were
under discussion in that legislature, the birds of ill-omen,
that deal in bank stock, hovered round that hall, and
watched the progress of this unholy proceeding with an
intense anxiety.

"But no farmers, no mechanics, were there. They had

not been consulted; they took no interest in the proceeding. They had no share at that time in this conspiracy of the state banks against their interest. They were delving at their labor, and slumbering in security, while these banks were forging the chains with which they have since bound them. Yes, sir, I was informed, and I believe it, that nightly, during the discussion of those resolutions, their supporters in the legislature met in conclave, in one of the principal banks in that city, to devise ways and means to carry them through. They were carried. These banks, with the aid of the party screws, proved too powerful for the independence and honesty of that body; and the result was proclaimed as the sense of the people of that great state against the United States Bank. This state bank, sir, had its reward — it shared the *spoils*. But, sir, my colleague (Mr. Foster) has taken occasion to eulogize his safety-fund system. He says it works like a charm. I shall not deny, sir, that it has some good qualities; but I am far from thinking it so charming as my honorable colleague. I doubt not it appears so, sir, to many who share in its golden harvest, and enjoy its exclusive privileges; but to the great majority of the people, who, like myself, deal not in bank stock, but occasionally see or feel the tyranny of these little *monsters*, the working of this political engine is anything but *charming*. Sir, I conceive it had its origin in the foul embraces of political ambition, and cunning, heartless avarice. ' It was conceived in sin, and brought forth in iniquity.' It has spread its baleful influence over that state, corrupting the fountains of power, and demoralizing the whole community, by the manner in which its privileges have been granted and its stock distributed. Banks have been granted, and the stocks distributed, to party favorites, as a reward for party services. They have been the mercenary bribe offered to the community to sap the foundations of moral honesty and political integrity. But I will not enter into the disgusting details. As to those who wish to see the *workings* of this *charming* system of my colleague, I will refer them to an examination of our state legislature, last winter, and the proceedings of that body upon the report of their committee upon a single bank. I believe the very day on which the report was made, it showed such abominable corruption and abuses, that a bill was introduced to repeal its charter, and, within one or two days, passed through all the forms of legislation in the popular branch without a dissentive vote; and also passed the senate with but three or four votes against it. Does my honorable colleague think that a system which produces banks like this works like a charm? But, sir, I perceive that this incestuous connection between the politics and banks of that state has been festering and corrupting until it is about to fall asunder from its own rottenness. I, for one, have no tears to shed at the dissolution. I only regret that many of these banks, since they were chartered, have passed into the hands of honest and honorable men. I fear that the odium which rests upon this corrupt system, and which, in my opinion, is in nowise necessarily connected with banking, will sink the whole, without discrimination. The vengeance of an insulted and oppressed community is

terrible and overwhelming in its course. It stops not always to discriminate between the 'just and the unjust,'
between the proper use and improper abuse of a particular
system ; but in the wild madness of popular fury, they
hurl the whole to destruction. I warn them to stay their
desolating hands. All sudden changes are dangerous.
Let us not destroy, but purify this odious system. We
cannot live without banks and banking. Credit in some
shape is indispensable to our prosperity. Were we reduced to a specie circulation, as now proposed by the
president, property would not be worth twenty-five per
cent. what it now is, and would soon be wholly absorbed
by the wealthy capitalists of our country. The debtor
part of the community would be utterly ruined. Then
let us purge this vile system of its corruptions and abuses,
and strip it of its odious monopoly, and open the privilege
of banking to all who comply with such prescribed rules
of the legislature as secure the bill-holder and public
generally from fraud and imposition. I hope, sir, to live
to see the day when this shall be done, and the moral
pestilence of political banks and banking shall be unknown."

*　　*　　*　　*　　*　　*　　*　　*

The foregoing speech was delivered at a time when
party spirit raged in the legislative halls of our country
with a fierceness rarely excelled in the annals of the republic. It was not directed against the United States Bank,
but against the bill before the house for the postponement
of the fourth installment, as before stated. A miscon-
struction having been placed upon it in the Congressional
Globe, Mr. Fillmore sent the subjoined note to the pub-

lishers of that paper, where, upon the bank subject, his views are sufficiently indicated:

> " HOUSE OF REPRESENTATIVES,
> September 27th, 1837.

"GENTLEMEN: My attention has been this moment drawn to a remark in the Globe of last evening, purporting to give the proceedings of the house on Monday evening, in which I find the following statement:

"'Mr. Fillmore resumed and continued his remarks on the subject, with the addition of a lengthy argument in favor of a Bank of the United States.'

"Passing over some evident misapprehensions of your reporter as to the purport of my remarks generally, I wish to say that he is entirely and most singularly mistaken in saying that I made a lengthy argument in favor of the United States Bank. I made no argument in favor of *the* United States Bank, nor of *a* United States Bank; but, on the contrary, expressly disclaimed ever having been the particular friend of the United States Bank, and expressed my sincere doubts whether the incorporation of a new United States Bank, at this time, would relieve the present embarrassments of the community. Will you do me the justice to correct the mistake?

> "Respectfully yours, MILLARD FILLMORE.

"Messrs. BLAIR and RIVES."

This speech, though not remarkable for its features of eloquence, embodies a vast fund of facts, showing the speaker to have been thoroughly informed upon the condition of the finances and matters of public interest gen-

erally.   During its delivery, he exhibited a tabular view
of the annual expenses of the government for twelve consecutive years, prepared with the exactest mathematical
precision.

We rarely have the good fortune to read a speech of no
greater length, that is so replete with evidences of research
and sound judgment.   I have inserted these extracts as a
specimen of his political oratory.

The bill, against the passage of which this speech was
made, passed the house, after being so amended as to spe-
cify the first of January, 1839, as the day of making the
transfer, and was approved the second day of October,
1837.   Mr. Clay's position in the senate in regard to this
measure was Mr. Fillmore's in the house.

The coincidence of the views of these gentlemen on
many subjects of vital interest can but be observed by
the student of their respective characters.   Mr. Clay
had assumed that leadership in the senate which, as we
shall presently see, Mr. Fillmore assumed in the house,
and though the excitement in regard to the bank question
was participated in by Mr. Clay to a much greater extent
than Mr. Fillmore conceived the circumstances justified
exhibiting himself, on many other subjects their views
were as similar as though they were colleagues acting in
concert upon them.   Subsequent events will show, too,
that there were feelings of unison between these two distinguished gentlemen, not restricted to the conventional
formalities of public station.

Petitions and memorials for the abolition of slavery in
the District of Columbia poured in upon the deliberations

of the present session of Congress from all quarters, and elicited no little controversy. The subject involved in these controversies was the right of petition upon the subject of slavery. On the eighteenth day of September, 1837, Mr. Wall, of New Jersey, presented a memorial in the senate from the ladies of New Jersey, praying for the abolition of slavery in the District. Many members, very tender upon this subject, were disposed to look unfavorably upon the memorial, and even went so far as to say that it was prompted by a spirit of fanaticism.

The right of petition has always, in the estimation of the wisest statesmen and purest patriots of our country, been regarded as sacred, and the petitioners as entitled to courtesy and respect, at least. To wise statesmen, who wish to pursue a peaceful, conciliatory course, prudence, if no higher consideration, should dictate the extension of respectful attention to such memorialists, on all occasions. And those who refuse such respect, unless of no ordinary nature, upon the ground that the petitioners are fanatics, merely because they presume, in the form of a memorial, to couch their wishes in regard to certain important measures, usually evince a much greater spirit of fanaticism themselves than do those who produce the petitions.

The memorial referred to by the New Jersey ladies, elicited quite an animated debate in the senate, commencing as follows :

" Mr. Hubbard moved to lay the motion on the table.

" Mr. Clay wished the motion withdrawn for a moment It was manifest that the subject of slavery in the Dis-

trict of Columbia was extending itself in the public
mind, and daily engaging more and more of the public
attention. His opinions, as expressed in the legislature
of the country, were, he believed, perfectly well known.
He had no hesitation in saying that Congress ought not
to do what was asked by the petitioners without the consent of the people of the District of Columbia. He was
desirous of inquiring of the senator from New Jersey, or
any other conversant with the subject, whether the feeling of abolition in the abstract was extending itself in
their respective states, or whether it was not becoming
mixed up with other matters — such, for instance, in the
belief that the sacred right of petition had been assailed.
It became the duty of the senate to inquire into this business, and understand the subject well.

" There were many, no doubt, of these petitioners, who
did not mean to assert that slavery should be abolished,
but were contending for what they understood to be a great
constitutional right. Would it not, then, under this
view of the subject, be the best course to allay excitement, and endeavor to calm down and tranquilize the
public mind ? Would it not be wiser to refer the subject to the committee for the District of Columbia, or
some other committee, that would elicit all the facts, reason coolly and dispassionately, presenting the subject in
all its bearings to the citizens of non-slaveholding states,
and in a manner worthy of the great subject ? Would
not such a proceeding be well calculated to insure harmony and amity in all parts of the Union ? On this subject there was, he was aware, a great diversity of opinion,

and he rose merely for the purpose of making these suggestions to the senate.

"Mr. Calhoun said he had foreseen what this subject would come to, he knew its origin, and that it lay deeper than was supposed; it grew out of a spirit of fanaticism, which was daily increasing, and, if not *in limine*, would, by and by, dissolve the Union. It was particularly our duty to keep the matter out of the senate — out of the halls of the national legislature. These fanatics were interfering with what they had no right. Grant the receptions of these petitions, and you will next be required to act upon them. He was for no conciliatory course — no temporizing; instead of yielding one inch, he would rise in opposition, and he hoped every man from the south would stand by him, to put down this growing evil. There was but one question that would ever destroy this Union, and that was involved in this principle. Yes; this was potent enough for it, and must be early arrested, if the Union was to be preserved. A man must see little into what is going on, if he did not see that this spirit was growing, and that the rising generation was becoming more strongly imbued with it. It was not to be stopped by reports on paper, but by action — very decided action."

Mr. Clay opposed the above remarks in a very mild, conciliatory manner, assuring the gentleman that the Union was in no danger of dissolution. No man ever understood better than Mr. Clay the effect of a conciliatory course. Bold and fearless as he was, when occasion required, he was always for cementing the bonds of union,

by the golden chain of national brotherhood ; and decided
as were his convictions on the subject treated of in the petitions that came into Congress, he knew that by their dis-
respectful repulsion, the very excitement they wished to
allay would be kindled into an intenser heat, and courteous petition be changed to indignant denunciation. Then,
besides the motives of policy and prudence, to the dictates of which all legislators should give watchful heed,
by which he was actuated to the defence of the memorialists, the right of petition he conceded as an inherent
one in the free exercise of which, no barrier should be
raised between legislators and the people—between the sen-
tinels and the camp. Such was the attitude, the right of
petition presented in the senate, with Mr. Clay for its
defender; it remains to be considered in what light it
was regarded in the house, and who was its defender
there.

On the twelfth of December, 1837, J. Q. Adams presented in the house a petition praying the abolition of
slavery in the District of Columbia.

This, in connection with former petitions presented by
that gentleman, was signed by fifty-thousand persons,
embracing the most influential of his constituency. He
moved that the memorials be referred to the committee
on the District of Columbia.

Mr. Wise moved that it be laid on the table. The
house voted on Mr. Wise's motion, which was carried by
a large majority, Mr. Fillmore voting with the minority
in the negative, sustaining the right of petition. Several
lengthy memorials were presented by the same gentle-

man, of the same nature, all of which, on motion of Mr. Wise, were tabled, Mr. Fillmore, with characteristic consistency, voting uniformly in the negative. Mr. Fillmore entertained the same views in regard to the right of petition that Mr. Clay did ; on the presentation of the memorials that flooded Congress during that session, though they were most usually tabled, he occupied grounds favorable to their reception and respectful consideration. Many of Mr. Fillmore's constituents, however, notwithstanding the uniformity of his votes in Congress sustaining the right of petition, were not satisfied with his views upon that and other subjects connected with the delicate question of slavery. There was then in Erie county an anti-slavery society, who regarded the considerations connected with that subject as paramount to all others, and when Mr. Fillmore was again placed by his fellow citizens before the people, for a seat in the twenty-sixth Congress, the chairman of a committee appointed by that society addressed the following interrogatories to Mr. Fillmore :

" 1st. Do you believe that petitions to Congress on the subject of slavery and the slave trade ought to be received, read, and respectfully considered by the representatives of the people ?

" 2d. Are you opposed to the annexation of Texas to this Union under any circumstances, as long as slaves are held therein ?

" 3d. Are you in favor of Congress exercising all the constitutional power it possesses to abolish the internal slave trade between the states ?

" Are you in favor of immediate legislation for the abolition of slavery in the District of Columbia ? "

From the subjoined reply to the above questions, Mr. Fillmore's views are fully ascertained and appreciated upon the subjects under consideration :

" BUFFALO, October 17th, 1838.

" SIR :— Your communication of the 15th inst., as chairman of a committee appointed by ' The Anti-slavery Society of the County of Erie,' has just come to hand. I am much engaged, and have no time to enter into an argument or to explain at length my reasons for my opinion. I shall, therefore, content myself for the present by answering all your interrogatories in the affirmative, and leave for some future occasion a more extended discussion of the subject. I would, however, take this occasion to say, that in thus frankly giving my opinion, I would not desire to have it understood in the nature of a pledge. At the same time that I seek no disguises, but freely give my sentiments on any subject of interest to those for whose suffrages I am a candidate, I am opposed to giving any pledges that shall deprive me hereafter of all discretionary power.

" My own character must be the guarantee for the general correctness of my legislative deportment. On every important subject I am bound to deliberate before I act, and especially as a legislator, to possess myself of all the information, and listen to every argument that can be adduced by my associates, before I give a final vote. If I stand pledged to a particular course of action, I cease to be a responsible agent, but I become a mere machine. Should subsequent events show, beyond all doubt, that the course I had become pledged to pursue was ruinous to my constituents and disgraceful to myself, I have no alternative, no opportunity for repentance, and there is no power to absolve me from my obligations. Hence the impropriety, not to say absurdity of giving a pledge.

" I am aware that you have not asked any pledge, and I believe I know your sound judgment and good sense too well to think you desire any such thing. It was, however, to prevent any misrepresentation on the part of others, that I have felt it my duty to say thus much on this subject.

" I am, respectfully, your most ob't servant,

"MILLARD FILLMORE.

" W. MILLS, Esq., Chairman, &c."

Here, by an emphatic, unequivocal affirmative reply to the questions proposed by the chairman, his views are fully elicited upon the right of petition on the subject of slavery in the District of Columbia. There is certainly an effective power of conciliation embraced in them. A courteous and respectful deference to the feelings and views of others, in both public and private stations, is much the surest way of quelling excitements, even though such views differ widely from our own.

If the northern and southern states would but take into consideration the important fact, that they are so many members of a united family, whose maternal derivative is liberty, and study their relative duties as such,

11

instead of being so excited upon the subject of each
other's peculiar institutions, much trouble and alarm
would be allayed. If, instead of croaking disunion, ruin,
slavery, and civil war, they would occupy liberal conservative ground, conceding to each their own views, and
manifest a respectful bearing to those entertaining them,
the storm clouds would soon roll from the political horizon,
and leave us with a clear national sky, each independent
star undimned. If the public servants of the country
would be willing, in the true spirit of liberality, to make
some concessions, instead of piercing each other with the
porcupine quills of sectional partisanship, our Congress,
instead of becoming a gladiatorial amphitheatre for ban-
dying opprobrious epithets and originating affairs of honor,
would be an assemblage of patriots studiously endeavoring
to promote the national welfare. When, in the spirit of
mutual concession and good-will, the north and the south
will shake hands across Mason & Dixon's Line, and bury
their animosities in the tomb of oblivion, we will certainly
have attained a " consummation devoutly to be wished."

Than Mr. Fillmore, no one has evinced a greater desire,
or manifested more solicitude in subduing all excitements
of a dangerous tendency. He is no partisan, though firm
in his views upon what tends to the public good. In a
long career of usefulness to his country, he has discharged
the duties of official station upon the soundest conservative principles, and in a spirit of liberality, showing
the greatest anxiety of equal rights to all, irrespective
of party faction or local prejudice. Mr. Fillmore, as a

statesman, though decisive and patriotic, is eminently conciliatory.

There is not in the Union another man so much of whose life has been devoted to public service, who can cull from his antecedents so many evidences of conciliatory capacities.

In the defence of the right of petition, side by side we again find him with the immortal Clay, earnestly, though in a minority party, defending those liberal conciliatory principles. His whole congressional career was an exhibit of earnest desire to be useful, and a casual retrospect of it when we arrive at its close will be sufficient to convince us of their gratification.

CHAPTER VII.

His views on the subject of public defence — The outrageous conduct
of British officers —Awful fate of the Caroline — Mr. Fillmore's
resolution urging redress — A committee reports upon the outrage — He opposes the report — Prompt, but not excitable —
His solicitude for the northern frontier — The celebrated Jersey
case — Its importance — Mr. Fillmore's determination to investigate it fairly— Proceedings of the committee on elections — Foul
play— Democratic contestants successful — Letter to his constituents — Twenty-seventh Congress — Great change — Party politics — Harrison and the Whig party— The nominal president —
John Tyler's treachery— Committee of ways and means — Distress of the country— Giant efforts of the twenty-seventh Congress — Equal to the emergency— Great innovations.

WE have before indicated that, as a legislator, Mr.
Fillmore felt the necessity in time of peace of being prepared for war, and making such arrangements for public
defence as would be necessary to protect the national
honor and prosperity against any sudden or unforeseen
attack or outrage. His course in the present Congress,
in regard to the requirement of redress from Great Britain,
for an outrage perpetrated upon the northern frontier,
shows his views upon the subject of public defence more
fully, and also furnishes evidence of his activity as a
member of Congress.

The cause for the demand for redress on the part of
Congress, originated in the dastardly conduct of a British
officer stationed at Chippewa, in Canada, in command of a

large body of troops, toward a citizen of Buffalo, in seiz-
ing a vessel belonging to him, then plying on Niagara
River.   It was during the Canadian insurrection, or the
Patriot war.   McNab, the British officer in command at
Chippewa, fitted out an expedition against the Caroline,
the vessel alluded to.   On the twenty-ninth of December,
they fired a heavy volley of musketry into the vessel at
Black Rock, on the American side.   She sustained no
injury, however, from this insult, and had the outrage
stopped here, no great harm would have been done.   But
after nightfall, while cabled at Schlosser's dock, and after
the larger part of the crew were asleep, she was boarded
by the piratical expedition of McNab, set on fire, and sent
over the rapids of Niagara, wrapped in flames, with
twelve souls on board.

On the 5th of January, 1838, Mr. Van Buren sent a
message to the senate and house of representatives, in
regard to the northern frontier, of which the following is
an extract : " Present experience on the southern boundary of the United States and the events now daily occurr-
ing on our northern frontier, have abundantly shown that
the existing laws are insufficient to guard against hostile
invasion from the United States of the territory of friendly
and neighboring nations."   In the senate, on the reception of the message,

" Mr. Clay rose to express his full conviction of the
necessity of some early action on this important subject.
No spectacle could be more revolting to the feelings of a
free people than either a war among themselves or with
another country.   The views of the executive met his

highest approbation ; but it was the duty of Congress to
examine, and if the existing laws were not adequate to
prevent the alleged interference of our citizens, others
should be forthwith enacted for the full accomplishment
of an object so desirable. He adverted in connection to
the vexatious and unsettled state of our northern boundary, which state of things tended to increase the danger
which now' threatened us. He had witnessed a similar
course of policy, on the part of our citizens, during recent
occurrences of a similar character in another quarter, on
which subject, however, he had never expressed his opinions, nor should he do so now." This, in the senate, was
a subject of very great interest, and the sentiments
embodied in the message were approved by most of the
leading members. The necessity of placing the northern
frontier in a position of protection, after the perpetration
of so flagrant an outrage against all neutrality relation-
ship, and revolting to humanity itself, was too paramount
to be overlooked. Canada, as the rendezvous of an
armed band of twenty-five hundred soldiers, led by such
hyenas as McNab, who would not hesitate to send an
unarmed crew, engaged in their daily avocation, in a
burning ship over the cataract of Niagara, was too contiguous to the territory of the United States not to excite
serious alarm on the part of the national legislatures.

The message coming up in Congress the same day, Mr.
Fillmore offered the following resolution :

" Resolved, that the president be requested to communicate to this house any information in his possession of
acts endangering the amicable relations between this

government and that of Great Britain, either by the subjects of Great Britain, or by our own citizens, on the Canada frontier, and what measures have been adopted by the executive to preserve our neutrality with said kingdom, or repel invasion from a foreign country ; and that he furnish the information called for by each of these resolutions, in separate communications."

Various resolutions and amendments were presented, among others an amendment by Mr. Adams, requiring of the president all documents and information in regard to the preservation of our neutrality with Mexico and the British provinces north of the United States.

An amendment to this was offered by Mr. Fillmore, as follows : " And that the president be requested to communicate to this house any additional information in his possession of acts endangering the amicable relations of this government and that of Great Britain, either by the subjects of Great Britain or by our own citizens, on the Canadian frontier, and what measures have been adopted by the executive to preserve our neutrality with that kingdom." In support of this amendment Mr. Fillmore remarked, that the house was aware that there had been, and now was, a great excitement existing on the Niagara frontier, and that there had been movements in Buffalo in reference to the revolution now raging in Canada. They were probably aware that an armament had been fitted out, mostly by American citizens, which had made a stand upon Navy Island, which is within British territory, in Niagara River, twenty miles from Buffalo, and two or three miles above the Falls, the lowest point at which a crossing can be safely effected from the main shore."

Mr. Fillmore here gave a full account of the outrage of McNab upon the United States government, in the destruction of the Caroline, and read letters containing full particulars of the same, and desired to know if the president was in possession of any information in regard to the proceedings. Mr. Adams made some remarks in support of his original amendment, indicating that the various suggestions and amendments were postponing the question, and deferring action upon it until it would be too late to accomplish their object.

In reply to the remarks of Mr. Adams, Mr. Fillmore said he " could not conceive how his proposition could possibly tend to embarrass the action of the house upon the resolution offered by the committee on foreign affairs. It was certainly very easy for the president to distinguish between the different kinds of information sought for by the different propositions. He had tried every other way to bring his proposition before the house, and could not present it in any form which would secure its immediate consideration, excepting that in which it now stood. For if it were offered as an independent resolution, it would take its place behind all others now on the speaker's table. Its great importance would not permit him to expose it to such a risk, and he had, therefore, offered it in the form of an amendment to the original resolution of the committee on foreign affairs, in which shape he hoped it would pass.

" As to the expression which he had used in relation

to the disturbances of the Niagara frontier, that this country was on the eve of a war with Great Britain, perhaps it was too strong an expression. But certainly all the facts demonstrated that there was imminent danger of such a result. The citizens of the United States, while in the peaceful pursuit of their business, had been attacked by an armed force from a foreign nation, and a portion of the militia of the country is even now ordered to repel such hostility.

"He well knew that the spirit of the people on the United States side of that frontier would not permit them to stand tamely by, and witness such assaults. These were facts, vouched for by respectable citizens as true and authentic; and he must ask if they were not such as to warrant the offering of such a proposition as he had moved. It makes no difference, he contended, whether one or one hundred miles of the territory of the United States has been invaded by the arms of a foreign nation; the jurisdiction of this country is coëxtensive with the utmost limits of her territory. Even if the vessel which was attacked had been carrying munitions of war to the revolutionists on Navy Island, she was only liable, he contended, to be attacked while within the British lines. As it was, he agreed with the gentleman from Massachusetts, (Mr. Adams,) that there was scarcely a parallel to this act upon the pages of our history as a nation; and it was to suppose an absolute impossibility, for a moment to imagine that the people on that frontier will ever submit to the occurrence of such acts, without complaint and redress. It was, therefore, in any view, highly important
11*

that the house should obtain all possible information upon a subject so important."

These extracts are sufficient indications of Mr. Fillmore's patriotism, in resisting the taunts and insults of a neighboring nation. Buffalo being so near the seat of strife during the insurrectionary movements of the Canadians in 1837-8, that it is not surprising, serious apprehensions should be felt by the citizens concerning her commercial interests, especially after such an outrage as had been committed upon the Caroline by McNab.

The following extract from some remarks of Mr. Fillmore's, delivered on a subsequent occasion in Congress, shows the views he entertained upon the necessity of preparing means of public defence. It was while urging the adoption of some resolutions he had presented relative to the northern frontier difficulties, and the neutrality of our government toward that of Great Britain. An individual had been arrested, who was a participant in certain disturbances, and the frontier excitement was raging most fiercely. The resolutions which he was urging before Congress passed, and resulted in the elicitation of all the correspondence between the two governments in regard to the transactions of the British troops, and the frontier difficulties generally. The occurrences growing out of the insurrections in Canada were of a very unpleasant nature. Buffalo, situated not much further than a stone's throw from Canada, of course was in incessant alarm, dreading a repetition of such outrages upon her commerce as was inflicted upon the unfortunate Caroline, by McNab, in the fall of 1837. After the correspondence had been laid before Congress, it was referred to the appropriate committee to report thereon. The report made by the committee to whom the correspondence was referred was so inflammatory, and coupled with it such evidences of bitter hostility, whose evident tendencies were to excite rather than allay the existing troubles, that many members of the house were decidedly against its adoption. Among these was Mr. Fillmore. Notwithstanding his patriotism, and the just cause which he felt his country had for being indignant at the infamous conduct of McNab, and other outrages she had endured, his conciliatory nature forbade his concurrence in a report whose tone was to excite, and not allay.   Satisfied his country had been insulted, with the truest dignity he was the first to resent it.   But there was a proper way to resent; and, with characteristic firmness and deliberation, that proper way he wished to be the executor of pacific negotiations.   And if all other means failed, *then* the sword.

These are his principles in regard to the adjustment of national difficulties — principles of which his whole public career has been an exemplification.   Prompt and conciliatory, he leaves no means untried to retain amicable relations ; but if those measures fail, equally prompt and decided, he is ready to meet the emergency.   In this case of the Canada troubles, he was first to introduce a resolution in the house, asking information, etc.   When the information was received, and the committee reported thereon, he opposed the report because its tone was fraught with too much excitement.   Try pacific, conciliatory measures first, if they fail, then resort to other expedients. No man has ever been more prompt in resenting national insults than has Mr. Fillmore, and by the sound judgment and spirit of conciliation he has manifested, none has evinced a happier combination of qualities, or those better adapted to awe into the profoundest respect, while they elicit the warmest esteem.

This is a combination rarely possessed to the same extent by the legislators of the country; yet it is certainly one of the most essential to correct statesmanship. The very tenor of the subjoined shows the man — while he is ready to make every consistent effort for peace, he is, in case of failure, equally ready for war:

"But one thing, at all events, should be borne in mind by all whose duty requires them to act on this subject here. There is a great state of excitement on that frontier, which *might by possibility lead to an outbreak.* My objection to the printing of the report was, that it was calculated to inflame the public mind; and I was governed in that vote by three reasons. In the first place, I did not wish that anything should be done here which might have a tendency to do injustice to the individual who is soon to be tried by the laws of the state of New York. I desire that the law should have its free action, that no excitement should be raised against McLeod, which might prevent a fair and impartial trial. In the second place, I do not desire that any action on the part of this house should compromise or control the executive of this nation in the negotiations now pending between the government of the United States and the government of Great Britain. I have all confidence in the incoming administration. If this controversy can be amicably and honorably settled between the two governments, I desire that it should. But there is a third and very strong reason in my mind against anything being done to exasperate the public mind on the subject of war with Great Britain. It is this: for three or four years I have used all the exertions in my power to induce this administration, which is responsible to the country, to provide some means of defence on our northern frontier. But all my efforts were in vain. And yet the gentleman from South Carolina (Mr. Pickens) now tells us that the course to be pursued to avoid a war with Great Britain is to stand up to her — to threaten her — to take a high stand; and *that*, he says, will avert a war. I may have been mistaken in the meaning. I know that those were not his words. But I would submit to him that the best way to avoid a war with Great Britain, is to show that we are prepared to meet her, if there is to be war; because reasonable preparations for defence are better than gasconading."

Mr. Fillmore then alluded to the defenceless condition of the northern frontier. He desired, and believed the whole country desired, that we should yield nothing to the demands of Great Britain, to which she was not fairly entitled. But, at the same time, he regarded it as rather the act of a madman, to precipitate the country into a war before it was prepared for it, than the act of a statesman. In his section of country, the people would yield nothing to Great Britain to which she was not justly entitled; or they would yield it only with the last drop of their blood. But he did not wish prematurely to be drawn into war; he did not wish to invite Great Britain to invade our defenceless coast. The true plan was to prepare for war if we had yet to come to it; but to do no'hing in the way of bragging. If it did come, gentlemen would not find his people shrinking from their just share of responsibility. All they had — their property, their lives, everything — they were willing to devote, if need be, to the service and honor of their country. But was it not the part of wisdom and prudence, before we made a declaration of war, to prepare for it? This was all he desired; and if this report was calculated to stir up a war feeling, without corresponding preparation being made to meet the consequences, he, for one, was opposed to it. He did not wish the country to be disgraced by defeat. When she must go to war, he desired to see her prepared for it; he desired to see her placed in a situation which would enable her to bid defiance to the power of any government on earth."

No member of Congress manifested the solicitude, in regard to fortifying and putting in a condition of defence the northern frontier that Mr. Fillmore did. The labors he put forth in that body for the attainment of this object were incessant. Living on that frontier himself, he had the fairest opportunities of understanding and appreciating the evils incident to their defenceless condition, open as it was to the inroads of an insurrectionary soldiery.

The deliberations of the twenty-sixth Congress commenced amid the greatest excitement engendered by the contest for their seats by the New Jersey members. On the second of December, the clerk of the house called the roll of the members, and when he got to the state of New Jersey, after pronouncing the name of one member from that state, he remarked that the seats of five of the six representatives of that state were contested. Considerable feeling upon the subject ensued immediately in the house, in regard to the claims of the New Jersey representation.

Mr. Fillmore, on the second day of the session, while various propositions were being made, arose and desired that all the facts and the law regulating the case be laid before the house before proceeding to debate the matter. This was a case of great importance, in which the rights of a sovereign state were involved, and he felt much interest in behalf of the Jersey members, and evinced a determination, at this early stage of the proceedings, to commence its investigation upon facts and laws regulating such cases. Had this wise course been pursued when subjected to the law and the evidence governing elections, the difficulties of the several claimants would have been easily adjusted, and, instead of deferring the organization of the house for weeks by an incessant wrangle over individual opinions, it would have been organized immediately.

That portion of the New Jersey members who presented certificates of election endorsed by the executive of the state averred they had a right to their seats under the laws of the country, and a right of participation in the proceedings of the house, until its organization was effected, and the oaths of office came to be administered.

On the third day of the session the clerk, who had interfered with the organization by a refusal to call the roll of the members from New Jersey, upon the ground of conflicting evidence, proposed reading a prepared document to the house, purporting to lay information before it concerning the case. Several members objected to the reading of this prepared document, on the ground that it was calculated to produce false impressions in regard to the claimants to seats from New Jersey.

On the 16th of December an organization of the house was effected, and still the investigation of the Jersey case had but fairly commenced. Mr. Fillmore was appointed one of the committee on elections, the responsibilities of which, next to those devolving upon that of ways and means were, in view of the contested Jersey case, the greatest belonging to any committee of the house. On the 28th of February the house adopted a resolution directing the committee on elections to report forthwith, which five of the ten delegates claiming seats from the state of New Jersey received the largest number of votes at the election in that state in the year 1838. Mr. Fillmore was anxious to amend the resolution, the substance of which is embraced above so as to read, the greatest number of *lawful* votes. He was anxious the case should be fairly investigated, and so adjusted as to do justice to all parties. In view of the above resolution, and the fact that in the adjudication of the case there was a disposition to take all sorts of votes into account, and of evidence in his possession that illegal votes had been polled at the election before mentioned, Mr. Fillmore introduced a subsequent resolution, in substance, as follows : That the committee take their report into consideration, with instructions to ascertain, with all possible dispatch, which five of the ten claimants to seats from New Jersey received the greatest amount of *lawful* votes at the preceding congressional election in that state.

The solicitude he felt in regard to that contest was exceeded by that of no member in the house ; but in this, he was determined that his great life principle should govern him, and that right should be his aim, in connection with its investigation.   The law and the facts were what he wished laid before the house, the second day of the session — the law and the facts were what he desired to ascertain still.   Indications of an unfair issue had become developed in the house, and to counteract them he threw his whole great talents and energies into a fair and lawful investigation of the whole affair, commencing at the ballot-box.   The report that had been made to Congress established the right of five claimants to seats, to the exclusion of some whose claims were evidently more valid than theirs, if subjected to the strictly legal investigation proposed by Mr. Fillmore's resolution.

On the tenth of March the democratic contestants from New Jersey were recognized as members of the twenty-sixth Congress, duly qualified, and took their seats, under a resolution to that effect, with a proviso that such recognition was not, in any way, to interfere with any subsequent investigations the committee might think proper to institute.   Their title to seats in that body was confirmed by the final adoption of the majority report of the committee on elections, the sixteenth of July. On the adoption of this report, the minority report of the committee was presented. A portion of the committee on elections, among whom was Mr. Fillmore, was satisfied that three of the gentlemen, (whigs,) excluded by the adoption of the majority report, were entitled to seats, and had been dealt with unfairly by being deprived of them through testimony believed to be incompetent. After being satisfied from all the evidence in the case, that these three whigs were the rightful claimants to seats, Mr. Fillmore became warmly interested in their behalf. But a majority of both the house and the committee were against him; the whole investigation was conducted upon party considerations, and in a legislative body where the majority was democratic, and on a committee where the majority were opposed to his views, the result was what might have been anticipated — the whigs, to a man, were excluded, and the democrats admitted.

The views he entertained in regard to the justness of the whig claimants, were endorsed by a respectable minority of the committee, who presented the report referred to, elaborately giving their views and convictions upon the whole case, the substance of a part of which is above enumerated. On the 6th of March preceding the final adoption of the majority report adjusting the Jersey contest, when the excitement in regard to it was raging in its fiercest heat, Mr. Fillmore, while making some remarks in reference to the superior claims to seats of those embraced in the minority report, was suddenly called to order. Appeal was made to the chair, who decided Mr. Fillmore was in order, and had a right to proceed with his remarks. The objector appealed from this decision of the chair to the members of the house. Mr. Fillmore then required the gentleman to reduce his point of order to writing, saying that he had been often enough put down by a mere numerical force in everything relating to this New Jersey election. Gentlemen on the other side would hear nothing — see nothing — but would decide everything.

The objector was sustained in his appeal from the decision of the chair, and Mr. Fillmore was silenced by a numerical force that was determined to over-leap all reason, propriety, and fairness, in securing seats in Congress for their favorite claimants. As a free-man, representing as high-toned a constituency in the national Congress as any over which that body exercised jurisdiction — one that had proven the highest appreciation by his third election as their representative — Mr. Fillmore felt indignant at this infringement upon the freedom of speech. It was not the first time during the exciting Jersey controversy a disposition had been manifested by the dominant party to render his talented opposition as inefficient as possible, by calls of previous questions and resorts to various tricks of legislative chicanery. The firm stand he took, on the second day of the session, to have the affair investigated by subjecting it to the infalli-ble test of law and facts, and his subsequent avowals and determined energy to have justice prevail, made him an antagonist much to be feared ; and the talents they could not compete with in argument, they resolved to silence by questions of order. Speaking of the unworthy manner in which Mr. Fillmore was treated on this occasion, a leading paper in New York made the following remarks: " When a party or faction, for the time being in the majority, are resolved to accomplish merely party objects, to break through all rules and trample on the laws and rights of the minority, it has always been deemed expedient to prostrate the freedom of speech, in order that the enormity of their acts may not be exposed on the spot. This has been eminently the fact in the management of the New Jersey case in the house of representatives. A few days since, Mr. Fillmore, a member of the committee on elections, in addressing the house, attempted to read a resolution passed by the committee, which was decided not to be in order. He then attempted to proceed in his speech without reading it, and the house decided he had lost his right to speak, except by their permission, which he scorned to accept, refusing to receive, as a matter of *grace* from a majority, what he claimed as a *right*."

Mr. Fillmore, after receiving such treatment from the house, and seeing the utter hopelessness of being heard in the halls of Congress, addressed a letter to his constituents, in which he went into a detailed elaboration of the Jersey case, and all the difficulties connected therewith. The letter is an able document, evincing the soundest judgment as a legislator, and the wisest patriotism as a statesman. The following extracts from it will indicate more fully his views in regard to that the most exciting sub ject of the twenty-sixth Congress. Speaking of the ourageous proceedings of the majority party, he says :

" Let us, like true philosophers, draw wisdom from this calamity, and turn to that revered charter of our liberties and calmly review its provisions, before we conclude its venerated authors contemplated a proceeding so revolting and dangerous as that which has just been witnessed. The constitution provides that, ' each house shall be the judge of the election returns and qualifications of its own members.' It is clear that this clause of the constitution created the house a high judicial tribunal to hear and finally determine; first, who was ' elected ;' secondly, who was ' returned ;' thirdly, whether the person thus elected and returned possessed the requisite ' qualifications.' I conceive that these three subjects of judicial investigation by the house are entirely distinct, and that any attempt to confound them must inevitably lead to confusion and error.

" It is obvious that one man may be duly elected, by receiving the greatest number of legal votes ; and that, by some accident or fraud, another may be duly returned ; and that a man may be duly elected and returned, and yet not be qualified ; for the constitution expressly declares, " that no person shall be a representative who shall not have attained the age of twenty-five years, and been seven years a citizen of the United States; and who shall not, when elected, be an inhabitant of that state in which he shall be chosen.' "

Mr. Fillmore continues his letter at some considerable length, showing that the parties, in the investigation raised no questions upon the most important of these constitutional requisitions. He shows that their inquiries were directed upon the election and return, without any attention to qualification whatever. After showing with great clearness the partiality evinced in the adjudication of the case, and the palpable violations of the constitution it developed, he says :

" I, therefore, submit it to you, as my immediate constituents, to whom I am responsible for my official act, to say whether I have done right in opposing this disorganizing and unlawful proceeding from the commencement; whether I have done right in insisting that the persons, only, returned should, in the first instance, take their seats; whether I have done right, after these returns and the laws and commissions from the executive of a sovereign state were trampled under foot, to insist on a full inquiry into all the frauds charged, to ascertain who was elected; and, finally, whether I did right, when I saw the most venerated and sacred principle of the constitution about to be desecrated, and the right of speech tyrannically suppressed, to stand up and resist the despotic assumption of power to the last."

His reëlection to the next Congress, by a larger majority than was ever given in his district to any congressional aspirant, told in the plainest terms that he was right.

Before going into the investigation of Mr. Fillmore's career in the twenty-seventh Congress, it is necessary to notice briefly the passing current of intermediate events, replete with glorious results to our common country, but which were afterwards a source of the most mournful melancholy.

Another political revolution had swept over the country and nipped the opening flower of progressive democracy with a withering blight. Van Burenism and the adherent principles of the Jacksonian administration had been eclipsed by the unprecedented triumph of the hero of Tippecanoe. The campaign of 1840, between Harrison and Van Buren, was, perhaps, the most exciting that ever occurred in our political annals. Unprecedented was the intensity of feeling that manifested itself on every hill and in every vale of the Union, from Maine to Texas.

Old party lines were destroyed ; the rivalrous feelings of factional antagonisms were subdued ; the adherents to democratic principles, so long in the ascendant, seemed to forget the hero of New Orleans, whose star, though resplendent with the halo of "battle target red," had gone down. Men of all parties seemed, for once, to bury the animosities of a radical partisanship, "Change," "change," the evanescence of whose label is stamped upon all earthly measures, seemed to be the watchword of each battalion, that, to the notes of "Tippecanoe and hard cider," marched into the political battle of 1840. The victory was a glorious one ; and, but for the perfidy of a partisan Iscariot, would have resulted in a triumphant establishment and vindication of conservative, time-honored principles.

Harrison was borne into executive power by the mightiest tide of revolution—of prosperity—to the whig

party that ever swelled the current of national politics
Whig principles had not only been successful in his
elevation to the presidency, but were brightly in the
ascendancy in both branches of the national legislature.
So triumphant had been the revolution, that the veteran
chief at the head of affairs could look down through a
long line of subordinate officials, and see a large majority
marshaled under the same banner. In Congress, a large
majority presented an array of patriotic talent, rendered
courageous by their success, to sustain his administration.

The senate, reinvigorated by the successful charge led
by their Clay, stood a Macedonian phalanx around
their civic chief, ready to vindicate his administration.
Of this administration the most glorious results had
been predicted; and, upon the terrific ruins of old institutions that marked the line of march pursued by Jacksonism, the sage of Ashland thought to build them up again
in all their primal purity. The great battle of 1840 had
been fought and won under banners flung to the breeze,
inscribed with the avowed principles of a party whose
maturity they presumed would be the result of victory.
After that victory had perched upon their banners, as the
surest means of putting those principles into successful
operation, on the thirty-first of May, 1841, an extra session
of Congress was called.

But, before the convention of that Congress that was
to be a realization of the hopes entertained by the whig
party, Harrison died, and in his grave was buried the
prospects of the whig party. Enshrouded in a winding-
sheet as dark—aye, darker, because it was the blackness of

treachery — as wrapped their lamented chief, their principles were buried.   John Tyler, like Judas Iscariot, betrayed his master; and, with a more horrid steel than Cascas' blade, murdered the party that placed him in power.

Tyler was *called* President at the time the twenty-seventh Congress first met.

By what right he was so designated, I shall not pretend to say.   By the same right, I presume, the famous Captain Kidd retained the name of Captain : he was commissioned to clear the seas of pirates; but, after getting among them, he buried his Bible, turned pirate himself, and he was still Captain Kidd.   In the cases, there is certainly some analogy.

Tyler was commissioned to assist in the promulgation of whig principles, and upon the endorsement of those principles was elected by his party; but when he came into power, like Kidd, he buried his creed, and plunged the stiletto of treason in its heart.   The infamous turpitude of Tyler, in the betrayal of his party, stands a blackened monument of political treachery that will tower conspicuously through distant ages.   And yet he was president.   But we must discriminate.   He was not president by election, nor was he president by the moral force of constitutional power.   He was elevated to the vice-presidency by the people; but to have been president, in the true sense of the term, he should have been reëlected upon the principles he endorsed, after his repudiation of those upon whose avowal he was elected. . After the death of Harrison, the constitution empowered him to

12

take his place as president. Did he do it? He took the chair, but murdered his principles; instead, therefore, of taking the place of Harrison, he took his chair merely; and as executive, occupied a position directly opposite to him, in the administration of the government.

The reversional revolution produced by the summerset of whig principles, under the treachery of Tyler, was almost as dark as the one of Harrison's election was glorious. The great measures, whose enactment the party anticipated with joyous gratification, were knocked off under the hammer of his veto with as little hesitancy as though he had been elected for their express repudiation. The old Harrison cabinet, who had been selected as a body-guard to the principles expected to be carried out by the administration, on seeing them cast to the four winds, resigned their places with unfeigned disgust. The language applied to him by a distinguished gentleman who witnessed with regret his dastardly conduct, for its peculiar applicability is worthy of insertion. Looking at the change in the aspect of affairs, and knowing the cause was the recreant Tyler, he exclaimed:

"False to his friends and to himself, he stands before the American people as a warning alike in the disinterestedness of a patriot, the fidelity of an associate, and the honor of a gentleman."

One of his earliest measures, after his inauguration, was the veto of the bank bill passed by the called session. The principle doings of his *mal*-administration consisted in his undoing. The most commendable quality he possessed, was a finely developed imbecility.

The most efficient services he rendered the country, were those he withheld. The consistency of his deceit was the only spot in his character sufficiently bright to be labeled with treason.   The only bright sun that shone upon his administration was the one that set on its last day. Rufus Choate would have to cull the vocabulary of language for its most opprobrious epithets, to write an eulogy for John Tyler.

> " Is there not some chosen curse,
>   Some hidden thunder in the storms of heaven,
>   Red with uncommon wrath, to blast the man,
>   Who owes his greatness to his country's ruin ? "

On the assemblage of the twenty-seventh Congress, in consequence of the experience and legislative capacity evinced on previous sessions, Mr. Fillmore was made chairman of the committee on ways and means, by far the most responsible position in that body.

The most important measure of the ever memorable twenty-seventh Congress was the passage of the tariff of 1842. The political revolution that placed the whigs in power had made them hope for the establishment of many other cherished measures belonging to the old whig creed. The bank bill, as we have seen, passed by Congress immediately after the convention of its extra session was vetoed. The distribution of the proceeds of the public lands was prevented through the faithless perfidy of the executive. Yet, than that body, never were legislators more faithful. They had been placed in power by the uprising masses of a people smarting under the lash of misrule, that

had marked the course of national officials for the period
of twelve years. A nobler array of talent and a wiser
embodiment of patriotism never convened in any congressional assembly. The vast amount of labor looming
before them required just such a Congress. Theirs was
emphatically a business of reconstruction. In 1823, the
country was in a prosperous condition under the safe guidance of first principles. Subsequent to that period, " bargain and intrigue " was saddled upon her purest patriots.
Old and time-honored institutions were toppled from their
base, and regal assumptions of power were exercised by
the national executive ; the currency of the country was
destroyed; the principles of Washington were forgotten;
another race arose up, " who knew not Joseph ;" and in
their progressive innovations had left a cancerated ulcer
upon the national system, that had been preying upon
its vitals for a dozen years, with the most destructive
virulence. The business of the present Congress was its
removal ; to them the people looked with hopeful expect-
ancy, as the great physician that was to extract the infectious seeds of extravagance and corruption that had
found their way into the very heart of the national system,
and were fast polluting every fibre of its delicately constituted organism. The administration of Jackson began
the work of demolition, and Van Buren, in the development
and elaboration of his stupendous sub-treasury schemes,
magnified the ruin. The awful extravagancies of these
administrations, the despotic assumptions incident to their
development, and the admirably concocted plans to secure
payment to all officials, were it not for names, times, and

places, the student of them would conclude he was reading the history of some consulate or triumvirate.

The enormous extravagance of government expenditures were so unparalleled that serious apprehensions were entertained on the part of the people in regard to a curtailment of their privileges, by the imposition of onerous taxations to maintain a tyrannous oligarchy, whose adhesive principles were the loaves and fishes. With the deepest solicitude, then, they looked for an alleviation of their distresses to the twenty-seventh Congress. The sequel will show they did not look in vain. The political revolution that placed a majority of whigs in the present Congress developed a distressing condition of American nationality, rarely, if ever, witnessed in times of peace. With as little compunction as Cæsar did, when, with sword in hand, he took the gold from the Roman guards to aid him in making war against his own commonwealth, the treasury had been robbed, and its contents pandered to the caprice of a corrupt official crew, until it was almost bankrupt. The old system of protective policy had been tattered and torn piece from piece, until but fragmental shreds remained scarce sufficient to indicate its once useful proportions. The reservoirs of specie circulation had, one by one, been effectually demolished, until from the happiest mediums of remittance and circulation, we had been hurled into the stagnant consequences of a broken-down currency. Commerce, trade, and manufactures, the great heart of national prosperity, to whose healthful pulsation a sound circulative currency is as essential as is the blood to the life-throb of the human heart, in consequence of the destruction of these arterial facilities, was in a state of hopeless inactivity. Gloom, distress, and national depression stared in the face of the twenty-seventh Congress, with the question, "Is there no balm in Gilead?" On that Congress devolved the arduous task of taking the old ship of state from the high and dry strand whereon she was run by Jackson and Van Buren, and reconstructing her after the old model. They had to pour the elixir of life into a jaundiced nationality, and reinvigorate it with healthful vitality. They proved themselves worthy; and, with the coöperation of an effective chief magistrate, of whom they had been deprived by Providence and treachery, they would have relieved the public distress entirely.

As before remarked, the business of this Congress was a reorganization of things that had been so transformed into a pell-mell, topsey-turvey heterogeneousness, that powers, prerogatives, accounts and salaries, were all amalgamated in indiscriminate confusion, without order or system. For years, nothing had been fixed or definite — salaries and expenditures had been particularly indefinite. The progressive rates of extravagant licentiousness developed in the few years preceding this Congress would have resulted, before now, in the conversion of official quarters into sumptuous seraglios. Right faithfully did they commence the work of investigation and retrenchment. Mr. Fillmore, from the peculiarity of his position, and with a natural acuteness of perception that sees anything " rotten in Denmark " almost by intuition, was enabled to assist in discoveries of a startling nature.

The universal complaint of a financial distress, that weighed like an incubus upon all departments of business and thrilled them with strokes of incurable paralysis, Congress very justly concluded must be attributable to some remedial cause. But on investigating the condition of the national system, the corruption which they knew was preying upon it was seen to have eaten much deeper than was imagined. It was an ulcer that would take time to heal. They instituted true searching committees to ascertain the extent of the corruptive influences exerted by the precedent administrations. In this duty, these committees were faithful to the very letter.

The first discovery resulting from this scrutiny was the *economical* proceedings of a Van Buren administration, Item first, showed two hundred and eighty-seven dollars and a quarter for each member's stationery, for a period of nine months, in a democratic Congress; item second, showed twenty-five dollars for each member's wafers, for the same length of time. These awful expenditures, and a perfect recklessness on the part of officials, had produced the great financial crisis.

They greatly diminished the amount of the annual appropriations, and boldly marched ahead in the commendable work of retrenchment. The closer the investigation, the deeper the infection of licentiousness became perceptible. Every department of the whole government machinery had become infected. The expenses of the government, it was seen, were twice as enormous as they had been in former years, and they resolved on effecting a reduction to their reasonable limits before the political

Robespiere and Danton commenced their Reign of Terror, and raised the guillotine to the head of American finance.

They spared neither time nor pains in these investigations, and counted by thousands in their curtailments of all extravagance developed by their scrutiny. The many instances, and the largeness of the amounts lopped off by these conservative financial excisors, would swell these remarks to too great a length by their enumeration. The military expenses were greatly curtailed, and the whole system remodeled.

By reference to the proceedings of that Congress, I find that a complete transformation was effected in a little time. The navy and the army were recipients of wise and judicious legislation; extra pays, contingent allowances, and loose means of doing government business, were all done away with. Everything, in fact, underwent a radical change. In all these reformations, Mr. Fillmore, as chairman of the committee of ways and means, led the van in the house, and helped to wipe out the traces of political vermin that had usurped the offices of government for a number of years.

CHAPTER VIII.

Tariff of 1842 — A remedy for an existing evil — Protective tariff as
a feature in politics — Tariff men in all parties — Jackson's views —
Early statesmen's views — Clay calls it the American system —
Mr. Fillmore's speech on the Tariff — Conclusions to be drawn
from his course in regard to the Tariff — His high position in Congress — The Morse Appropriation — Cave Johnson — Close of his
congressional career—J. Q. Adams and Mr. Fillmore—Campaign of
1844 — Prospects of the whig party — Mr. Fillmore urged as a
candidate for the vice-presidency— Defeat of Clay— Causes which
led to that result — Mr. Fillmore nominated for governor —
Letter to Thurlow Weed — Foreign influence — Letter to Henry
Clay— Extracts showing the cause of defeat — The Comptroller-
ship — Its arduous duties — His report to the state — Its ability—
His sympathy for the sufferers of the Emerald Isle.

THE tariff of 1842 is too well known to require an
enumeration of its principles in this connection. Then
it was regarded a wise measure, and denominated by Mr.
Clay, The American system. The friends of the measure
were prompted by the immediate remedy for the distress
of the times, to lend it their support. Like the old bankrupt law enacted by the same session, it was to meet the
demand of an existing, but very undesirable necessity.
Mr. Fillmore, though the author of that measure, was not
ultra, or prompted by any spirit of partisanship, in his
advocacy of it. He saw the financial distress, and thought
the measure would be remedial of it, and true to his
12*

nature, he wished to test his conviction. The origination of that measure by Mr. Fillmore, then, instead of being construed into an endorsement of the peculiar views of a party in regard to protective policy, should be regarded as an earnest desire to remedy the existing evils. Men of all parties, from the earliest days of the republic, have been friends of *a* protective policy, though they have differed widely in regard to the establishment of such systems. It has been a leading feature in the history of party politics, from the earliest administrations. The country has, time and again, been convulsed with disastrous revulsions, that have made the enactment of different protective principles imperatively necessary. Periods of financial depression have existed, the only remedial agency of which consisted in certain enactments to protect the revenue. These tariffs, and tariff modifications, have resulted as did the one of 1842, from the absolute necessities of the case. Jackson himself was a protectionist, convinced of its propriety from the wants of the country at a particular time.

The advocacy of a protective tariff has been regarded as belonging to the whigs, exclusively, and that measure as an article in the whig creed, that received the repudiation of all other parties. The following extract of a letter from Jackson shows that men may entertain views favorable to protective principles, and not be whigs. It shows, from peculiar exigencies, men may advocate such a measure, as an immediate operative remedy, without reference to the abstract principles involved in it, as a plank in the platform of a great party. The letter was written to a friend of the General's, in North Carolina, in August, 1824.

"I will ask, what is the real situation of the agriculturist? Where has the American farmer a market for his surplus produce? Except for cotton, he has neither a foreign nor a home market. Does not this clearly prove, when there is no market at home or abroad, that there is too much labor employed in agriculture? Common sense at once points out the remedy. Take from agriculture in the United States six hundred thousand men, women, and children, and you will at once give a market for more breadstuffs than all Europe now furnishes us with.

"In short, sir, we have been too long subject to the policy of British merchants. It is time we should become a little more AMERICANIZED, and, instead of feeding paupers and laborers of England, feed our own; or else, in a short time, by continuing our present policy, we shall be paupers ourselves.

"It is, therefore, my opinion, that a careful and judicious tariff is much wanted, to pay our national debt and to afford us the means of that defence within ourselves on which the safety of our country and liberties depend; and last, though not least, to give a proper distribution of our labor, which must prove beneficial to the happiness, wealth, and independence of the community.

"I am very respectfully, your odedient servant,

"ANDREW JACKSON."

Jefferson, and all the early presidents, irrespective of party, saw clearly the necessity of establishing some pro tective measures, to remedy the evils of a defective revenue. The frauds practiced for years upon the country by foreign speculators, and the imposition of heavy duties upon our people, showed to all parties the importance of some protective system. From the subjoined remarks of Mr. Fillmore, delivered in the advocacy of his bill, it will be seen that, as the originator of it, he took no ultra partisan grounds upon the measure whatever. The remarks are clearly indicative of the fact, that he viewed it as a remedy for existing evils :

" I prefer my own country to all others, and my opinion is that we must take care of ourselves ; and while I would not embarrass trade between this and any foreign country by any illiberal restrictions, yet, if by legislation or negotiation an advantage is to be given to one over the other, I prefer my own country to all the world besides. I admit that duties may be so levied, ostensibly for revenue, yet designedly for protection, as to amount to prohibition, and consequently to the total loss of revenue. I am for no such protection as that. I have no disguise of my opinions on this subject. I believe that if all the restrictive systems were done away with, here and in every other country, and we could confidently rely on continued peace, that would be the most prosperous and happy state. The people of every country would then produce that which their habits, skill, climate, soil, or situation enable them to produce to the greatest advantage ; each would then sell where he could obtain the most, and buy where he could purchase cheapest ; and thus we should see a trade as free among the nations of the world as we now witness among the several states of this Union. But, however beautiful this may be in theory, I look for no such political millennium as this. Wars will occur until man changes his nature ; and duties will be imposed upon our products in other countries, until man shall cease to be selfish, or kings can find a more convenient mode of raising revenue than by imposts.

"These, then, form the true justification for laying duties in a way to protect our own industry against that of foreign nations: First, a reasonable apprehension of war — for no nation can always hope to be at peace. If, therefore, there is any article that is indispensably necessary for the subsistence of a nation, and the nation can produce it, that nation is not independent if it do not. If it is necessary, the production should be encouraged by high duties on the imported article. This should be done, not for the benefit of persons who may engage in the manufacture or cultivation of the desired article, but for the benefit of the whole community : what though each pays a little higher for the article in time of peace than he otherwise would , yet he is fully compensated for this in time of war. He then has this necessary, of which he would be wholly deprived had he not provided for it by a little self-sacrifice. We all act upon this principle individually ; and why should we not as a nation ? We accumulate in time of plenty for a day of famine and distress. Every man pays, from year to year, a small sum to insure his house against fire, submitting willingly to this annual tax, that, when the day of misfortune comes, (if come it shall,) the overwhelming calamity of having all destroyed may be mitigated by receiving back from the insurer a partial compensation for the loss. It is upon the same principle that we maintain an army and a navy in time of peace, and pour out millions annually for their support: not because we want them, but because it is reasonable to apprehend that war may come, and then they will be wanted; and it is a matter of economy to provide and discipline them in time of peace, to mitigate the evils of war when it does come. The same reason requires us to encourage the production of any indispensable article of subsistence. I shall not stop now to inquire what these articles are. Every one can judge for himself. But that there are many such, no one can doubt.

*　*　*　*　*　*　*　*

" But I make a distinction between the encouragement and protection of manufacturers. It is one thing for the government to encourage its citizens to abandon their ordinary pursuits and engage in a particular branch of industry; and a very different thing whether the government is bound to protect that industry by laws similar to those by which it encouraged its citizens to embark in it. In the first case there is no obligation on the part of the government. Its act is entirely voluntary and spontaneous. It may or may not encourage the production or manufacture of a particular article, as it shall judge best for the whole community. Before attempting it, the government should weigh well the advantages and disadvantages which are likely to result to the whole, and not to the particular class which may be tempted to engage. If a particular branch of industry is so important in its bearings upon the public wants, on account of its providing in time of peace for some necessary article in time of war, then, as the strongest advocates of free trade themselves admit, the government may and should legislate with a view to encourage its establishment; and so, likewise, if it be necessary to provide a home market for our products in consequence of the prohibitory duties levied upon them by foreign countries. But all these are questions to be decided according to the circumstances of each particular case; and the decision should be made with a view to the benefit of all, and not of a few, or of any particular class or section of the country. But when the government has decided that it is best to give the encouragement, and the citizen has been induced by our legislation to abandon his former pursuits, and to invest his capital and apply his skill and labor to the production of the article thus encouraged by government, then a new question arises — for another party has become interested — and that is, whether we will, by our subsequent legislation, withdraw our protection from the citizen whom we have thus encouraged to embark his all in a particular branch of business for the good of the public, and overwhelm him with ruin by our unsteady, not to say perfidious, legislation. I can consent to no such thing. It seems to me to be manifestly unjust. Our act in the first instance is free and voluntary. We may give the encouragement or not; but, having given it, the public faith is, to a certain extent, pledged. Those who have accepted our invitation, and embarked in these new pursuits, have done so under the implied promise on our part that the encouragement thus given should not be treacherously withdrawn, and that we would not tear down what we had encouraged them to build up. This I conceive to be a just, clear, and broad distinction between encouragement beforehand and protection afterward. The former is voluntary, depending wholly upon considerations of public policy and expediency; the latter is a matter of good faith to those who have trusted to the national honor."

The high position occupied by Mr. Fillmore in the twenty-seventh Congress, and the absolute leadership assumed in that body, is evinced by the following letter, published in a leading paper of the metropolis. We can but think of the "legislative portrait," elsewhere published in this work, while he was a member of the assembly at Albany, where it was predicted he could never be a political leader. Though both letters are highly commendatory of Mr. Fillmore, there is considerable difference in their tones; not more, however, than circumstances justified:

"Millard Fillmore is the distinguished representative from the city of Buffalo, and at present chairman of the committee of ways and means, a situation both arduous and resposible. He stands in the same relation to the United States government in the house of representatives that the chancellor of the exchequer does to the government of Great Britain in the houses of Parliament. He is emphatically the financial organ of the legislature. In the house of representatives all bills affecting the revenue originate. These are presented by the ways and means committee—matured by it—and its chairman has to explain their object and the data upon which they are based. He is obliged to make himself thoroughly acquainted with the situation of the national treasury; has to examine its details; become familiar with its wants, its expenditures, its income, present and prospective; and be ever ready to give the house a full exposition of all the measures he may present for consideration. To discharge the duties which this post enjoins, faithfully, requires both physical and mental capacity of a high order; and I believe they could not have devolved upon an individual better qualified than the subject of this notice. In every respect will he be found equal to the task assigned him.

*　*　*　*　*　*　*　*　*

" His judgment is very clear, and he has no emotions which ever over-ride it; is always to be relied upon, and whatever he undertakes he will master. He never takes a stride without testing his foothold. He belongs to that rare class whose merits are developed with every day's use; in whose minds new beauties and new riches are discovered as they are examined into. He has a high legal reputation; possesses great industry; is agreeable in conversation, and his information upon general subjects, without being profound, is varied and extensive. As a shrewd, sagacious politician—by this I do not mean that he is particularly skilled in mere partisan strategy — there are few men in the country superior to him—perhaps none.

*　*　*　*　*　*　*　*　*

"As a public man, I know of none—not one—of greater promise than Mr. Fillmore. He has many of the highest attributes of greatness, and is still a young man, not to exceed forty-one years of age, and must continue to rise in public estimation as his character shall be developed. He has been a member of Congress some six years, and was previously an active member of the state assembly. As a useful, practical, efficient, and enlightened legislator, he has no superior, and very few equals among his associates."

His career in Congress was drawing to a close. As indicated above, he had been four sessions a member of that body, and served with distinguished ability to the country and the greatest credit to himself. The twenty-seventh Congress was a very active one; many useful measures had been passed; the sub-treasury act was repealed, and useful appropriations had been made. One appropriation was made, against much opposition, that deserves notice. Prof. Morse was just on the eve of making a successful experiment of his telegraph, by putting a line in operation from Baltimore to Washington City. He asked Congress for an appropriation. Much depended on his getting it. He was there with scarcely a dollar in his pocket, and the lightnings of heaven at bay. Mr. Fillmore became his warmest friend, and, through the great influence he had with that body, procured the Morse appropriation.

It was violently opposed by many members of the house. Cave Johnson was furious at the result, and publicly declared that the appropriation of the same amount by Congress for the purpose of investigating mesmerism, would have been more useful. Time has shown who had the soundest judgment in regard to it.

Mr. Fillmore addressed a letter to his constituents, in the summer of 1842, containing his determination not to be a candidate for reëlection. Notwithstanding this letter, however, he was nominated by acclamation, in their ensuing convention. But he adhered to his determination. From his letter of declension, the following extracts may prove interesting:

"FELLOW CITIZENS: Having long since determined not to be a candidate for reëlection, I have felt that my duty to you required that I should give you seasonable notice of that determination. The chief causes which have brought me to this resolution, being mostly of a personal character, are unimportant, and would be uninteresting to you or the public. It is sufficient to say that I am not prompted to this course by anything in the present aspect of political affairs. Many of you know that I desired to withdraw before the last congressional election, but, owing to the importance of that contest, the desire for unanimity, and the hope that, if the administration were changed, I might render some essential local service to my district and those generous friends who had so nobly sustained our cause, I was induced to stand another canvass. But how sadly have all been disappointed! How has that sun, which rose in such joyous brightness to millions, been shrouded in gloom and sorrow! The lamented Harrison, around whom clustered a nation's prayers and blessings, is now no more. For reasons inscrutable to us, and known only to an all-wise Providence, he was cut down in a moment of triumph, and in his grave lie buried the long-cherised hopes of a suffering nation.

*   *   *   *   *   *   *   *   *

"It is now nearly fourteen years since you did me the unsolicited honor to nominate me to represent you in the state legislature. Seven times have I received renewed evidence of your confidence, by as many elections, with constantly increasing majorities; and, at the expiration of my present congressional term, I shall have served you three years in the state, and eight years in the national councils. I can not call to mind the thousand acts of generous devotion from so many friends who will ever be dear to my heart, without feeling the deepest emotion of gratitude. I came among you a poor and friendless boy. You kindly took me by the hand, and gave me your confidence and support. You have conferred upon me distinction and honor, for which I could make no adequate return but by an honest and untiring effort faithfully to discharge the high trusts which you confided to my keeping. If my humble efforts have met your approbation, I freely admit, that, next to the approval of my own conscience, it is the highest reward which I could receive for days of unceasing toil, and nights of sleepless anxiety.

"I profess not to be above or below the common frailties of our nature. I will, therefore, not disguise the fact that I was highly gratified at my first election to Congress; yet I can truly say that my utmost ambition has been satisfied. I aspire to nothing more, and shall retire from the exciting scenes of political strife to the quiet enjoyments of my own family and fireside with still more satisfaction than I felt when first elevated to this distinguished station.

" In conclusion, permit me again to return you my warmest thanks for your kindness, which is deeply engraven upon my heart.

" I remain, sincerely and truly,

" Your friend and fellow citizen,

" MILLARD FILLMORE."

The close of the twenty-seventh Congress placed Mr. Fillmore again in retirement. Laden with honors, he returned to the shades of private life, with the complacent consciousness of having done his duty. A number of years he had spent in public life, to the entire satisfaction of the people. It is a little remarkable that, as much as Mr. Fillmore has served in public life, he has never given a vote but was approved by his constituents. Of his career in Congress, J. Q. Adams bore the following testimony : speaking of Mr. Fillmore, he said, he was was one of the ablest, most faithful, and fairest-minded men with whom it had been his lot to serve in public life. Subsequent to that time, Lewis Cass has made some similar expressions, and declared, in substance, that his patriotism, ability, and correct judgment are above all question. During the summer of Mr. Fillmore's residence at home, after the close of his congressional labors, and not long before that old and patriot statesman was seized, while at his post, in Congress, with a paralysis that terminated in death, and called from his lips, "I am content," J. Q. Adams visited Buffalo. Mr. Fillmore was deputed by the committee of arrangements, who had made preparations to give him a reception. A large concourse of people had assembled to witness the occasion. The following is Mr. Fillmore's address:

"SIR: I have been deputed by the citizens of this place to tender you a welcome to our city. In the discharge of this grateful duty, I feel that I speak not only my own sentiments, but theirs, when I tell you that your long and arduous public services — your lofty independence — your punctilious attention to business, and, more than all, your unsullied and unsuspected integrity, have given you a character in the estimation of this republic, which calls forth the deepest feelings of veneration and respect.

"You see around you, sir, no political partisans seeking to promote some sinister purpose; but you see here assembled the people of our infant city, without distinction of party, sex, age, or condition — all — all anxiously vying with each other to show their respect and esteem for your public services and private worth.

"Here, sir, are gathered in this vast multitude of what must appear to you strange faces, thousands whose hearts have vibrated to the chord of sympathy which your written speeches have touched. Here is reflecting age, and ardent youth, and lisping childhood, to all of whom your venerated name is as familiar as household words — all anxious to feast their eyes by a sight of that extraordinary and venerable man of whom they have heard and read and thought so much — all anxious to hear the voice of that 'old man eloquent,' on whose lips wisdom has distilled her choicest nectar — here, sir, you see them all, and read in their eager and joy-gladdened countenances and brightly beaming eyes a welcome — a thrice-told, heart-felt, and soul-stirring welcome, to 'the man whom they delight to honor.'"

The occasion was an interesting one. Mr. Adams, in a long life of usefulness to the country, was an impersonation of the "awful virtues of the Pilgrim fathers." Venerable and experienced, he had stood on the battle-field of many a political struggle. Between him and Mr. Fillmore, from the congeniality of their virtuous patriotism evinced in years of public service, a warm friendship existed. There was a peculiar fitness in Mr. Fillmore being selected to deliver the address of welcome. The following is from the reply of Mr. Adams:

"MR. FILLMORE, MR. MAYOR, AND FELLOW CITIZENS: I must ask your indulgence for a moment's pause to take breath. If you ask me why I ask this indulgence, it is because I am so overpowered with the eloquence of my friend, (the chairman of the committee of ways and means, whom I have so long been accustomed to refer to in that capacity, that, with your permission, I will continue so to denominate him now,) that I have no words left to answer him. For so liberal has he been in bestowing that eloquence upon me which he himself possesses in so eminent a degree that, while he was ascribing to me talents so far above my own consciousness in that regard, I was all the time imploring the god of eloquence to give me, at least at this moment, a few words to justify him before you in making that splendid panegyric which he has been pleased to bestow upon me ; and that the flattering picture which he has presented to you, may not immediately be defaced before your eyes by what you should hear from me.

*　　*　　*　　*　　*　　*　　*　　*　　*

" I congratulate you again upon your possession of another dear and intimate friend of mine, in the person of the gentleman who has just addressed me in your name, and whom I have taken the liberty of addressing as chairman of the committee of ways and means — the capacity in which he has so recently rendered services of the highest importance to you his constituents, by whose favor he was enabled to render them — to us, and our common country. And I cannot forbear to express here my regret at his retirement in the present emergency from the councils of the nation. There, or elsewhere, I hope and trust he will soon return ; for, whether to the nation or to the state, no services can be, or ever will be, rendered by a more able or a more faithful public servant."

The regret expressed by Mr. Adams in the above, at Mr. Fillmore's withdrawal from the national councils, was universal among all classes of his fellow-citizens. He remained true to his purpose. The close of the twenty-seventh Congress left him in possession of the brightest civic laurels. His political career had been a glorious one. He remained, after the close of that Con-

gress, in the shade of private life, and in the duties of
his profession, until other events called him again to the
service of his country.

It is now my duty to notice very briefly another political revolution, pregnant with the most disastrous results,
one of which was the infliction into the heart of the
whig party of its eventual death-stab. The whig national
convention met at Baltimore, for the purpose of nominat-
ing candidates for the presidency and vice-presidency of
1844. The result of the deliberations of that convention
was the selection of Henry Clay, of Kentucky, for president, and Frelinghuysen for vice-president. Clay was
nominated by acclamation. Never did a party enter a
political contest more sanguine of success than did the
whigs in 1844. Never was a nomination more enthusi-
astically received. From northern New York to the
Carolinas, a simultaneous outburst of joy arose from the
ranks of the whig party. Banners were flung to the
breeze in a thousand cities, and along the line pæans of
victory were heard, and the blaze of triumph gleamed on
every countenance. But, fair as were all these indications, Clay was beaten. Which were the more surprised
at this result, the whigs or the democrats, would be difficult to say. Among the causes that led to the defeat of
Henry Clay may be enumerated the annexation question ;
the bankrupt law ; and the efforts of Cassius M. Clay in
the north. Tyler had some influence, which 'he exerted
against Clay's election. The large amount of abolition
votes in the north contributed to his defeat. The want
of efficient party organization did much harm. The too
13

sanguine hopes of the party was another cause ; the outbursts of enthusiasm prevented their zealous coöperative
labors.   Corruption, in the large cities, at the ballot-box
exerted considerable influence.   These are some of the
minor causes that led to the defeat of Clay ; but the
great and true cause was foreign influence.   The fraudulent issue of naturalization papers was developed to an
alarming   extent.   In Georgia, Louisiana, Maryland,
Pennsylvania, and New York City, this and other illegal
means were resorted to, for the purpose of electing
Polk in 1844.

At the Baltimore convention Mr. Fillmore was put in
nomination for the vice-presidency ; it was regarded by
many as unfortunate that he did not get it.   It was well
known that the result of the presidential election, in 1844,
depended greatly upon the state of New York.   Mr.
Fillmore was the choice for vice-president throughout
that state.   On the ticket with Clay, the state, it was
thought, could have been carried.   Disappointed in their
desires to place him before the people as a candidate for
the vice-presidency, the voters of New York, of his party,
were unanimous in their wishes to place him on the ticket
as candidate for governor.   Mr. Fillmore felt no desire to
engage in political struggles, and expressed himself
opposed to complying with the wishes of the people.
The following extracts from a letter published in the
Albany Journal, edited by Thurlow Weed, shows his
feelings in regard to the gubernatorial canvass of 1844 :

NEW YORK, May 16th, 1844.

THURLOW WEED, ESQ.— My Dear Sir: Being here in attendance upon the supreme court, my attention has been called to an article in your paper of the 8th instant, and to some extracts from other journals in yours since that time, in which my name is mentioned as a candidate for nomination to the gubernatorial office in this state. You do me the justice to say that ' I have never desired the office of governor, though I admit the right of the people to the services of a public man in any station they may think proper to assign him.' My maxim has always been that individuals have no claim upon the public for official favors, but that the public has a right to the service of any and all of its citizens. This right of the public, however, must in some measure be qualified by the fitness and ability of the person whose services may be demanded for the station designed, and the propriety of his accepting the trust can only be properly determined when all his relations, social and political, are taken into account. Of the former, I am ready to concede that the public must be the proper and only judge. In regard to the latter, the individual himself has a right to be consulted. These notices of the public press are from such sources, and so flattering, as to leave no doubt either of the sincerity or friendship of the authors. And the office itself, in my estimation, is second in point of dignity, honor, and responsibility only to that of president of the United States. When we reflect that it has been held by a Jay, a Tompkins, and a Clinton, who in the discharge of its various and responsible duties, acquired a fame that has connected them with the history of our country, and rendered their names immortal, all must agree that its honors are sufficient to satisfy the most lofty ambition. For myself, I can truly say, that they are more than I ever aspired to.

*　　*　　*　　*　　*　　*　　*

" But the whig party of this state now presents an array of talent and of well-tried political and moral integrity not excelled by that of any state of the Union. From this distinguished host it can not be difficult to select a suitable candidate for the office of governor — one who is capable, faithful, true to the cause and the country, and who will call out the enthusiastic support of the whole whig party. To such a candidate I pledge in advance my most hearty and zealous support. Let us add his name to those of Clay and Frelinghuysen, and our success is certain.

"But while I thus withdraw from competition for the honors, be assured that I do not shrink from the labors or responsibilities of this great contest. We have a work to perform in this state which calls for the united effort and untiring exertion of every true whig. Here the great battle is to be fought. For myself, I am enlisted for the war. Wherever I can be of most service, there I am willing to go; I seek no distinction but such as may be acquired by a faithful laborer in a good cause. I ask no reward but such as results to all from a good government well administered; and I desire no higher gratification than to witness the well merited honors with which victory will crown my numerous whig friends.

> " I am truly yours,
>
> "MILLARD FILLMORE."

But, notwithstanding the reasons advanced in the foregoing letter, and the unequivocally expressed preference to remain in private life, he was nominated by the state convention for governor, by acclamation. The pride they felt in presenting him as the candidate of their choice, is evinced in the following resolution, adopted among others by that convention :

"Resolved, that we announce to the people of this great commonwealth, with peculiar and triumphant satisfaction, the name of our candidate for the chief magistracy of the state — a nomination which we were called together not to suggest but to declare, as the previously expressed will of the people — a nomination which we have therefore made unanimously without a moment's delay, and without a thought of dissent — and that we rejoice in the opportunity thus to show a grateful people's high appreciation of the modest worth, the manly public virtue, the spotless integrity, and unchangeable fidelity of that eminent champion of whig principles, the dauntless vindicator of the outraged popular suffrage in the case of the insulted 'broad seal' of New Jersey in 1850, the valiant and victorious leader of the patriotic whigs of the immortal twenty-seventh Congress in their long and trying warfare against corruption and despotism, the laborious author and eloquent defender of the whig tariff — Millard Fillmore."

Mr. Fillmore was beaten and shared the general fate of whig principles in 1844. The same agencies enumerated in the causes of Clay's defeat, had been actively worked against Mr. Fillmore. This is the only instance in which Mr. Fillmore has ever known defeat, and to him, so far as he was concerned personally, it was no source of regret; but the great pang to him was, it sealed the doom of Henry Clay. Depressed under a consciousness of *this* fact, immediately after the result, he wrote the following letter to Mr. Clay:

"BUFFALO, November 11th, 1844.

"MY DEAR SIR: I have thought, for three or four days, that I would write you, but really I am unmanned. I have no courage or resolution. All is gone. The last hope, which hung first upon the city of New York and then upon Virginia, is finally dissipated, and I see nothing but despair depicted on every countenance.

"For myself I have no regrets. I was nominated much against my will, and though not insensible to the pride of success, yet I feel a kind of relief at being defeated. But not so for you or for the nation. Every consideration of justice, every feeling of gratitude conspired in the minds of honest men to insure your election; and though always doubtful of my own success, I could never doubt yours, till the painful conviction was forced upon me.

"The abolitionists and foreign catholics have defeated us in this state. I will not trust myself to speak of the vile hyprocrisy of the leading abolitions now. Doubtless, many acted honestly but ignorantly in what they did. But it is clear that Birney and his associates sold themselves to locofocoism, and they will doubtless receive their reward.

" Our opponents, by pointing to the native Americans and to Mr. Frelinghuysen, drove the foreign catholics from us, and defeated us in this state.

" But it is vain to look at the causes by which this infamous result has been produced. It is enough to say that all is gone, and I must confess that nothing has happened to shake my confidence in our ability to sustain a free government so much as this. If with such issues and such candidates as the national contest presented, we can be beaten, what may we not expect? A cloud of gloom hangs over the future. May God save the country, for it is evident the people will not."

We have stated that the main cause of these defeats were the effects of foreign influence; in support of this assertion, read the following extracts of letters to Mr. Clay immediately afterwards, by distinguished gentlemen, and notice the corroborative evidence contained in the foregoing letter, from Mr. Fillmore himself:

From Ambrose Spencer, of New York:

" The foreign vote destroyed your election.　＊　＊　＊ One sentiment seems to prevail universally, that the naturalization laws must be altered; that they must be repealed, and the door forever shut on the admission of foreigners to citizenship, or that they undergo a long probation. I am for the former.

" The Germans and Irish are in the same category;

those who know not our language, and are as ignorant as the lazzaroni of Italy, can never understandingly exercise the franchise ; and the other, besides their ignorance, are naturally inclined to go with the loafers of our population."

From Philip Hone, of New York city :

"Foreigners who have 'no lot or inheritance' in the matter, have robbed us of our birth-right, the 'sceptre has departed from Israel.' Ireland has re-conquered the country which England lost; but never suffer yourself to believe that a single trace of the name of Henry Clay is obliterated from the swelling hearts of the whigs of New York."

From John H. Westwood, of Baltimore :

"It was foreign influence, aided by the Irish and Dutch vote, that caused our defeat. As a proof, in my native city alone, in the short space of two months there were over one thousand naturalized. Out of this number, nine-tenths voted the loco-foco ticket. Thus men who could not speak our language were made citizens and became politicians too, who, at the polls were the noisy revilers of your fair fame. Thus you have been well rewarded for the interest you ever took for the oppressed of other nations. Notwithstanding the ingratitude of the Irish and German voters, if the abolitionists of New York had done their duty, all would have been well."

From Mr. Frelinghuysen, of New-Jersey :

"The foreign vote was tremendous. More than three thousand, it is confidently said, have been naturalized in this city, (New-York) alone, since the first of October. It is an alarming fact, that this foreign vote has decided the great questions of American policy, and counteracted a nation's gratitude."

These extracts, showing the great cause to which the disastrous results of 1844 were attributable, are fully corroberated by numerous other letters from distinguished men from all parts of the Union, to Mr. Clay. By reference to Colton's life and times of Henry Clay, many letters of the above nature are found, but we have published enough for our purpose. The conclusions naturally arrived at, at this time, by the perusal of the above extracts, are connected with the formation of a great American party. These letters are suggestive of an imperative necessity of a resort to some national step to counteract the pernicious effect of foreign influence. But more of this in the proper place.

In 1847 Mr. Fillmore was elected to the comptrollership of the state of New York, by a large majority. He endeavored by every means in his power to refuse the solicitations of his fellow citizens to become an incumbent of that office, and when he eventually signified his acceptance it was with extreme reluctance. As superintendent of the bank department in the Empire State of the Union, the duties devolving upon him were numerous and of the most onerous nature. Over the various funds belonging to the state, he exercised entire control, as being at the head of her finance. The plain, matter-of-fact, practical qualities of Mr. Fillmore's mind, and his untiring industry, eminently qualified him to fill that office with service to the country, and credit to himself. The precise accuracy of all his calculations rendered him

13*

well fitted for the discharge of the duties of an office
exclusively financial in its nature. The following letter, published in one of the ablest conducted papers of
the state, indicates both the nature of these duties, and
the faithful manner in which they were discharged :

" There is no officer of the state whose duties and powers are so diversified, so extensive, and complicated, as
those of the comptroller; nor is there any who is placed
in a more commanding position for exercising a political
influence. From a simple auditor of accounts, and a
watch upon the treasury, he has sprung up into an officer
of the first eminence in the administration ; supplanting,
by degrees, some departments which were once of equal,
if not higher, regard, as auxiliaries and advisers of the
executive power. He is the one-man of the government.
He is not simply an officer, but a bundle of officers.
There is hardly a branch of the administration of which
he is not a prominent member — so prominent, in some
cases, that the affairs of that branch cannot be conducted
without his actual presence, although personally, he may
be a minority of those having it in charge. He is the
chief of the finances ; the superintendent of the banks ;
and the virtual quorum of the commissioners of the canal
fund, with all the power which such a position gives him
in the canal board. While other state departments have
no more than maintained their original sphere of authority,
or have suffered material diminution, particularly of influence, the office of the comptroller has been a favorite of
the legislature, and the chief object of its confidence,

entrusted with high, if not extraordinary, powers of government.

"To form an adequate idea of the mass of duty he has in charge, it is necessary not only to survey the summary contained in the revised code of our laws, but to trace out the statutes from year to year; to review the reports of his office; and to follow him and his numerous assistants in the actual discharge of their various labors in the financial, banking, and tax bureaus of his department. But it is inconsistent with the designed brevity of these papers to enter into the details which alone can convey a suitable notion of the magnitude and responsibility of his trust and influence.   As the department is now organized, it is overgrown and cumbersome; and to perform with intelligence and conscientiousness, without error or delay, all its requisite offices of supervision and of action, requires the sight of an Argus, with his hundred eyes, and the activity of a Briareus, with his hundred hands."

Herein consists the infinite advantages of having such men as Mr. Fillmore for public servants — plain, business, practical men.   In every capacity in which Mr. Fillmore has been placed, he has proven himself to be a working man.   Such men are of practical utility to the country. This office of comptroller was one which required those peculiar kind of talents which Mr. Fillmore possessed to such an eminent degree.   In all the duties he has had to discharge, the greatest amount of labor to be accomplished in the least time, has been his desire.   Instead of laboring for display and show, he has labored to be useful.   In his speeches, he says as little as possible, and says it as plain as possible. In his writings he is careful to make everything plain and accurate. The faithful and correct performance of duty in any and all stations, has been the great aim of his life. The report he made, as comptroller of the state, showed the exact condition of the finances, exhibited with mathematical precision. Much clearness and financial capacity is exhibited in the comptroller's report, prepared by Mr. Fillmore. The very great amount of attention he devoted to the duties of the office is clearly indicated in the report of its condition. The following is a portion of the report:

" The comptroller believes that the safest way to make a sound paper currency is to have, at all times, ample security for its redemption in the possession of the state. In order to make this security ample, it should be not only sufficient in amount, but should be of such a nature that it may be readily converted into cash without loss. It is not enough that the security be ultimately good or collectable; delay in redeeming the circulation causes it to depreciate, and is almost as fatal to the poor man who cannot wait, as ultimate insolvency. He becomes at once the victim of the broker.

"A bond and mortgage may be good — that is the whole amount secured by them may be collectable; 'but the bill-holder can not wait for this. They must be convertible into cash by sale; and if, for any reason, this can not be done, they are not of that kind of security which should be required. All the experience of this department shows that bonds and mortgages are not the best security for this purpose, and while better security can be had, it is deeply to be regretted that they were ever received. The apprehension that there may be a defect of title, that the lands mortgaged may have been appraised too high, or that there may be some legal defence to a suit of foreclosure, all conspire to depreciate their value in the estimation of purchasers, when offered for sale at auction on the failure of a bank.

"Capitalists are cautious about purchasing, and the consequence is that they have sometimes sold for less than twenty per cent. on the amount received by them; and the average amount for which all have been sold, for the last ten years, is only thirty-seven and seventy-one hundredths per cent., while the average amount for which the five per cent, stocks of this state have sold is ninety-two and eighty-six one-hundredths per cent., or ninety-two dollars and eighty-six one hundredths for every hundred dollars of stock. This shows that a six per cent. stock, such as is now required, would doubtless have sold at par, and the bill-holder would have received dollar for dollar for the circulation.

"Should the country remain at peace, it can not be doubted that the stocks of the United States will be a safe and adequate security. The comptroller would, therefore, recommend that the law be so changed as to exclude bonds and mortgages from all free banks which shall hereafter commence business, and to prevent the taking of any more from those now in operation, and to require that ten per cent. per annum of those now held as security be withdrawn, and their places supplied by stocks of this state, or of the United States. If this recommendation be adopted, at the end of ten years the whole security will be equal to a six per cent. stock of this State, or of the United States, which it is presumed will be ample security for the redemption of all bills in circulation.

"Could this system of banking be generally adopted in the several states, it can hardly be doubted it would prove highly beneficial. It would create a demand for their own state stocks. The interest paid upon them would be paid to their own citizens. Every man who held a bank-note, secured by such stock, would have a direct interest in maintaining inviolate the credit of the state. The blasting cry of *repudiation* would never again be heard, and the plighted faith of the state would be as sacred as national honor; and lastly, it would give them a sound and uniform currency.

"If then, in addition to this, Congress would authorize such notes as were secured by stocks of the United States to be received for public dues to the national treasury, this would give to such notes a universal credit, coëxtensive with the United States, and leave nothing further to be desired in the shape of a national paper currency. This would avoid all objection to a national bank, by obviating all necessity for one, for the purpose of furnishing a national currency. The national government might be made amply secure. The law might provide that all bills secured by United States stock should be registered and countersigned in the treasury department, as the notes circulated by the banks in this state are registered and countersigned in this office. This would enable every collector, postmaster, or other receiver of public moneys, to know that they were receivable for public dues.

"The stock of the United States by which their redemption was secured, might be so transferred to the state officer holding the same, that it could not be sold or transferred by him without the assent of the secretary of the treasury; and, in case of the failure of the bank to redeem its notes, it might be optional with the secretary of the treasury to exchange the notes held by the government for an equal amount of United States stock held for their redemption, or let it be sold and receive the government's share of the dividends. In this way the national government would always be secure against loss.

" But this suggestion is foreign from the chief object of this report, and is merely thrown out to invite attention to the subject. But in conclusion, the comptroller has no hesitation in recommending that the free bank system be modified in the particulars above suggested, and that it be then adopted, in preference to the safety-fund system, as the banking system of this state.

" It can not be supposed that the banking under this system will be as profitable as it has been under the safety-fund system. It is therefore desirable that every facility should be given to capitalists who engage in it that can be granted consistent with the security of the public, and that no unreasonable or unjust system of taxation should be adopted which discriminates invidiously against them; but persons engaged in banking should be taxed like all other citizens."

It was about this time when the calamitous results of

famine were sweeping over the land of Erin, and philanthropy was appealing across the waters to the humane
feelings of Americans, for their manifestations of liberality
in behalf of the sufferers.

These appeals were not made in vain to a people ever
alive to the dictates of an active benevolence. Meetings
were held all over the land, and the most munificent spirit
of liberality prevailed throughout the entire Union.
Among the places of the North that responded with open
hands and hearts to her distressing appeal was the gener-
our city of Buffalo. A meeting was held in that place
expressive of their sympathy for the sufferers of the
Emerald Isle. Mr. Fillmore, ever alive to the calls
of humanity, addressed a letter upon that subject,
expressive of entire approval of the spirit manifested in
their behalf, and breathing the purest sentiments of
philanthropy.

CHAPTER IX.

Another national convention — Great changes — Military glory —
General Taylor nominated for the presidency — Millard Fillmore
for the vice-presidency — Their election — Sketch of the U. S.
Senate — Illustrious names — California asks admission — Sectionalism in the senate — ONE MAN at the head — The " omnibus
bill "— Death of President Taylor — Mr. Fillmore communicates
the fact to the senate — Proceedings of the two houses — Mr.
Fillmore takes the oath — Assumes the chief magistracy —
Funeral obsequies.

DURING the time he was incumbent of the comptroller-
ship another whig national convention assembled at Philadelphia, for the purpose of selecting political standard-
bearers for the campaign of 1848. Previous to the
assemblage of that convention, much had been said in
regard to the presidential candidate. Great changes had
taken place since it met four years before. War had
raged with a neighboring nation, and victory perched
upon the banners that waved in triumph over the peaks of
the Cordilleras. Texas had come into the Union as a
state, and the territorial acquisition of California had
fringed that side of our possession with its golden colors.
Banks and bank excitements had been silenced in the din
of progress. The sage of Ashland had been defeated.
The fame of Taylor had dazzled, on the fields of Palo
Alto, the heights of Monterey, and rose to its acme at
Buena Vista. Scott had placed the American flag upon
the heights of San Juan d' Ulloa, flashed like a meteor

over the crests of Cerro Gordo, Molina Del Rey, and erected his trophies in the halls of the Montezumas. The proud Tlascalan's land, the domain of the Aztecs, had submitted to the American arms. These two heroes circled in the halo of military fame, were looked upon with a view to the presidency. A strong feeling prevailed throughout the country favorable to Taylor; but so much of his life had been spent in the field and around the camp fire, that they were ignorant of his political creed, or whether he had any creed other than pertained to military tactics. The following letter in reply to previous inquiries on the subject, which was circulated throughout the country, was far from being satisfactory upon the subject of his political faith:

"BATON ROUGE, LA., January 30th, 1848.

" SIR : In reply to your inquiries, I have again to repeat, I have neither the power nor the desire to dictate to the American people the exact manner in which they should proceed to nominate candidates for the presidency of the United States. If they desire such a result, they must adopt the means best suited, in their opinion, to the consummation of the purpose ; and if they think fit to bring me before them for this office, through their legislature, mass meetings, or conventions, I can not object to their designating these bodies as whig, democrat, or native. But in being thus nominated, I must insist on the condition — and my position on this point is immutable — that I shall not be brought forward as the candidate of their party, or considered as the exponent of their party doctrines.

" In conclusion, I have to repeat, that if I were nominated for the presidency, by any body of my fellow citizens, designated by any name they might choose to adopt, I should esteem it an honor, and should accept such nomination, provided it had been made entirely independent of party considerations.

" I am, sir, very respectfully,

" Your obedient servant,

" Z. Taylor.

" Peter S. Smith, Esq., Philadelphia."

The following, known as the Allison letter, is a little more explicit:

"I will proceed now to respond to your inquiries :

" 1. I reiterate what I have so often said: I am a whig. If elected, I would not be the mere president of a party. I would endeavor to act independent of party dominion. I should feel bound to administer the government untrameled by party schemes.

" 2. The Veto Power. The power given by the constitution to the executive to interpose his veto is a high conservative power; but, in my opinion, should never be exercised except in cases of clear violation of the constitution, or manifest haste and want of consideration by Congress. Indeed, I have thought that for many years past the known opinions and wishes of the executive have exercised undue and injurious influence upon the legislative department of the government; and for this cause I have thought that our system was in danger of undergoing a great change from its true theory. The personal opinions of the individual who may happen to occupy the executive chair ought not to control the action of Congress upon questions of domestic policy; nor ought his objections to be interposed where questions of constitutional power have been settled by the various departments of government, and acquiesced in by the people.

"3.   Upon the subject of the tariff, the currency, the improvement of our great highways, rivers, lakes, and harbors, the will of the people, as expressed by their representatives in Congress, ought to be respected and carried out by the executive."

One point was pretty well settled by the above letter, viz., that if he *was* a military chieftain, in case of his election to the presidency, he would not be a Jackson, and in the assumption of the regal powers of the executive, forget the democratical ones of Congress.

Taylor, Scott, Clay, Webster, McLean, and Clayton, were presented before the convention as candidates for the presidency.   On the fourth ballot Taylor was declared the nominee of the convention, over Scott, Clay, and Webster — McLean and Clayton being scarcely considered.   After the selection of a candidate for president, Millard Fillmore and the late Abbott Lawrence were put in nomination for the vice-presidency.   On the second ballot, Mr. Fillmore was declared the nominee, having received more votes than were given to Taylor.   This announcement was received with unbounded delight.   Proud of Fillmore, New York had long been advocating his claims to that office ; a happier selection could not have been made.   Mr. Fillmore was informed of the result of the Philadelphia convention, and made the following reply :

"ALBANY, N. Y., June 17th, 1848.

" SIR : — I have the honor to acknowledge the receipt of your letter of the 10th inst., by which I am notified that at the late whig convention held at Philadelphia, Gen. Zachary Taylor was nominated for president, and myself for vice-president, and requesting my acceptance.

" The honor of being thus presented by the distinguished representives of the whig party of the Union for the second office in the gift of the people — an honor as unexpected as it was unsolicited — could not fail to awaken grateful emotions, which, while they can not be suppressed, find no appropriate language for utterance.

"Fully persuaded that the cause in which we are enlisted is the cause of the country ; that our chief object is to secure peace, preserve its honor, and advance its prosperity ; and feeling, moreover, a confident assurance that in General Taylor, whose name is presented for the first office, I shall always find a firm and consistent whig, a safe guide and an honest man, I can not hesitate to assume any position which my friends may assign me.

" Distrusting, as I well may, my ability to discharge satisfactorily the duties of that high office, but feeling that in case of my election, I may with safety repose upon the friendly aid of my fellow whigs, and that efforts guided by honest intentions will always be charitably judged, I accept the nomination so generously tendered, and I do this the more cheerfully, as I am willing, for such a cause and with such a man, to take my chances of success or defeat, as the electors, the final arbiters of our fate, shall, in their wisdom, judge best for the interests of our country.

"Please accept the assurance of my high regard and esteem, and permit me to subscribe myself

"Your friend and fellow citizen,

"MILLARD FILLMORE."

The result of this nomination was an election by a large majority.

Cass and Butler, the democratic candidates, were beaten by thirty-six electoral votes, Mr. Fillmore was immediately, after this result became known, honored in New York City by the general committee, giving him their congratulations, and an address through their chairman. In a private letter, written immediately afterwards, Mr. Fillmore makes the following remarks :

"The cordiality and unanimity with which the whig ticket has been sustained everywhere, north and south, east and west, is a just cause of national felicitation. It proves that the great whig party is truly a national party — that it occupies that safe and conservative ground which secures to every section of the country all that it has a right to claim under the guarantee of the constitution — that such rights are inviolate — and as to all other questions of mere policy, where Congress has the constitutional right to legislate, the will of the people, as expressed through their representatives in Congress, is to control, and that will is not to be defeated by the arbitrary interposition of the veto power.

" This simple rule, which holds sacred all constitutional guarantees, and leaves the law-making power where the constitution placed it, in Congress, relieves the party at once from all the embarrassing questions that arise out of sectional differences of opinion, and enables it to act harmoniously for the good of the country. When the president ceases to control the law-making power, his individ ual opinions of what the law ought to be, become comparatively unimportant. Hence we have seen General Taylor, though attacked as a slaveholder and a pro-slavery man at the north, cordially supported and triumphantly elected by men opposed to slavery, in all its forms ; and though I have been charged at the south, in the most gross and wanton manner, with being an abolitionist and an incendiary, yet the whigs of the south have cast these calumnies to the winds, and, without asking or expecting any thing more than what the constitution guarantees to them on this subject, they have yielded to me a most hearty and enthusiastic support. This was particularly so in New Orleans, where the attack was most violent.

" Really, these southern whigs are noble fellows Would you not lament to see the Union dissolved, if for no other cause than that it separated us from such true, noble, and high-minded associates ? But I regard this election as putting an end to all ideas of disunion. It raises up a national party, occupying a middle ground, and leaves the fanatics and disunionists, north and south, without the hope of destroying the fair fabric of our constitution. May it be perpetual !"

Let the attention of all parties, in both extremes of our union, be called to the noble, patriotic sentiments contained in the foregoing. Men of the south, let them sink into your hearts and become impressed upon your minds.

"Really, these southern whigs are noble fellows. Would you not lament to see the Union dissolved, if for no other cause than that it separated us from such true, noble, and high-minded associates?"

Look again at the closing sentence of this patriotic letter. It was a private letter, never intended for the public eye; hence, it must be admitted as a true index of the man.

Mr. Fillmore resigned the comptrollership in February, 1849, to assume the responsible duties of the vice-presidency, and on the fifth of March was inaugurated as the incumbent of that office. The occasion was one of solemnity and importance. Vast multitudes assembled at the capitol to witness the ceremony. The following are Mr. Fillmore's remarks to the senate on the occasion:

" SENATORS : Never having been honored with a seat on this floor, and never having acted as the presiding officer of any legislative body, you will not doubt my sincerity, when I assure you that I assume the responsible duties of this chair, with a conscious want of experience, and a just appreciation that I shall often need your friendly suggestions, and more often your indulgent forbearance. I should, indeed, feel oppressed and disheartened, did I not recollect that the senate is composed of eminent statesmen, equally distinguished for their high intellectual endowments and their amenity of manners, whose persuasive eloquence is so happily tempered with habitual courtesy, as to relieve your presiding officer from all that would be painful in the discharge of his duty, and render his position as agreeable as it must be instructive.

"Thus encouraged and sustained, I enter upon the duties assigned me, firmly resolved to discharge them with impartiality, and to the best of my ability. But I should do injustice to the grateful emotions of my own heart, if I did not, on this occasion, express my warmest thanks for the distinguished honor that has been conferred upon me, in being called by the voice of the nation to preside over your deliberations.

" It will not, I trust, be deemed inappropriate to congratulate you on the scene now passing before us. I allude to it in no partisan aspect, but as an ever-recurring event contemplated by the constitution. Compare the peaceful changes of chief magistrate of this republic with the recent sanguinary revolutions in Europe.

" There the voice of the people has only been heard amid the din of arms and the horrors of domestic conflicts; but here, in our own favored land, under the guidance of our constitution, the resistless will of the nation has, from time to time, been peaceably expressed, by the free will of the people, and all have bowed in obedient submission to their decree.

" The administration which but yesterday wielded the destinies of this great nation, to-day quietly yields up its power, and, without a murmur, retires from the capitol.

" I congratulate you senators, and I congratulate my country, upon these oft-recurring and cheering evidences

14

of our capacity for self-government. Let us hope that the sublime spectacle we now witness may be repeated as often as the people shall desire a change of rulers, and that this venerated constitution, and this glorious Union may endure forever."

At the time this administration came into power, many changes had just taken place of no ordinary nature, and numerous discordant elements were about wrapping the political horizon in a blaze of fire. It was on the eve of the fierce struggle relating to the balance of power, between the slaveholding states of the south, and the non-slaveholding states of the north. Secession conventions were being held in the south, and anti-slavery meetings in the north. Led by Rhett, Sharkey, and others, the southern secessionists were fomenting the wildest excitements, and were beginning to advocate disunion. Headed by Hale and others, the anti-slavery adherents of the north were creating animosity of the bitterest nature, and saying to slavery, "Thus far and no farther shalt thou come."

Disunion conventions were beginning to be agitated, and the southern disunionists subsequently met in convention, in the city of Nashville, with delegated representatives from most of the southern states. The whole political organism had begun to rock and heave with convulsive throes, preceding the mighty shock that was to pour its eruptive lava upon the green vales of union. Lightnings of fanaticism flashed in the heavens, and the muttering thunders of the approaching storm rolled their awful peals in the distance. Quick, and wild with the

o

fitful blaze of excitement, the national leaders looked on each other as rivals instead of colleagues, and kindled instead of allayed the furies of the coming crisis. Sectional strifes and fanatical discords of different natures, diffused with the most rancorous irritation, sparkled their fierceness from under the panoply of the Wilmot Proviso. It was on the eve of the mighty storm, pregnant with such fearful bolts, that Mr. Fillmore assumed the speakership of the senate.

Let us glance, for a moment, at the elements of that august body, over which he had to preside. There was the venerable Clay, who had for years been woven with his country, by the web of destiny. From Ashland he bent his steps again to the scenes of his early triumphs. Though venerable in years, he was an intellectual giant that nothing could overcome. Curtius-like, he had gone there to throw his virtue and patriotism into the breach that was opening about his country's capitol, and to die, a self-immolated martyr to patriotism. The immortal Webster was there, thundering forth his lion-tones of " I know no north, no south," upon the ears of a captive senate. Benton was there, enthroned upon " thirty years' " experience, a pillar of firmness, fixed as the poles. Dickenson was there, with his great perceptive powers, to raise his arm and voice for union. The patriot Cass was there, exhibiting the stern inflexibility of justice and right.

J. R. Underwood was there, side by side with Clay, throwing his talents into the task of pacification, with a spirit of patriotic virtue, true as steel. Foote was there the great antagonist of Benton, the Phocion of the south. What a seven were *these.* Imagine them stirred into strife, as they were destined to be. Imagine how vast the mental volcano, when lit with the phrenzies of discord. Imagine how resistless the torrent, when that realm of mind boiled over with excitement, and wonder how they passed the ordeal of 1849–50. They had ONE MAN at their head fit to be their pilot. Such was the senate — the memorable senate of that fearful epoch.

The first measure that tended to fan the elements of discord into an unexampled fury, was the application of California to be admitted as a state into the Union. Before coming as a sister into the family of Union, it was insisted that the mantle of the Wilmot Proviso had to wrap her fair proportions. Here the whole subject of slavery began to roll its dark evolvements thick about the political sky. California, spreading her lap, a golden El Dorado, lured to her plains the restless adventurers from all parts of the world, and became densely populated, with unprecedented rapidity. So fast had she been settled, that under a state constitution adopted by the people, she was knocking at the door for admission into the Union.

Her admission, as the admission of many other states into the Union, involved the slavery question. Was she to come in as a free or a slave state? She demanded admittance as a free state. This the South, of course, opposed; and the only way of conciliating them was to *compromise* by the introduction of some measure possessing the merits of mutual concession. This resulted in the elaboration of the compromise measures of Mr. Clay. We have before remarked that Mr. Clay well understood the principles of conciliation. By a masterly stroke of the most consummate statesmanship, he demonstrated this attribute in the present emergency. He was opposed to California's admission into the Union as a free state without a corresponding area of territory to maintain the balance of power in the senate. The compromise he introduced specified that certain parcels of territory which it organized into governments should decide by the voice of the people upon the subject of slavery. Here was a concession to the south, in the event of California's ultimate admission as a free state. His measure also settled the Texas boundary question, and embraced certain portions of the fugitive slave law, which was afterwards adopted by congress. Embracing as it did all these designs, it was denominated the " omnibus bill."

The great quality it possessed was that of mutual concession on the part of the North and South, so as not to endanger the balance of power. Had the senate endorsed these sentiments, the terrific excitements of that session would have been allayed in the incipient stages of their development. Webster, Cass, Underwood, and others, came to the rescue, and rendered patriotic services. While excited over this question, and that excitement still on the increase, as if to strike an awful bolt of " beware ! " into their deliberations, General Taylor died. General Taylor was a great and a good man, though politics were evidently not his sphere. The reins of government, in this instance, instead of passing from old hands into new, passed from the hands of inexperience into those of skill, ability, and experience. They could have found no safer repository. Taylor died on the 9th of July, 1850, exclaiming, *"I am prepared — I have tried to do my duty."* On the next day, the following communication was sent to the senate and house by Mr. Fillmore:

"WASHINGTON, July 10th, 1850.

"Fellow citizens of the Senate and of the House of Representatives: I have to perform the melancholy duty of announcing to you that it has pleased Almighty God to remove from this life Zachary Taylor, late President of the United States. He deceased last evening at the hour of half-past ten o'clock, in the midst of his family, and surrounded by affectionate friends, calmly, and in the full possession of all his faculties. Among his last words were these, which he uttered with emphatic distinctness: 'I have always done my duty — I am ready to die; my only regret is for the friends I leave behind me.'

"Having announced to you, fellow citizens, this most afflicting bereavement, and assuring you that it has penetrated no heart with deeper grief than mine, it remains for me to say, that I propose this day, at twelve o'clock, in the hall of the house of representatives, in the presence of both houses of Congress, to take the oath prescribed by the constitution, to enable me to enter on the execution of the office which this event has devolved on me.

"Yours, respectfully,

"MILLARD FILLMORE."

The senate, pursuant to previous arrangements, of a committee appointed under resolutions for that purpose, proceeded to the hall of the house, where Judge Cranch administered the oath of office to Mr. Fillmore.

The following message was then received from the president:

"WASHINGTON, July 10th, 1850.

"Fellow citizens of the Senate and of the House of Representatives : A great man has fallen among us, and a whole country is called to an occasion of unexpected, deep, and general mourning.

"I recommend to the two houses of Congress to adopt such measures as their discretion may seem proper, to perform with due solemnity the funeral obsequies of Zachary Taylor, late President of the United States; and thereby to signify the great and affectionate regard of the American people for the memory of one whose life has been devoted to the public service; whose career in arms has not been surpassed in usefulness or brilliancy; who has been so recently raised by the unsolicited voice of the people to the highest civil authority in the government, which he administered with so much honor and advantage to his country; and by whose sudden death so many hopes of future usefulness have been blighted forever.

"To you, senators and representatives of a nation in tears, I can say nothing which can alleviate the sorrow with which you are oppressed.

"I appeal to you to aid me under the trying circumstances which surround us in the discharge of the duties, from which, however much I may be oppressed by them, I dare not shrink; and I rely upon Him, who holds in His hands the destinies of nations, to endow me with the requisite strength for the task, and to avert from our country the evils apprehended from the heavy calamity which has befallen us.

" I shall most readily concur in whatever measures the wisdom of the two houses may suggest, as benefitting this deeply melancholy occasion.

" MILLARD FILLMORE."

The funeral obsequies of the late president were performed with great solemnity, on the 13th of July. Like Harrison, Taylor died immediately after he commenced the duties of his office. But, *un*like Harrison, he left the sacred trust reposed in his keeping in safe and reliable hands.

CHAPTER X.

MR. FILLMORE'S ADMINISTRATION — He selects a cabinet — Wisdom of his selection — Excitement in the senate — Defeat of the omnibus bill — The North and the South — Struggle for supremacy — Three parties in the senate — Wisdom and patriotism — The great crisis — Mr. Fillmore's firmness and patriotism — Difficulties in New Mexico and Texas — Passage of the compromise measures — Their submission to the president — A civic Callimachus — Fugitive Slave Law — Attorney General — Mr. Fillmore signs the compromise measures — Is violently assailed in consequence — Judge McLean's opinion — First annual message — Its ability.

THE first duty devolving upon Mr. Fillmore was the selection of his cabinet. Appreciating, to its fullest extent, the importance of unison of feeling · between president and cabinet, he made the selection with great care, and with reference to the immediate adjustment of the measures that bid fair to be so exciting. His cabinet was composed of the following gentlemen :

DANIEL WEBSTER, of Massachusetts, Secretary of State.

THOMAS CORWIN, of Ohio, Secretary of the Treasury.

JAMES A. PEARCE, of Maryland, Secretary of the Interior.

WILLIAM A GRAHAM, of North Carolina, Secretary of the Navy.

EDWARD BATES, of Missouri, Secretary of War.

NATHAN K. HALL, of New York, Postmaster-General.

JOHN J. CRITTENDEN, of Kentucky, Attorney-General.

14*

In addition to the eminent talent and ability combined in this selection, we see an entire absence of all local prejudices. From Lake Erie to Carolina, from Kentucky to Boston, and from Maryland to Missouri, this able cabinet was brought together, to aid him in the administration of the government.

Simultaneously with the elevation of Mr. Fillmore to the presidency, commenced the fiercest political struggle recorded in the annals of American history. The difficulties originating in the demand of California for admission into the Union as a state increased in number and magnitude, until the North and the South stood up in deadly conflict. Two powerful rivals, they seemed to sever the bond of union, and in fierce hostility to struggle for supremacy. There was a party in Congress who opposed the measures embodied in the compromise, upon the grounds that it was too much concession to the South. There was another party who averred that it was too much concession to the North. While in the midst of these sectionalists stood a Spartan band of Union patriots, led by Clay, Webster, and others, and encouraged by Fillmore, laboring to conciliate with the mild measures of the compromise, requiring mutual concession, and guaranteeing mutual protection. But the very mutuality of these measures was what tended to elicit such incessant opposition. It was a crisis — a very great crisis — in the struggle between North and South. The smallest advantage gained by either party could be turned to great account. Each wanted to gain some supremacy, and, as long as all the adjustment measures presented precluded the possibility of any ascendency by either party of sectionalists, both parties were arrayed against it. Adjustment was not what they desired so much as ascendency. Clay, Webster, and the whole administration party threw themselves into the breach, with the determined spirit of martyrs. I call this the administration party, because their views were the same as entertained by the administration. Of these compromise measures, it may be said they were the only means of quelling the troubles of the nation. The lofty intellects and penetrating sagacity of those who originated them have never been excelled. The towering eloquence of Clay, Webster, and others, thrilled every part of the Union, and vibrated in the old world.

The conciliatory measures of the compromise, or the omnibus bill, as it was derisively called by the opponents, were submitted to the senate, shortly after Mr. Fillmore's accession to the presidency. That measure was defeated by a vote taken amid the wildest excitement. After the defeat of this measure, the feeling became still more intense, until signs of red revolution began to indicate themselves. A blaze of fanaticism flashed across the Union like a bolt of destruction. The thunders of discord rolled their notes, with a terrific shock, that threatened to upheave the whole superstructure of our republican system. The great ocean of politics were ploughed from the very bottom, and foamed with all the rage of sectional strife. The old ship of state would sink beneath the surge, and bend her spars to the gale, then again she would rise above the blast unharmed. Amid the storm that wrapped her mast, the pilot was at the helm, unmoved by the raging tempest, determined to guide her into port. Men of all parties felt the shock, and all eyes were turned to him with intense anxiety. Calm and patriotic he breasted the tempest, and guided the vessel true to the star of national freedom. "He was the man for the crisis," was the opinion of patriots in all parts of the country. The nation was groaning under the fearful anticipations as to what might be the result. Disunion was spread from Maine to Texas. Party strife opened wide the breach between North and South. Fanatics, with an Alexander sword, stood ready to cut the Gordian knot of union, and rip out the heart of freedom. The stars and stripes of liberty were being torn to fragmental shreds, and furled about their shattered staff. Demarkation lines were being drawn across the tomb of Vernon. The banners that waved where Warren fell seemed ready to dip in intestine blood. America shrieked a wild pang, as she saw sectionalism weave the winding sheet of her independence. Columbia gasped convulsive throes of agony, as she lay half-prostrate, to see fanatics place a cypress wreath about her pale brow. Freedom no longer sped her holy message, but, quivering with anguish, hovered about the capitol, pierced with an hundred darts, ready to shriek her death gutterel.

At the head of the union party as the nation's chief, stood Mr. Fillmore, unmoved, erect and patriotic, destined to rule the storm, and to whisper "peace, be still." With prompt energy he commenced the task of allaying the excitement by ordering such military preparations as was necessary to suppress the civil war between New Mexico and Texas, who stood with daggers drawn for fight, in regard to their boundaries, and advised Congress of the necessity of immediate action in reference to the difficulties in that quarter. Congress responded by taking adequate steps to meet the emergency. In the meantime the great difficulties originating in the application of California were beginning to be amicably adjusted. The compromise, a pillar of patriotism, of which Clay, Cass, Webster, Underwood, and others were the architects, after passing a Red Sea of terrific excitement, were begining to be regarded more favorably. The compromise embraced the following measures : 1. California came into the Union as a free state; 2, the boundary between New Mexico and Texas was settled; 3, governments were organized for the territories of New Mexico and Utah; 4, the slave trade abolished in the District of Columbia; 5, the Fugitive Slave Law, which provided for the recovery of fugitives from labor.

Of these measures and their several utilities, it is not my province to speak. Their great services to the country are full well appreciated. All friends to the country are friends to these measures. They have been the subjects of much comment and controversional excitements.

After the passage of these measures, they were submitted to President Fillmore for approval. What an awful responsibility was this. He could make them the laws of his country, or he could dash to pieces by the refusal of his signature the giant structure of months.

He was, emphatically, the Polemarch of the Union, the Callimachus of the great American civic battle. He was no Van Buren or Tyler, to leave the veto upon the great measures of the American Congress.

Mr. Fillmore's having signed the fugitive slave law, should endear him to the hearts of the people as their favorite son. They should take into consideration the exalted patriotism that induced the act. The violence with which he knew he would be assailed by men of the North,—by those, too, who had been his friends,—exerted no influence in his action. Like Washington, as Millard Fillmore, he could pay some attention to the wishes of personal friends, but, as president of the Union, HER interests were the only dictates he obeyed.

Some points in the Fugitive Slave Law Mr. Fillmore feared were not constitutional. The wisdom of some such measure he did not doubt. Circumstances transpiring over the country continually demonstrated the necessity of such an enactment. Such necessities have always existed. During the administration of Washington, such an enactment was found to be necessary, and resulted in the somewhat similar law of 1793 ; then how much more so in 1850. The sectional feelings between the North and South had become so great, that the efforts of the owners to recover their fugitives were not only futile, but attended with expence and insult. On some occasions, when the legitimate owner of the fugitives pursued them to the state to which they fled, and took them before the proper tribunals, the officials would refuse to investigate the case ; and if, without an investigation, he took his property back to his state, he was indicted for violating law, and sometimes convicted, and would have to appeal to the supreme court for release.

Such were some of the absolute necessities of the act. The clause in the constitution in reference to fugitives certainly contemplates some such law as the one under consideration.   But the necessities for such a law and the constitutionality of some of its peculiar provisions, when passed, are widely different; upon the first, Mr. Fillmore was well satisfied — upon the other he was not.   With that profound regard for the constitution which he has always manifested, he was determined to become satisfied upon that point, and to withhold his signature until it was thoroughly investigated.   He studied it himself and submitted it to his attorney-general.   Mr. Crittenden delivered a long and able opinion in support of its constitutionality.   After becoming satisfied of its constitutionality, Mr. Fillmore signed all the measures of the Compromise.

Here we are tempted into a brief review.   Mr. Fillmore was seen in childhood making peace among his companions; in the commencement of his profession, he was on the side of the people; in the assembly, laboring for the people's rights, he removed the law that imprisoned for debt; in Congress, when universal distress prevailed, as chairman of the committee of ways and means, he labored for the people, and retrenched government extravagance; in the comptroller's office, a friend to the people, he guarded their funds, and systematized their state finances; as vice-president, he maintained the dignity of their laws, and ruled with order ; as president, looking at the distresses of the people, he gave relief, and preserved their freedom.   Who can present such antecedents as these, in a life of public service ?   Who else can point to a career so replete with evidences of devotion to the people — the whole people?

As might have been expected, the Fugitive Slave Law created great excitement in the North, and was violently assailed by the sectionalists. Seward, especially, poured his denunciations against it. Mr. Fillmore came in for a large share of the abuse — thick and heavy was it heaped upon him. But, with the consciousness of having performed his duty, he never felt their bitter malignity. In Boston, and other places, so hostile were the demonstrations against the enforcement of the law, that they opposed it with mob resistance. On learning these facts, Mr. Fillmore issued his proclamation, calling on all good citizens to suppress the riot. The law had been passed, and, as the law of the land, he was determined it should be effectually enforced.

The prompt and patriotic manner in which he commenced the enforcement of the compromise measures, contributed greatly to restore the country to tranquillity, after the terrible agitation that had shaken it from centre to circumference.   The main basis of the arguments advanced against the Fugitive Slave Law, and the denunciations heaped upon Mr. Fillmore, for having signed it, was its alleged unconstitutionality.   The following able and elaborate opinion by Judge McLean puts that question effectually to rest ; and, he being a prominent man among the anti-slavery party, it is certainly unbiased by any prejudices, and slavery predilections.

" It is contended that the law authorizing the reclamation of fugitives from labor is unconstitutional; that the constitution left the power with the states, and vested no power on the subject in the federal government.

" This argument has been sometimes advanced, and it may have been introduced into one or more political platforms. In regard to the soundness of this position, I will first refer to judicial decisions. In the case of Prigg *v.* The State of Pennsylvania, 16 Peters' R. 539, the judges of the supreme court of the United States, without a dissenting voice, affirmed the doctrine, that this power was in the federal government. A majority of them held that it was exclusively in the general government. Some of the judges thought that a state might legislate in aid·of the act of Congress, but it was held by no one of them, that the power could be exercised by a state, except in subordination of the federal power.   *   *   *

" Every state court which has decided the question, has decided it in accordance with the view of the supreme court. No respectable court, it is believed, has sustained the view that the power is with the state. Such an array of authority can scarcely be found in favor of the construction of any part of the constitution, which has ever been doubted. But this construction, sanctioned as it is by the entire judicial power, state as well as federal, has also the sanction of the legislative power.

" In a very few years after the constitution was adopted by the states, the fugitive act of 1793 was passed. That law is still in force, except where the act of 1850 contains repugnant provisions. In the Congress which enacted the act of 1793, it is believed that some of the members had been members of the convention. They could not have been ignorant of the provision of that instrument. And by the passage of that act they exercised the power, as one that belonged to the federal government. Here is a force of authority, judicial and legislative, which can not be found on any other seriously litigated point in the constitution.

" Such a weight of authority is not to be shaken. If the question is not to be considered authoritatively settled, what part of that instrument can ever be settled ? The surrender of fugitive slaves was a matter deeply interesting to the slave states. Uuder the confederation there was no provision for their surrender. On the principles of comity amongst the states, the fugitives were delivered up; at other times they were protected and defended. This state of things produced uneasiness and discontent in the slave states. A remedy of this evil, as it was called, was provided in the constitution.

" An individual who puts his opinion, as to the exercise of this power, against the authority of the nation in its legislative and judicial action, must have no small degree of confidence in his own judgment. A few individuals in Massachusetts may have maintained, at one time, that the power was with the states; but such views were, it is believed, long since abandoned, and they are re-asserted now, more as a matter of expediency than of principle.

" But whether we look at the weight of authority

against state power, as asserted, or at the constitutional provision, we are led to the same result. The provision reads : " No person held to service or labor in one state, under the laws thereof, escaping into another, shall, in consequence of any law or regulation therein, be discharged from such service or labor, but shall be delivered up on claim of the party to whom such service may be due."

" This, in the first place, is a federal measure. It was adopted by the national convention, and was sanctioned, as a federal law, by the respective states. It is the supreme law of the land. Now a provision which cannot be enforced, and which has no penalty for its violation, is no law. The highly respectable gentleman who read an ingenious argument in support of these views, is too good a theologian to contend that any rule of action which may be disregarded without incurring a penalty, can be a law. This was the great objection to the articles of confederation. There was no power to enforce its provisions. They were recommendatory, and without sanctions.

" There is no regulation, divine or human, which can be called a law, without a sanction. Our first parents, in the garden, felt the truth of this. And it has been felt by violators of the divine or human laws throughout the history of our race.

" The provision in the constitution is prohibitory and positive. It prohibits the states from liberating slaves which escape into them, and it enjoins a duty to deliver up such fugitives on claim being made. The constitution vests no special power in Congress to prohibit the first, or to enforce the observance of the second. Does it, therefore, follow that effect can be given to neither, if a state shall disregard it?

" Suppose a state declares a slave who escapes into it shall be liberated, or that any one who shall assist in delivering him up shall be punished. If this power belongs to the states, and not to the federal government, these regulations would be legal, as within the exercise of their discretion. This is not an ideal case. The principle was involved in the Prigg case, and the supreme court held the act of the state unconstitutional and void.

" It is admitted that there is no power in the federal government to force any legislative action on a state. But, if the constitution guarantees a right to the master of a slave, and that he shall be delivered up, the power is given to effectuate that right. If this be not so, the constitution is not what its framers supposed it to be. It was believed to be a fundamental law of the Union. A federal law. A law to the states and to the people of the states. It says that the states shall not do certain things. Is this the form of giving advice or recommendation? It is the language of authority, to those who are bound to obey. If a state do the thing forbidden, its acts will be declared void. If it refuse to do that which is enjoined, the federal government, being a government, has the means of executing it.

" The constitution provides, 'that full faith shall be given to public acts, records, and judicial proceedings,' of one state in every other. If an individual claiming this provision as a right, and a state court shall deny it, on a writ of error to the supreme court of the Union, such judgment would be reversed. And the provision that, 'the citizens of each state shall be entitled to all privileges and immunities of citizens in the several states.' Congress unquestionably may provide in what manner a right claimed under this clause and denied by a state, may be enforced. And if a case can be raised under it, without any farther statutory provisions, so as to present the point to the supreme court, the decision of a state court denying the right would be reversed. So a state is prohibited from passing a law that shall impair the obligations of a contract. Such a law the supreme court has declared void. In these cases, and in many others, where a state is prohibited from doing a thing, the remedy is given by a writ of error under the legislation of Congress. The same principle applies in regard to fugitives from labor.

"A fugitive from justice may be delivered up under a similar provision in the constitution. It declares that, 'a person charged in any state with treason, felony, or other crime, who shall flee from justice and be found in another state, shall, on demand of the executive authority of the state from which he fled, be delivered up, to be removed to the state having jurisdiction of the crime.' This is contained in the same section as the clause in relation to fugitives from labor, and they both stand upon the same principle. In both cases Congress has provided a mode in which effect shall be given to the provision. No one, it is believed, has doubted the constitutionality of the provision in regard to fugitives from justice.

" The men who framed the constitution were adequate to the great duties which devolved upon them. They knew that a general government was essential to preserve the fruits of the revolution. They understood the necessities of the country. The articles of confederation had been found as a rope of sand, in all matters of conflict between the different states, and the people of the different states. Without a general government, commerce could not be regulated among the states, or with foreign nations; fugitives from labor could not be reclaimed; state boundaries could not be authoritatively established.

"I am aware it has been stated that the subject of slavery was not discussed in the convention, and that the reclamation of fugitives from labor was not, at that time, a subject of much interest. This is a mistake. It was a subject of deep and exciting interest, and without a provision on the subject no constitution could have been adopted. I speak from information received from the late Chief-justice Marshall, who was one of the chief actors in that day, than whom no man then living was of higher authority.

*   *   *   *   *   *   *

"Various objections are stated to the Fugitive Slave Law of 1850. The duties of the commissioners, the penalties inflicted, the bribe secured to the commissioner for remanding the fugitive, are all objected to as oppressive and unconstitutional. In regard to the five dollars, in addition, paid to the commissioner, where the fugitive is remanded to the claimant in all fairness, it can not be considered as a bribe, or as so intended by Congress; but as a compensation to the commissioner for making a statement of the case, which includes the facts proved, and to which his certificate is annexed. In cases where the witnesses are numerous, and the investigation takes up several days, five dollars would scarcely be a compensation for the statement required. Where the fugitive is discharged, no statement is necessary.

" The powers of the commissioner, or the amount of the penalties of the act, are not involved in this inquiry. If there be an unconstitutional provision in an act, that does not affect any other part of the act. But I, by no means, intimate that any part of the act referred to is in conflict with the constitution. I only say that the objections made to it do not belong to the case under consideration.

" The act of 1850, except by repugnant provisions, did not repeal the act of 1793. The objection, that no jury is given, does apply to both acts. From my experience in trying numerous actions for damages against persons who obstructed an arrest of fugitives from labor, or aided in their escape, I am authorized to say, that the rights of the master would be safe before a jury. I recollect an instance, where a strong anti-slavery man, called an abolitionist, was on the jury in a case for damages, but who, being sworn to find as the evidence and the law required, agreed to a verdict for the plaintiff. He rightly determined that his own opinions could not govern him in deciding a controversy between parties, but that, under his oath he was bound by the law and the evidence of the case.

"It was the power of Congress to give a jury in cases like the present; but the law contains no such provision, and the question raised is, whether the act without it is constitutional.

"This question has been largely discussed in Congress, in the public press, and in conventions of the people. It is not here raised as a question of expediency or policy, but of power. In that aspect only is it to be considered.

"The act of 1793 has been in operation for about sixty years. During that whole time it has been executed as occasion required; and it is not known that any court, judge, or other officer has held the act, in this, or any other respect, unconstitutional. This long course of decisions, on a question so exciting as to call forth the sympathies of the people, and the acuteness of lawyers, is no unsatisfactory evidence that the construction is correct.

"Under the constitution and act of Congress, the inquiry is not, strictly, whether the fugitive be a slave or a freeman, but whether he owe service to the claimant. This would be the precise question in the case of an apprentice. In such a case, the inquiry would not be, whether the master had treated the apprentice so badly as to entitle him to his discharge. Such a question would more probably arise under the indenture of apprenticeship, and the laws under which it was executed. And if the apprentice be remanded to the service of his master, it would, in no respect, affect his right to a discharge where he is held, for the cruelty of his master, or any other cause.

"The same principle applies to fugitives from labor. It is true, in such cases, evidence is heard that he is a freeman. His freedom may be established by acts done or suffered by the master, not necessarily within the jurisdiction where he is held as a slave. Such an inquiry may be made as is required by the justice of the case. But on whatever ground the fugitive may be remanded, it cannot, legally, operate against his right to liberty. That right, when presented to a court in a slave state, has generally been acted upon with fairness and impartiality. Exceptions to this, if there be exceptions, would seem to have arisen on the claims of heirs or creditors, which are governed by local laws, with which the people of other states are not presumed to be acquainted."

Emanating, as it does, from the highest authority, the above opinion should put to rest all ideas of the unconstitutionality of the Fugitive Slave Law. Those of the anti-slavery party who censure Mr. Fillmore for signing that measure, should look to this opinion, from one of their ablest men, who was spoken of as their candidate for the presidency, and see the true principle of the law. But, in addition to the foregoing and other decisions of the supreme court, the act of 1793 stands upon the American archives as a witness to the constitutionality of the Fugitive Slave Law. That act was passed 12th Feb., 1793, and provided, first, the right of the owner to arrest his fugitive slave wherever he may be found; second, the owner of such fugitive was allowed, after the arrest, to

15

take his slave before a magistrate, to have his claim investigated; third, it required such magistrate to investigate the case without a jury, and to deliver up the fugitive to his master; fourth, it established the right of the owner to remove such fugitive slave to his residence. This law was approved by George Washington, and remained in force nearly sixty years.

Those who censure Mr. Fillmore for having signed the Fugitive Slave Law of 1850, might, with the same propriety, denounce the Father of their country, for having signed the law for the recovery of fugitives, passed in 1793, especially, when the necessities for the latter were so much greater than for the former.

Our present Fugitive Slave Law passed the senate by a vote of twenty for, to twelve against it — the purest patriots of the land voting affirmatively. Among those voting for it, were Houston, Bell, Underwood, Berrien, Butler, and others. To attach motives in the least unpatriotic to Mr. Fillmore for having signed that act, would be equivalent to saying that Clay, Webster, Cass, and the greatest men of our country were no patriots. The idea is preposterous.

The following extracts from the first annual message of Mr. Fillmore to Congress are so replete with the patriotic wisdom characteristic of the author, that their publication is not deemed amiss. In these pages we are endeavoring to delineate the qualities of the man about whom we write, instead of the events transpiring in his time, especially, if, in such events, he did not participate. We have refrained from the relation of occurrences not connected with Mr. Fillmore's career, unless such relation was considered essential to a correct understanding of his position.   But to the extracts :

"Among the acknowledged rights of nations is that which each possesses of establishing that form of government which it may deem most conducive to the happiness and prosperity of its own citizens ; of changing that form, as circumstances may require ; and of managing its internal affairs according to its own will.   The people of the United States claim this right for themselves, and they readily concede it to others.   Hence it becomes an imperative duty not to interfere in the government or internal policy of other nations ; and, although we may sympathize with the unfortunate or the oppressed, everywhere, in their struggles for freedom, our principles forbid us from taking any part in such contests.   We make no wars to promote or to prevent successions to thrones ; to maintain any theory of a balance of power ; or to suppress the actual government which any country chooses to establish for itself.   We instigate no revolutions, nor suffer any hostile military expedition to be fitted out in the United States to invade the territories or provinces of a friendly nation.   The great law of morality ought to have a national, as well as a personal and individual application.   We should act toward other nations as we wish them to act toward us ; and justice and conscience should form the rule of conduct between governments, instead of mere power, self-interest, or the desire of aggrandizement.   To maintain a strict neutrality in foreign wars, to cultivate friendly relations, to reciprocate every noble and generous act, and to perform punctually and scrupulously every treaty obligation — these are the duties which we owe to other states, and by the performance of which we best entitle ourselves to like treatment from them; or if that, in any case, be refused, we can enforce our own rights with justice and with a clear conscience.

"In our domestic policy, the constitution will be my guide; and in questions of doubt, I shall look for its interpretation to the judicial decisions of that tribunal which was established to expound it, and to the usage of the government, sanctioned by the acquiescence of the country. I regard all its provisions as equally binding. In all its parts it is the will of the people, expressed in the most solemn form, and the constituted authorities are but agents to carry that will into effect. Every power which it has granted is to be exercised for the public good; but no pretence of utility, no honest conviction, even, of what might be expedient, can justify the assumption of any power not granted. The powers conferred upon the government, and their distribution to the several departments, are as clearly expressed in that sacred instrument as the imperfection of human language will allow; and I deem it my first duty, not to question its wisdom, add to its provisions, evade its requirements, or nullify its commands.

* * * * * * *

"Over the objects and subjects intrusted to Congress, its legislative authority is supreme. But here that authority ceases, and every citizen who truly loves the constitution, and desires the continuance of its existence and its blessings, will resolutely and firmly resist interference in those domestic affairs which the constitution has clearly and unequivocally left to the exclusive authority of the states. And every such citizen will also deprecate useless irritation among the several members of the Union, and all reproach and crimination tending to alienate one portion of the country from another. The beauty of our system of government consists, and its safety and durability must consist, in avoiding mutual collisions and encroachments, and in the regular separate action of all, while each is revolving in its own distinct orbit.

*   *   *   " The law is the only sure protection of the weak, and the only efficient restraint upon the strong. When impartially and faithfully administered, none is beneath its protection, and none above its control. You, gentlemen, and the country, may be assured, that to the utmost of my ability, and to the extent of the power vested in me, I shall, at all times, and in all places, take care that the laws be faithfully executed. In the discharge of this duty, solemnly imposed upon me by the constitution and by my oath of office, I shall shrink from no responsibility, and shall endeavor to meet events as they may arise, with firmness, as well as with prudence and discretion.

" The appointing power is one of the most delicate with which the executive is vested. I regard it a sacred trust, to be exercised with the sole view of advancing the prosperity and happiness of the people. It shall be my effort to elevate the standard of official employment, by selecting for places of importance individuals fitted for the posts to which they are assigned, by their known integrity, talents, and virtues. In so extensive a country, with so great a population, and where few persons appointed to office can be known to the appointing power, mistakes will sometimes unavoidably happen, and unfortunate appointments be made, notwithstanding the greatest care. In such cases, the power of removal may be properly exercised; and neglect of duty or malfeasance in office will be no more tolerated in individuals appointed by myself than in those appointed by others.

* * * * * * * *

" Citizens of the United States have undertaken the connection of the two oceans by means of a railroad across the Isthmus of Tehauntepec, under grants of the Mexican government to a citizen of that republic. It is understood that a thorough survey of the course of the communication is in preparation, and there is every reason to expect that it will be prosecuted with characteristic energy, especially when that government shall have consented to such stipulations with the government of the United States as may be necessary to impart a feeling of security to those who may embark their property in the enterprise. Negotiations are pending for the accomplishment of that object; and a hope is confidently entertained that, when the government of Mexico shall become duly sensible of the advantage which that country can not fail to derive from the work, and learn that the government of the United States desires that the right of sovereignty of Mexico in the isthmus shall remain unimpaired, the stipulations referred to will be agreed to with alacrity.

*　　*　　*　　*　　*　　*　　*　　*

"All experience has demonstrated the wisdom and policy of raising a large portion of revenue, for the support of government, from duties on goods imported. The power to lay these duties is unquestionable, and its chief object, of course, is to replenish the treasury. But if, in doing this, an incidental advantage may be gained by encouraging the industry of our own citizens, it is our duty to avail ourselves of that advantage.

"A duty laid upon an article which can not be produced in this country — such as tea or coffee — adds to the cost of the article, and is chiefly or wholly paid by the consumer. But a duty laid upon an article which may be produced here, stimulates the skill and industry of our own country to produce the same article, which is brought into the market in competition with the foreign article, and the importer is thus compelled to reduce his price to that at which the domestic article can be sold, thereby throwing a part of the duty upon the producer of the foreign article. The continuance of this process creates the skill, and invites the capital which finally enables us to produce the article much cheaper than it could have been procured from abroad, thereby benefiting both the producer and the consumer at home. The consequence of this is, that the artisan and the agriculturalist are brought together, each affords a ready market for the produce of the other, the whole country becomes prosperous, and the ability to produce every necessary of life renders us independent in war as well as in peace.

*   *   *   *   *   *   *

" The papers accompanying the report of the secretary of the treasury will disclose frauds attempted upon the revenue, in variety and amount so great as to justify the conclusion that it is impossible, under any system of *ad valorem* duties levied upon the foreign cost or value of the article, to secure an honest observance and an effectual administration of the laws. The fraudulent devices to evade the law which, have been detected by the vigilance of the appraisers, leave no room to doubt that similar impositions not discovered, to a large amount, have been successfully practiced since the enactment of the law now in force. This state of things has already had a prejudicial influence upon those engaged in foreign commerce. It has a tendency to drive the honest trader from the business of importing, and to throw that important branch of employment into the hands of unscrupulous and dishonest men, who are alike regardless of law and the obligations of an oath. By these means, the plain intentions of Congress, as expressed in the law, are daily defeated. Every motive of policy and duty, therefore, impel me to ask the earnest attention of Congress to this subject. If Congress should deem it unwise to attempt any important changes in the system of levying duties, at this session, it will become indispensable to the protection of the revenue that such remedies, as in the judgment of

Congress may mitigate the evils complained of, should be at once applied.

*   *   *   *   *   *   *

"The unprecedented growth of our territories on the Pacific in wealth and population, and the consequent increase of their social and commercial relations with the Atlantic states, seem to render it the duty of the government to use all its constitutional power to improve the means of intercourse with them.   The importance of open-' ing 'a line of communication, the best and most expeditious of which the nature of the country will admit,' between the valley of the Mississippi and the Pacific, was brought to your notice by my predecessor, in his annual message ; and as the reasons which he presented in favor of the measure still exist in full force, I beg leave to call your attention to them, and to repeat the recommendations then made by him.

*   *   *   *   *   *   *

"I also beg leave to call your attention to the propriety of extending, at an early day, our system of land laws, with such modifications as may be necessary, over the state of California and the territories of Utah and New Mexico.

*   *   *   *   *   *   *

"More than three-fourths of our population are engaged in the cultivation of the soil. The commercial, manufacturing, and navigating interests are all, to a great extent, dependent on the agricultural. It is, therefore, the most important interest of the nation, and has a just claim to the fostering care and protection of the govern-

15*

ment, so far as they can be extended consistently with the provisions of the constitution. As this can not be done by the ordinary modes of legislation, I respectfully recommend the establishment of an agricultural bureau, to be charged with the duty of giving to this leading branch of American industry the encouragement which it so well deserves.

*   *   *   *   *   *   *   *   *

"I commend, also, to your favorable consideration the suggestion contained in the last mentioned report, and in the letter of the general-in-chief, relative to the establishment of an asylum for the relief of disabled and destitute soldiers. This subject appeals so strongly to your sympathies that it would be superfluous in me to say anything more than barely to express my cordial approbation of the proposed object.

*   *   *   *   *   *   *   *   *

"I invite your attention to the view of our present naval establishment and resources presented in the report of the secretary of the navy, and the suggestions therein made for its improvement, together with the naval policy recommended for the security of our Pacific coast, and the protection and extension of our commerce with Eastern Asia. Our facilities for a larger participation in the trade of the east, by means of our recent settlements on the shores of the Pacific, are too obvious to be overlooked or disregarded.

*   *   *   *   *   *   *   *

"I also earnestly recommend the enactment of a law authorizing officers of the army and navy to be retired from the service, when incompetent for its vigorous and active duties, taking care to make suitable provision for those who have faithfully served their country, and awarding distinctions, by retaining in appropriate commands those who have been particularly conspicuous for gallantry and good conduct. While the obligation of the country to maintain and honor those who, to the exclusion of other pursuits, have devoted themselves to its arduous service, this obligation should not be permitted to interfere with the efficiency of the service itself.

"I am grateful in being able to state, that the estimates of expenditure for the navy in the ensuing year are less, by more than one million of dollars, than those of the present, excepting the appropriation which may become necessary for the construction of a dock on the coast of the Pacific, propositions for which are now being considered, and on which a special report may be expected early in your present session.

*　*　*　*　*　*　*　*

"I entertain no doubt of the authority of Congress to make appropriations for leading objects in that class of public works comprising what are usually called works of internal improvement. This authority I suppose to be derived chiefly from the power of regulating commerce with foreign nations, and among the states, and the power of levying and collecting imposts. Where commerce is to be carried on, and imposts collected, there must be ports and harbors, as well as wharves and custom-houses. If ships, laden with valuable cargoes, approach the shore, or sail along the coast, lighthouses are necessary at

suitable points for the protection of life and property.
Other facilities and securities for commerce and naviga-
tion are hardly less important; and those clauses of the
constitution, therefore, to which I have referred, have
received, from the origin of the government, a liberal and
beneficial construction.

*   *   *   *   *   *   *   *

"I recommend that appropriations be made for com-
pleting such works as have been already begun, and for
commencing such others as may seem to the wisdom of
Congress to be of public and general importance.

*   *   *   *   *   *   *   *

"It was hardly to have been expected that the series
of measures passed at your last session, with the view
of healing the sectional differences which had sprung
from the slavery and territorial questions, should at once
have realized their beneficent purposes.   All mutual concessions in the nature of a compromise must necessarily
be unwelcome to men of extreme opinions.   And though
without such concessions our constitution could not have
been formed, and can not be permanently sustained, yet
we have seen them made the subject of bitter controversy
in both sections of the Republic.   It required many
months of discussion and deliberation to secure the concurrence of a majority of Congress in their favor.   It
would be strange if they had been received with immediate approbation by people and states, prejudiced and
heated by the exciting controversies of their representatives.   I believe those measures to have been required

by the circumstances and condition of the country. I believe they were necessary to allay asperities and animosities that were rapidly alienating one section of the country from another, and destroying those fraternal sentiments which are the strongest supports of the constitution. They were adopted in the spirit of conciliation, and for the purpose of conciliation. I believe that a great majority of our fellow citizens sympathize in that spirit, and that purpose, and, in the main, approve, and are prepared, in all respects, to sustain, these enactments. I can not doubt that the American people, bound together by kindred blood and common traditions, still cherish a paramount regard for the Union of their fathers, and that they are ready to rebuke any attempt to violate its integrity, to disturb the compromise on which it is based, or to resist the laws which have been enacted under its authority.

"The series of measures to which I have alluded are regarded by me as a settlement, in principle and substance — a final settlement of the dangerous and exciting subjects which they embraced. Most of these subjects, indeed, are beyond your reach, as the legislation which disposed of them was, in its character, final and irrevocable. It may be presumed, from the opposition which they all encountered, that none of those measures were free from imperfections; but, in their mutual dependence and connection, they formed a system of compromise, the most conciliatory and best, for the entire country, that could be obtained from conflicting sectional interests and opinions.

" For this reason I recommend your adherence to the adjustment established by those measures, until time and experience shall demonstrate the necessity of farther legislation to guard against evasion or abuse.

" By that adjustment we have been rescued from the wide and boundless agitation that surrounded us, and have a firm, distinct, and legal ground to rest upon. And the occasion, I trust, will justify me in exhorting my countrymen to rally upon, and maintain, that ground as the best, if not the only, means of restoring peace and quiet to the country, and maintaining inviolate the integrity of the Union.

" And now, fellow citizens, I can not bring this communication to a close without invoking you to join me in humble and devout thanks to the Great Ruler of nations, for the multiplied blessings which he has graciously bestowed upon us. His hand, so often visible in our preservation, has stayed the pestilence, saved us from foreign wars and domestic disturbances, and scattered plenty throughout the land.

" Our liberties, religious and civil, have been maintained; the fountains of knowledge have all been kept open, and means of happiness widely spread and generally enjoyed, greater than have fallen to the lot of any other nation. And, while deeply penetrated with gratitude, for the rest, let us hope that his all-wise Providence will so guide our counsels, as that they shall result in giving satisfaction to our constituents, securing the peace of the country, and adding new strength to the united government under which we live."

The tone of the foregoing extracts is conservative and patriotic, and indicates a feeling, than which none could be more desirable in a chief magistrate. With a com prehensive, vigorous perception, in his message, he em· braces all the great subjects then agitating the country, and in their elucidation, expresses the soundest national sentiments. In the messages and writings of Mr. Fill- more there is one remarkable fact developed: bitter and hostile as may be the feelings of party strife, political opponents have never been able to cull from them a sin- gle expression that could be tortured into the semblance of anything unpatriotic. They can not find a feature in his whole political career, upon which they can consist- ently heap abusive denunciation. The message from which the extracts are taken, as a state paper, is unsur- passed in its ability and correct views of national policy, by any document on the American archives. It is a paper that will live among the records of ability, and be regarded a "model message."

CHAPTER XI.

Fillibustering — The Cuban movement — Proclamation of the president — Progress of the adventurers — Their delusion — General Quitman — The Lopez expedition — Condensed history of that movement — Its disastrous termination — The Crescent City and Captain General of Cuba — European interference — Their proposals in regard to Cuba — Mr. Fillmore's views — A second Hulsemann letter — Mr. Fillmore's course in regard to Cuba — Kossuth — His mission — His interviews with Mr. Fillmore and Mr. Clay — Their views of his mission — Sound views in regard to foreign and domestic policy—Wisdom of Mr. Fillmore's administration —The American party—Its rise and progress —Causes that led to the defeat of the whig party— Mr. Fillmore's Americanism — His tour to Europe — Reflections, etc.— His nomination for the Presidency— Mr. Fillmore at home.

THE spirit of fillibustering, that has since resulted in the almost entire conquest of Nicaragua, began to manifest itself in the early part of Mr. Fillmore's administration. The sound conservative doctrine communicated to Congress, indicated the course he would take, in case executive interposition should be deemed necessary to quell the restless spirit of adventure, on the part of American citizens. A strict conformity to our neutrality laws was very desirable, and by a perusal of the message, it will be seen from sentiments embodied therein, that in regard to them, he entertained sound and patriotic views.

In various parts of the Union, demonstrations of no

very pacific nature were made, in regard to the island of Cuba. These demonstrations, and speculations as to their ultimate result, furnished fruitful themes for newspaper comment, and created quite an excitement. Adventurers, whose fortunes could not be worsted, but stood some chance of being benefited, were ready to embark in any lawless enterprise. The invasion of Cuba was interdicted by our existing neutrality laws, and embroilment with Spain and European affairs generally, would have been the result, in case of no official action on the subject. As soon as indications became sufficiently manifest that an invasion of Cuba was to be the object of the fillibusterers, the president issued the following proclamation :

" Whereas, there is reason to believe that a military expedition is about to be fitted out in the United States with intention to invade the island of Cuba, a colony of Spain, with which this country is at peace ; and whereas, it is believed that this expedition is instigated and set on foot chiefly by foreigners, who dare to make our shores the scene of their guilty and hostile preparations against a friendly power, and seek, by falsehood and misrepresentation, to seduce our own citizens, especially the young and inconsiderate, into their wicked schemes — an ungrateful return for the benefits conferred upon them by this people in permitting them to make our country an asylum from oppression, and in flagrant abuse of the hospitality thus extended to them.

" And whereas, such expeditions can only be regarded as adventures for plunder and robbery, and must meet the condemnation of the civilized world, whilst they are derogatory to the character of our country, in violation of the laws of nations, and expressly prohibited by our own. Our statutes declare, 'that, if any person shall, within the territory or jurisdiction of the United States, begin or set on foot, or provide or prepare the means for any military expedition or enterprise, to be carried on from thence against the territory or dominions of any foreign prince or state, or of any colony, district, or people, with whom the United States are at peace, every person so offending shall be deemed guilty of a high misdemeanor, and shall be fined not exceeding three thousand dollars, and imprisoned not more than three years.'

"Now, therefore, I have issued this, my proclamation, warning all persons who shall connect themselves with any such enterprise or expedition, in violation of our laws and national obligations, that they will thereby subject themselves to the heavy penalties denounced against such offenders, and will forfeit their claim to the protection of this government, or any interference on their behalf, no matter to what extremities they may be reduced in consequence of their illegal conduct. And, therefore, I exhort all good citizens, as they regard our national reputation, as they respect their own laws and the laws of nations, as they value the blessings of peace and the welfare of their country, to discountenance, and by all lawful means prevent, any such enterprise ; and I call upon every officer of this government, civil or military to use all efforts in his power to arrest for trial and punishment every such offender against the laws of the country

" Given under my hand the twenty-fifth day of April, in the year of our Lord one thousand eight hundred and fifty-one, and the seventy-fifth of the independence of the United States.

" MILLARD FILLMORE.

" By the President :

" W. S. DERRICK, Acting Secretary of State."

This timely proclamation, however, did not suppress the operations of the fillibusters. The work of fitting out an expedition still went on, though with great caution. General Quitman, of Mississippi, was implicated in the movement, and many other men of note advanced means and gave aid to these adventurers. The movement continued to gain strength until the equipment of the unfortunate Lopez was ready to embark for Cuba, carrying many deluded adherents to a fate awful to contemplate. With such secrecy and enterprise had the movement been conducted, that the officials were ignorant, at the time, of the extent of their preparations. Through the faithless collector at the port of Orleans, the Pampero, bearing the ill-fated crew of the Lopez expedition, got under way before day-light on the third of August. The followers of Lopez were misled ; they had been made to believe that the island of Cuba was on the eve of a rebellion, and that the appearance of a band of United States troops on the island would produce general insurrection on the part of the Creoles. This they found to be a great mistake, and paid for their folly with the forfeit of their lives or liberties. The following, from the president's message, in regard to the Cuba difficulties, furnishes a condensed

history of the expedition, and some very patriotic views
in regard to our domestic policy and foreign relations:

"Very early in the morning of the third of August,
a steamer called the Pampero departed from New Orleans
for Cuba, having on board upwards of four hundred
armed men, with evident intentions to make war upon
the authorities of the island. The expedition was set
on foot in palpable violation of the laws of the United
States. Its leader was a Spaniard, and several of the
chief officers, and some others engaged in it were foreigners. The persons composing it, however, were mostly
citizens of the United States.

"Before the expedition set out, and probably before it
was organized, a slight insurrectionary movement, which
appears to have been soon suppressed, had taken place
in the eastern quarter of Cuba. The importance of this
movement was, unfortunately, so much exaggerated in
the accounts of it published in this country, that these
adventurers seem to have been led to believe that the
Creole population of the island not only desired to throw
off the authority of the mother country, but had resolved
upon that step, and had begun a well-concerted enterprise for effecting it. The persons engaged in the expedition were generally young and ill-informed. The
steamer in which they embarked left New Orleans
stealthily and without a clearance. After touching at
Key West, she proceeded to the coast of Cuba, and, on
the night between the eleventh and twelfth of August,
landed the persons on board at Playtas, within about
twenty leagues of Havana.

"The main body of them proceeded to, and took possession of, an inland village, six leagues distant, leaving others to follow in charge of the baggage, as soon as the means of transportation could be obtained. The latter, having taken up their line of march to connect themselves with the main body, and having proceeded about four leagues into the country, were attacked, on the thirteenth, by a body of Spanish troops, and a bloody conflict ensued; after which they retreated to the place of disembarkation, where about fifty of them obtained boats and reëmbarked therein. They were, however, intercepted among the keys near the shore, by a Spanish steamer cruising on the coast, captured, and carried to Havana, and, after being examined before a military court, were sentenced to be publicly executed, and the sentence was carried into effect on the sixteenth of August.

"On receiving information of what had occurred, Commodore Foxhall A. Parker was instructed to proceed, in the steam frigate Saranac, to Havana, and inquire into the charges against the persons executed, the circumstances under which they were taken, and whatsoever referred to their trial and sentence. Copies of the instructions from the department of state to him, and of his letters to the department, are herewith submitted.

"According to the record of the examination, the prisoners all admitted the offences charged against them of being hostile invaders of the island. At the time of their trial and execution, the main body of the invaders

was still in the field, making war upon the Spanish authorities and Spanish subjects.   After the lapse of some days,
being overcome by the Spanish troops, they dispersed on
the twenty-fourth of August.

" Lopez, their leader, was captured some days after,
and executed on the first of September.   Many of his
remaining followers were killed, or died of hunger and
fatigue, and the rest were made prisoners.   Of those, none
appear to have been tried or executed.   Several of them
were pardoned upon application of their friends and
others, and the rest, about one hundred and sixty in number, were sent to Spain.   Of the final disposition made
of these we have no official information.

" Such is the melancholy result of this illegal and ill-
fated expedition.   Thus, thoughtless young men have
been induced, by false and fraudulent representation, to
violate the law of their country, through rash and un-
founded expectations of assisting to accomplish political
revolutions in other states, and have lost their lives in
the undertaking.   Too severe a judgment can hardly be
passed, by the indignant sense of the community, upon
those who, being better informed themselves, have yet
led away the ardor of youth, and an ill-directed love of
political liberty.   The correspondence between this
government and that of Spain, relating to this transaction is herewith communicated.

"Although these offenders against the laws have for-
feited the protection of their country, yet the government may, so far as is consistent with its obligations to
other countries, and its fixed purpose to maintain and

enforce the laws, entertain sympathy for their unoffending
families and friends, as well as a feeling of compassion
for themselves. Accordingly, no proper effort has been
spared, and none will be spared, to procure the release
of such citizens of the United States, engaged in this
unlawful enterprise, as are now in confinement in Spain ;
but it is to be hoped that such interposition with the
government of that country may not be considered as
affording any ground of expectation that the government
of the United States will, hereafter, feel itself under any
obligation of duty to intercede for the liberation or pardon
of such persons as are flagrant offenders against the law
of nations and the laws of the United States. These
laws must be executed. If we desire to maintain our
respectability among the nations of the earth, it behooves
us to enforce steadily the neutrality acts passed by Congress, and to follow, as far as may be, the violation of
those acts with condign punishment.

"But what gives a peculiar criminality to this invasion
of Cuba is, that under the lead of Spanish subjects, and
with the aid of citizens of the United States, it had its
origin, with many, in motives of cupidity. Money was
advanced by individuals, probably in considerable
amounts, to purchase Cuban bonds, as they have been
called, issued by Lopez, sold, doubtless, at a very large
discount, and for the payment of which the public lands
and public property of Cuba, of whatever kind, and the
fiscal resources of the people and government of that
island, from whatever source to be derived, were pledged,
as well as the good faith of the government expected to

be established. All these means of payment, it is evident, were only to be obtained by a process of bloodshed, war, and revolution. None will deny that those who set on foot military expeditions against foreign states by means like these, are far more culpable than the ignorant and the necessitous whom they induce to go forth as the ostensible parties in the proceeding. These originators of the invasion of Cuba seem to have determined, with coolness and system, upon an undertaking which should disgrace their country, violate its laws, and put to hazard the lives of ill-informed and deluded men. You will consider whether further legislation be necessary to prevent the perpetration of such offences in future.

"No individuals have a right to hazard the peace of the country, or to violate its laws, upon vague notions of altering or reforming governments in other states. This principle is not only reasonable in itself, and in accordance with public law, but is engrafted into the codes of other nations as well as our own. But while such are the sentiments of this government, it may be added that every independent nation must be presumed to be able to defend its possessions against unauthorized individuals banded together to attack them. The government of the United States, at all times since its establishment, has abstained, and has sought to restrain the citizens of the country, from entering into controversies between other powers, and to observe all the duties of neutrality. At an early period of the government, in the administration of Washington, several laws were passed for this purpose. The main provisions of these laws were reënacted by the act of April, 1818, by which, amongst other things, it was declared that, if any person shall, within the territory or jurisdiction of the United States, begin, or set on foot, or provide or prepare the means for any military expedition or enterprise, to be carried on from thence against the territory or dominion of any foreign prince or state, or of any colony, district, or people, with whom the United States are at peace, every person so offending shall be deemed guilty of a high misdemeanor, and shall be fined, not exceeding three thousand dollars, and imprisoned not more than three years; and this law has been executed and enforced, to the full extent of the power of the government, from that day to this.

"In proclaiming and adhering to the doctrine of neutrality and non-intervention, the United States have not followed the lead of other civilized nations; they have taken the lead themselves, and have been followed by others. This was admitted by one of the most eminent of modern British statesmen, who said in Parliament, while a minister of the crown, that, 'if he wished for a system of neutrality, he should take that laid down by America in the days of Washington and the secretaryship of Jefferson;' and we see, in fact, that the act of Congress of 1818 was followed, the succeeding year, by an act of Parliament of England, substantially the same in its general provisions. Up to that time there had been no similar law in England, except certain highly penal statutes passed in the reign of George II, prohibiting English subjects from enlisting in foreign service, the avowed object of which statutes was, that foreign armies,

16

raised for the purpose of restoring the house of Stuart to the throne, should not be strengthened by recruits from England herself.

"All must see that difficulties may arise in carrying the laws referred to into execution in a country now having three or four thousand miles of sea-coast, with an infinite number of ports, and harbors, and small inlets, from some of which unlawful expeditions may suddenly set forth, without the knowledge of government, against the possessions of foreign states.

"Friendly relations with all, but entangling alliances with none, has long been a maxim with us. Our true mission is not to propagate our opinions, or impose upon other countries our form of government, by artifice or force: but to teach by example, and show by our success, moderation and justice, the blessings of self-government, and the advantages of free institutions. Let every people choose for itself, and make and alter its political institutions to suit its own condition and convenience. But, while we avow and maintain this neutral policy ourselves, we are anxious to see the same forbearance on the part of other nations, whose forms of government are different from our own. The deep interest which we feel in the spread of liberal principles and the establishment of free governments, and the sympathy with which we witness every struggle against oppression, forbid that we should be indifferent to a case in which the strong arm of a foreign power is invoked to stifle public sentiment and repress the spirit of freedom in any country."

With the disastrous result of the Cuban expedition the

country is too well acquainted to need any recapitulation here. Many of them suffered the cruelest deaths; some were sent to the chain gang as prisoners, who were subsequently released by the interposition of Congress. The faithless collector was dismissed, and the vessel that carried the expedition to Cuba was condemned, as the penalty of her offence.

Such was the conclusion of the famous Lopez invasion of Cuba. One would have thought, from the disasters that attended it, and the prompt efficiency of the executive in quelling such excitements, that further attempts of that sort would not be contemplated. But such was not the case. Subsequent to the Lopez affair, the Crescent City and Purser Smith excitement created no small sensation. The governor of Cuba prevented the steamer Crescent City from landing at the port of Havana, upon the allegation that the purser of the vessel, Smith, had been inciting the citizens of the United States against the island. With the demand of the governor to remove that gentleman, as the only conditions by which he could land the vessel, the commander refused to comply. From this affair considerable difficulty originated, and it finally became a subject of executive attention. In the estimation of the president, the conduct of both the commander of the Crescent City and the governor of Cuba was reprehensible. The former was informed that in case of a forfeiture of his ship in consequence of violating the law, by endeavoring to force his entry into a foreign port, he could expect no remuneration from the government. The conduct of the captain-general was made a subject of investigation before the tribunals of his country. The excitement growing out of these fillibustering expeditions to the colony began to excite alarm in Europe, and elicited the considerations of the crowned heads. The voluntary mediation of France and England resulted in the proposition to the United States, through her secretary, for a treaty between the three powers, a stipulation of which forever prevented either of the parties from interfering in the affairs of Cuba. It is almost needless to say, from the expressed and demonstrated views of Mr. Fillmore in regard to our policy with reference to other countries, that he was opposed to such an "entangling alliance," as this proposed treaty would create. The following is a portion of Hon. Edward Everett's reply, as secretary of state, to the proposition. It is an able document, and indicates the views of the administration upon the proposition, and sets forth some of the objections to its favorable entertainment :

" But the president has a graver objection to entering into the proposed convention. He has no wish to disguise the feeling that the compact, although equal in its terms, would be very unequal in substance. England and France by entering into it would disable themselves from obtaining the possession of an island so remote from their seats of government, belonging to another European power, whose natural right to possess it must always be as good as their own — a distant island in another hemisphere, and one which by no ordinary or peaceful course of things could ever belong to either of them. If the present balance of power should be broker up — if Spain should become unable to maintain the island in her possession, and England and France should be engaged in a death struggle with each other, Cuba might then be the prize of the victor. Till these events all take place, the president does not see how Cuba can belong to any European power but Spain. The United States, on the other hand, would by the proposed convention disable themselves from making an acquisition which might take place without any disturbance of existing foreign relations, and in the natural order of things.

" The island of Cuba lies at our doors ; it commands the approach to the Gulf of Mexico, which washes the shores of five of our states; it bars the entrance to that great river which drains half the North American continent, and, with its tributaries, forms the largest system of water communication in the world ; it keeps watch at the doorway of our intercourse with California by the Isthmus. If an island like Cuba, belonging to the Spanish crown, guarded the entrance to the Thames, or the Seine, and the United States should propose a convention like this to England and France, those powers would assuredly feel that the disability assumed by ourselves was far less serious than that which we asked them to assume.

" The opinion of American statesmen, at different times and under varying circumstances, have differed as to the desirableness of the acquisition of Cuba by the United States. Territorially and commercially, it would, in our hands, be an extremely valuable possession. Under certain contingencies, it might be almost essential to our safety ; still, for domestic reasons on which, in a communication of this kind, it might not be proper to dwell, the President thinks that the incorporation of the island into the Union at the present time, although effected with the consent of Spain, would be a hazardous measure, and he would consider its acquisition by force, except in a just war with Spain, should an event so greatly to be deprecated take place, as a disgrace to the civilization of the age. The President has given ample proof of the sincerity with which he holds these views. He has thrown the whole force of his constitutional power against all illegal attacks upon the island. It would have been perfectly easy for him, without any seeming neglect of duty, to allow projects of a formidable character to gather strength, by connivance. No amount of obloquy at home, no embarrassments caused by the indiscretions of the colonial government of Cuba, have moved him from the path of duty. In this respect the captain-general of the island, an officer apparently of upright and conciliatory character, but probably more used to military command than the management of civil affairs, has, on a punctilio in reference to the purser of a private steamship, who seems to be entirely innocent of the matters laid to his charge, refused to allow passengers and the mails of the United States to be landed from a vessel having them on board. This is certainly a very extraordinary mode of animadverting upon a supposed abuse of the liberty of the press by the subject of a foreign government in his native country. The captain-general is not permitted by his government, three thousand miles off, to hold any diplomatic intercourse with the United States. He is subject in no degree to the direction of the Spanish minister at Washington ; and the president has to choose between a resort to force to compel the abandonment of this gratuitous interruption of commercial intercourse, which would result in war — and a delay of weeks and months, necessary to a negotiation with Madrid, with all the chances of the most deplorable occurrences in the interval, and all for a trifle that ought to have admitted of a settlement by an exchange of notes between Washington and Havana. The president has, however, patiently submitted to these evils, and has continued faithfully to give to Cuba the advantage of those principles of the public law, under the shadow of which she has departed, in this case, from the comity of nations. But the incidents to which I allude, and which are still in the train, are among many others which point decisively to the expediency of some change in the relations of Cuba; and the president thinks that the influence of England and France with Spain, would be well employed in inducing her so to modify the administration of the government of Cuba, as to afford the means of some prompt remedy for evils of the kind alluded to, which have done much to increase the spirit of unlawful enterprise against the island.   That a convention such as is proposed would be a transitory arrangement, sure to be swept away by the irresistible tide of affairs in a new country, is, to the apprehension of the president, too obvious to require a labored argument. The project rests on principles, applicable, if at all, to

Europe, where international relations are, in their basis, of great antiquity, slowly modified for the most part in the progress of time and events, and not applicable to America, which but lately a waste, is filling up with intense rapidity, and adjusting on natural principles, those territorial relations which, on the first discovery of the continent, were, in a good degree, fortuitous. The comparative history of Europe and America, even for a single century shows this."

The following extracts from Webster's famous Hulsemann letter, indicate the views of the administration. While it manifests an active sympathy and a lively interest for those struggling for freedom in all countries, it conveys an avowed determination to maintain inviolate all neutrality relationships, and to keep aloof from all foreign alliances :

    *   *   *   " But the interest taken by the United States in those events, has not proceeded from any disposition to depart from that neutrality toward foreign powers, which is among the deepest principles and the most cherished traditions of the political history of the Union.   *   *   *   *

" The power of this republic, at the present moment, is spread over a region, one of the richest and most fertile on the globe, and of an extent in comparison with which the possessions of the House of Hapsburg are but as a patch on the earth's surface. Its population, already twenty-five millions, will exceed that of the Austrian empire within the period during which it may be hoped

that Mr. Hulsemann may yet remain in the honorable
discharge of his duties to his government. Its naviga-
tion and commerce are hardly exceeded by the oldest and
most commercial nations; its maritime means and its
maritime power may be seen by Austria herself, in all
seas where she has ports, as well as it may be seen, also,
in all other quarters of the globe. Life, liberty, property, and all personal rights, are amply secured to all
citizens, and protected by just and staple laws; and
credit, public and private, is as well established as in
any government of Continental Europe. And the country, in all its interests and concerns, partakes most
largely in all the improvements and progress which distinguish the age. Certainly the United States may be
pardoned, even by those who profess adherence to the
principles of absolute governments, if they entertain an
ardent affection for those popular forms of political
organization which have so rapidly advanced their own
prosperity and happiness; which enabled them, in so
short a period, to bring their country, and the hemisphere
to which it belongs, to the notice and respectful regard,
not to say the admiration, of the civilized world. Nev-
ertheless, the United States have abstained, at all times,
from acts of interference with the political changes of
Europe. They cannot, however, fail to cherish always
a lively interest in the fortunes of nations struggling for
institutions like their own. But this sympathy, so far
from being necessarily a hostile feeling towards any of
the parties to these great national struggles, is quite
consistent with amicable relations with them all."

16*

The course pursued by Mr. Fillmore, in regard to the Cuban movements, elicited the universal approval of his countrymen of all parties, not infected with a spirit of fillibustering enterprise. From his action in regard to those movements, a full appreciation of his views upon the subject of our foreign and domestic policy may be derived. It was a sound, conservative, patriotic course, prompt in action, and conciliatory in effect, and affords an instructive example for chief executives of our country. Another event, important from subsequent events whose maturity it tended to accellerate, affords an opportunity of ascertaining Mr. Fillmore's view upon foreign alliances. I allude to the visit of Louis Kossuth to America, during his administration.

Kossuth came to this country to plead for Hungary, his 'fatherland.' The condition of that unhappy country was of itself sufficient to excite sympathy. Robbed of her jewels, deprived of her freedom, disrobed of her independence, quivering with the Austrian bayonet in her heart, and weeping over the fragments of her nationality, she presented a spectacle well calculated to arouse sympathy. But when, in all their magnitude, her sufferings were portrayed to Americans by the burning words of her exiled chief, the picture possessed a double potency. Never did a warmer embrace of a nation, extend a more heartfelt welcome than did we to him. The deep, wide-spread sympathy manifested for him wherever he went, was unparalleled; but he misconstrued it, and was much chagrined when forced to discriminate between sympathy and policy. To unsettle the national policy of a country consolidated on the maxims of Washington and Jefferson, was a task he could not accomplish. He visited our extensive cities,.and created sympathy everywhere. But the wily chief, from the elicitation of that, directed his hopes to "material aid." He was invited to Washington City, by a resolution of Congress. Accepting this invitation, he visited the capital. There he had an interview with Henry Clay and President Fillmore. Among the last acts of Clay's life was to extend to him a true sympathy, and to utter an emphatic protest against his designs, in regard to bringing the United States, as a party, into the difficulties of Europe. Let America engrave with a diamond pen upon her heart of hearts, this almost dying advice of Henry Clay. On the last day of the year, Kossuth was introduced to Mr. Fillmore by Daniel Webster. In the presence of the nation's executive, the Hungarian delivered the following address:

"President: I stand before your Excellency a living protestation against the violence of foreign interference, oppressing the sovereign right of nations to regulate their own domestic concerns.

"I stand before your Excellency a living protestation against centralization oppressing the state right of self-government.

"May I be allowed to take it for an augury of better times, that, in landing on the happy shores of this glorious republic, I landed in a free and powerful country, whose honored chief magistrate proclaims to the world that this country can not remain indifferent when the strong arm of a foreign power is invoked to stifle public sentiment and repress the spirit of freedom in any country.

"I thank God that he deemed me not unworthy to act and to suffer for my fatherland.

"I thank God that the fate of my country became so intimately connected with the fate of liberty and independence of nations of Europe, as formerly it was intimately connected with the security of Christendom.

"I thank God that my country's unmerited woe and my personal sufferings became an opportunity to seek a manifestation of the spirit and principles of your republic.

"May God the Almighty bless you with a long life, that you may enjoy the happiness to see your country great, glorious, and free, the corner-stone of international justice, and the column of freedom on the earth, as it is already an asylum to the oppressed.

"Sir, I pledge to your country the everlasting gratitude of Hungary."

To the above Mr. Fillmore made the following appropriate reply:

"I am happy, Governor Kossuth, to welcome you to this land of freedom; and it gives me pleasure to congratulate you upon your release from a long confinement in Turkey, and your late arrival here. As an individual, I sympathize deeply with you in your brave struggle for the independence and freedom of your native land. The American people can never be indifferent to such a contest; but our policy as a nation in this respect has been uniform, from the commencement of the government; and my own views, as the chief magistrate of this nation, are fully and freely expressed in my recent message to Congress. They are the same whether speaking to Congress here or to the nations of Europe.

"Should your country be restored to independence and freedom, I should then wish you, as the greatest blessing you could enjoy, a restoration to your native land; but should that never happen, I can only repeat my welcome to you and your companions here, and pray that God's blessing may rest upon you wherever your lot may be."

Mr. Fillmore viewed Kossuth's mission as one having dangerous tendencies if encouraged beyond the limits of sympathy. He took the same view of it that Clay did. It was evidently the design of Kossuth, from the moment he set foot upon our shores, to appeal to the hearts of a people, who, he knew, were lovers of liberty, and after arousing their sympathies to procure the assistance of men or money, or perhaps both, for Hungary. Had he succeeded, and we had become entangled just at that time in foreign broils, no human sagacity can tell where we would have been placed by the storm that has just blown over the trans-Atlantic world. But with men at the head of affairs, entertaining the sentiments embodied in Mr. Fillmore's reply to Kossuth's address, and demonstrated throughout his entire administration, there is not the remotest chance of bringing about such a result. It was during this administration that the oppressed Madiais were groaning under the cruel tyranny of the papal hierarchy. Mr. Fillmore wrote to the Grand Duke of Tuscany, through his secretary of state, Hon. Edward Everett, to have that unfortunate family released. His active sympathy in their behalf was, doubtless, what elicted the denunciatory effusions of Archbishop Hughes' journal, of which the following is a specimen :

" It does not escape the independent judgment of the universe, that the administration, now happily defunct, has been as bigoted as it has been imbecile. The universe congratulates the country upon having elected a statesman (Pierce!) for president, and for permitting the Unitarian ex-preacher, late secretary of state, to return to his pulpit to proclaim that Jesus is not God, and Mr. Fillmore himself to become a village lawyer."

Under the broad shield of our constitution, there is certainly no true American who can endorse such a sentiment as the above. Among true patriots, in regard to Mr. Fillmore's administration, there exists but one opinion — that in wisdom, virtue, and patriotism, it has never been excelled.

Many wise and important measures were adopted during Mr. Fillmore's administration. Among others were extensive exploring expeditions, that were highly creditable to the nation. The commerce to Japan was opened. A three cent letter postage was established, and a number of measures of infinite utility to the country. Never did a chief magistrate close an administration with more unbounded approbation. Never did one retire from office clothed with brighter lustre.

Never did official term weave for man a nobler, civic crown. Never did an individual more firmly enthrone hmself in the grateful hearts of his countrymen. Never did one wear more fadeless laurels, and never were they more proudly worn.

We now propose giving a brief notice to the American party, as being to some extent associated with the great man of whom we are writing, and figuring conspicuously in the measures of the country. Native Americanism had its origin in the almost utter prostration of the ballot-box, and the grossest abuses of the elective franchise in the municipal elections of our extensive cities.

The first American movement was in the city of New York in 1834. The intolerant frauds practiced upon the city by foreigners, and the immense influx into that city of the thousands annually disgorged from the old world, resulted in an organization for the purpose of counteracting their influence. Prof. Morse was run by that party for mayor of the city, and received a very respectable vote. The appeals made by the young party to the people in behalf of the sacredness of the ballot box, and warning them against foreign influence, had a powerful effect, and it gained many adherents.

This party, however, began, so far as the organization was concerned, to die away without having accomplished much more than the avowal of principles that were eventually to take deeper hold upon the masses. The American feeling received a startling impetus again in 1840, by the endeavors of Archbishop Hughes and Gov. Seward to set aside a portion of New York's cherished school fund for the support of catholic schools. This was the most dangerous innovation, as they conceived, that had yet indicated itself, and to counteract it and other abuses they re-organized in 1843. This time they published their principles, calling on other cities to follow their example. Many cities responded to the call and pursued the same course, and several succeeded in discomfiting the foreigners entirely. In 1844, the city of New York elected their mayor upon the American ticket, and most of the city council. The native American feeling was again lost sight of amid the smoke of battle in the presidential canvass of 1844, to remain in comparative quiet until 1851–52, when it assumed a more prominent aspect than it had at any time previous, and continued to increase until 1854 and 1855 it was *the* question of the day· The resuscitation and rapid progress of the principles of the party from that date may be attributed to a variety of concurrent causes. The compromise had just passed, and, the difficulties adjusted that had caused such fearful agitation, the minds of the people were called to the more immediate investigation of foreign influence, and were brought to see the necessity of some counteracting efforts. The defeat of Clay in 1844 was, to a great extent, the effect of naturalization frauds and the foreign vote, and people began to open their eyes and become alarmed at the fearful balance of power exerted by them. The campaign of 1852 and the excitement occasioned by and over the foreign vote, tended to accelerate the development of the party's strength. The political demagoguery and chicanery that had been manifest for years, and the prospect afforded for checking its influence, advanced and gave stability to the party. The death of the whig party created a national vacuum where the disaffected and those who had become convinced of the folly of partisan strife of all parties could marshal under the broad banners of Americanism. As whig has been mentioned, it may not be improper to advert to some of the causes that led to the eventual decay and disruption of that party. One thing that operated against the whigs, even in their palmiest days, was the attitude in which they placed their candidates. Instead of having that confidence in the man that circumstances justified, and regarding his past course as a sufficient guarantee for his future, they required pledges and indorsements, until they complicated with a multiplicity of national and local measures.

They required too much at the hands of their leaders — so much, that infalibility would not more than satisfy some of the party. They lacked consolidated, active organization in their campaigns, necessary to insure success. These, however, and various others, needless to enumerate, were secondary causes. The great cause of that party's destruction was the defeat of Clay in 1844. The acknowledged leader of his party, through many a hard-fought battle — thrice rejected by his countrymen, the people lost all confidence in their party. They thought if such men as Clay and Webster could not elicit the support of their party, that ability and patriotism were wholly unappreciated, and losing all confidence in the success of measures being carried in other hands, that had failed in Clay's, they bowed with the ruins of their party. The campaign of 1844 was an epoch in American politics, — the result of Clay's defeat was not unforeseen. From the very day the result became known a spirit of "all is lost" hung in gloom over the party. No signs indicated renewed energies at another time. A perfect "give up" disposition pervaded the entire party. Such was the result of the defeat of Henry Clay.

The vacuum thus produced by the defection of the old whig, was very appropriate for the re-organization of the American party. Reared upon the ruins of its great predecessor, it gained strength from 1851, continually, until 1854 and 1855 it swept like an avalanche over several entire states. Of its principles, aims, and objects, I need not speak here, they are known all over the country; suffice it to say, they are essentially American in letter and spirit, and number among their adherents the ablest men from all parties.

Mr. Fillmore became formally identified with the American order in 1855. If any additional evidences were needed, to those transpiring around him, to convince him of the utility of the American movement, they were furnished by the conduct of Kossuth, who, finding himself unable to make any impressions other than sympathy upon the native born citizens of our country, commenced appealing to the foreign voters.

The following is a sample of these appeals, and their results; it is a portion of a speech he made to the Germans of New York City in 1852:

"You are strong enough to effect the election of that candidate for the presidency who gives the most attention to the European cause. I find that quite natural, because between both parties there is no difference as regards the internal policy, and because only by the inanity of the German citizens of this country, the election will be such, that, by and by, the administration will turn their attention to other countries, and give every nation free scope. No tree, my German friends, falls with the first stroke; it is therefore necessary, that, inasmuch as you are citizens, and can command your votes, you support the candidate who will pursue the external policy in our sense, and endeavor to effect that all nations become free and independent, such as is the case in happy America."

The following resolutions are the result of a similar effusion a short time afterwards:

"Resolved, that as American citizens, we will attach ourselves to the democratic party, and will devote our strength to having a policy of intervention in America carried out.

"Resolved, that we expect that the candidates of the democratic party will adopt the principles of this policy, which has been sanctioned by all distinguished statesmen of this party.

"Resolved, that we protest against the manner in which, heretofore, the government of the United States has interpreted and applied the policy of neutrality, which is a violation of the spirit of the constitution of the United States.

"Resolved, that we ask that every American citizen, not being attached to the soil, may support the strength of any other people in the sense as the juries have interpreted the principles of the American constitution, and especially of the policy of neutrality."

And here again is his secret circular in *very* strict keeping with his " President: I stand before your excellency a living protestation against the violence of foreign interference, oppressing the sovereign right of nations to regulate their own concerns." Then he was addressing President Fillmore. In this circular he addressed himself to the Germans, and thought it best to play on a harp of another string :

"NEW YORK, June 28th, 1852.

" SIR : I hope you have read already my German farewell speech, delivered June 23d, in the Tabernacle at New York, and also the resolution of the meeting, which was passed subsequently.

" I hope, further, that the impression which this matter has made upon both political parties has not escaped your attention.

" Indeed, it is not easy to be mistaken, that the German citizens of America will have the casting vote in the coming election, if they are united in a joint direction upon the platform of the principles set forth in the speech before mentioned.

" They may decide upon the exterior policy of the next administration of the United States, and with that the triumph or the fall of liberty in Europe."

Whether Kossuth's mission, and such effusions as the foregoing, had effect upon Mr. Fillmore's feelings with immediate reference to his identification with the American party, or not, they were circumstances well calculated to induce serious reflection on the part of all.   Mr.

Fillmore's convictions on these principles had been pretty well settled for a number of years ; they were the results of a palpable necessity, of whose existence he had long been satisfied.

The following letter, from Mr. Fillmore to a friend residing in Philadelphia, gives his views more fully upon the principles of the American party :

"BUFFALO, New York, Jan. 3d, 1855.

" RESPECTED FRIEND ISAAC NEWTON :

*   *   *   " I return you many thanks for your information on the subject of politics. I am always happy to hear what is going forward ; but, independently of the fact that I feel myself withdrawn from the political arena, I have been too much depressed in spirit to take an active part in the late elections. I contented myself with giving a silent vote for Mr. Ullman for governor.

" While; however, I am an inactive observer of public events, I am by no means an indifferent one ; and I may say to you, in the frankness of friendship, I have for a long time looked with dread and apprehension at the corrupting influence which the contest for the foreign vote is exciting upon our elections. This seems to result from its being banded together, and subject to the control of a few interested and selfish leaders. Hence, it has been a subject of bargain and sale, and each of the great political parties of the country have been bidding to obtain it ; and, as usual in all such contests, the party which is most corrupt is most successful. The consequence is, that it is fast demoralizing the whole country; corrupting the very fountains of political power; and converting the ballot-box — that great palladium of our liberty — into an unmeaning mockery, where the rights of native-born citizens are voted away by those who blindly follow their mercenary and selfish leaders. The evidence of this is found not merely in the shameless chaffering for the foreign vote at every election, but in the large disproportion of offices which are now held by foreigners, at home and abroad, as compared with our native citizens. Where is the true hearted American whose cheek does not tingle with shame and mortification, to see our highest and most coveted foreign missions filled by men of foreign birth, to the exclusion of native born? Such appointments are a humiliating confession to the crowned heads of Europe, that a republican soil does not produce sufficient talent to represent a republican nation at a monarchical court. I confess that it seems to me, with all due respect to others, that, as a general rule, our country should be governed by American-born citizens. Let us give to the oppressed of every country an asylum and a home in our happy land; give to all the benefits of equal laws and equal protection; but let us at the same time cherish as the apple of our eye the great principles of constitutional liberty, which few who have not had the good fortune to be reared in a free country know how to appreciate, and still less, how to preserve.

"Washington, in that inestimable legacy which he left to his country — his farewell address — has wisely warned us to beware of foreign influence as the most baneful foe of a republican government. He saw it, to be sure, in a different light from that in which it now presents itself; but he knew that it would approach in all forms, and hence he cautioned us against the insidious wiles of its influence. Therefore, as well for our own sakes, to whom this invaluable inheritance of self-government has been left by our forefathers, as for the sake of the unborn millions who are to inherit this land — foreign and native — let us take warning of the father of his country, and do what we can to preserve our institutions from corruption, and our country from dishonor; but let this be done by the people themselves in their sovereign capacity, by making a proper discrimination in the selection of officers, and not by depriving any individual, native or foreign-born, of any constitutional or legal right to which he is now entitled.

"These are my sentiments in brief; and although I have sometimes almost despaired of my country, when I have witnessed the rapid strides of corruption, yet I think I perceive a gleam of hope in the future, and I now feel confident that, when the great mass of intelligence in this enlightened country is once fully aroused, and the danger manifested, it will fearlessly apply the remedy, and bring back the government to the pure days of Washington's administration. Finally, let us adopt the old Roman motto, 'Never despair of the republic.' Let us do our duty, and trust in that providence which has so signally watched over and preserved us for the result. But I have said more than I intended, and much more than I should have said to any one but a trusted friend, as I have no desire to mingle in political strife. Remember me kindly to your family, and, believe me,

            "I am truly yours,

                 "MILLARD FILLMORE."

Since the close of Mr. Fillmore's administration, he has been visited with the severest domestic afflictions that fell with a crushing weight upon his heart. He has continued to reside in Buffalo, a pattern for the old, and an example for the young. He recently took a tour to Europe, and visited the places in the old world hallowed by their historic associations. He was everywhere an object of respect and admiration. The plain, unostentatious manner of his traveling, won the approval of his countrymen at home, and demonstrated our republican principles abroad. He had personal interviews with Queen Victoria, Louis Napoleon, the Pope of Rome, and other crowned heads of Europe, and was on all occasions the recipient of marked respect. The reflections he made upon the governments of the old world were favorable to the highest appreciation for the beloved institutions of his own country. Mr. Fillmore is essentially American in manners, looks, and feelings, and in his intercourse with the friends of royalty evinced his purely American principles on all occasions. At a convention of his countrymen, wholly unsolicited and unexpected, held some time since at Philadelphia, he was nominated by acclamation as a candidate for the chief magistracy of the United States — the position he filled with such distinguished ability and patriotism through the struggle of 1850-51. He received notice of his nomination at Venice, in Italy, by a communication from the committee appointed for that purpose. From Paris he replied, signifying his acceptance, and giving his past as a guarantee for his future course. He is now, in obedience to the wishes of the American people, before the country as a candidate for the highest office in their power to bestow.

On the eleventh of June he left Liverpool for his native land. On reaching New York City, banners were flung to the breeze, and the entire population of the metropolis joined in mass, to give him a heart-felt welcome. New York's ovation to her favorite son excelled anything of the kind ever witnessed in America — ever witnessed anywhere, for it was the spontaneous outburst of freemen. From New York City homeward to Buffalo, his journey was a triumphal march. Not the march of a Cæsar, with a coronet on his brow, and captive kings at his car; not the march of a Salladin, with the red scimitar in one hand, and the trophies of vanquished empires in the other; it was the tread of a freeman, in reunion with his fellow citizens and his boyhood companions. In Buffalo the same imposing manifestations of " welcome home " awaited him. The ovation of his friends in Buffalo was, indeed, indicative of the lasting regard felt for him by his friends and neighbors. He is now at his home, on Franklin Street, in Buffalo, in the quietude of repose, enjoying excellent health, cheerful and contented.

17

CHAPTER XII.

Character of Mr. Fillmore as a domestic man — His adaptation for the family circle — Amiability and industry of Mrs. Fillmore — Mr. Fillmore as a philanthropist — As a neighbor — His love of home — Mr. Fillmore as a husband — As a parent — His residence and its sociabilities — His manners — His order and regularity — His industry — His temperance — His morality — Mr. Fillmore as a statesman — As a patriot — And as a man — Conclusion.

No man has ever sustained in all the domestic relations of life a character more worthy of emulation than has Mr. Fillmore. His spotless reputation in a long career of success and usefulness to his country has been tarnished by no misdeed calculated to subject him to sensorious remarks and criticism from those to whom his every day actions have been open to inspection. In looking over his past life, in so strict a conformity to the golden rule has it been, that the retrospect, instead of being disagreeable — instead of having to commune with the whisperings of remorse, is extremely pleasant, for it is accompanied with the plaudits of an approving conscience. As a domestic man, Mr. Fillmore is most happily constituted by nature to appreciate the blessings of the family circle. The most delightful enjoyments — those most calculated to animate his bosom with liveliest emotions — are those that eradiate around the fireside of his own home. Studiously careful to make his home the abode of love and happiness, he looked to that alone for the solid enjoyments of life. After the arduous duties of his professional labors, home as the Eden of his heart, he would turn, where, in the bosom of his family he forgot the cares and toils of life. After a conclusion of services in a public capacity, with delightful emotions he turned to the same haven, and in the cup of domestic bliss, would be sure to find an anodyne for his weariness. In the domestic circle, the amiability of his temperament shines most conspicuously. The gentleness of his nature and the mild dignity of his manners seem to infuse themselves into the minds of all present, until an harmonious assimilation of feeling pervades the entire circle. His cheerfulness is of such a nature as to convey an idea of the most perfect felicity of feeling. So manifest is his cheerfulness, that his entrance into the circle is sufficient to dispel all gloomy feelings, unless they are the result of an universal cause. He loves the family circle, and the peaceful quietude of home better than the grandeur of the palace, though decorated in all the ensignia of royalty. His home has ever been the centre of his deepest affections, and those to his family regarded as his highest duties. In the bosom of his family, surrounded by those he loved, he has experienced happier feelings and holier comforts than when in the halls of the great. Often, after the clouds of adversity began to disperse from the horizon of his future, were the smiles of welcome to his home from those he loved prized more highly than the world's applause.

So admirably adapted to the enjoyment of domestic life is his temperament, that, in the seclusion of his family, performing little duties as its head, he has spent days, in preference to mingling with the great, where he would have been so justly welcome. The family history of Mr. Fillmore is a very quiet one. Quiet, from the fact that it is entirely divested of pride and ostentatious display, and has exhibited no faults that could subject it to the criticisms of the community. The plain simplicity of Mr. Fillmore's taste in the arrangement of family comforts, while it combines neatness and utility, avoids extravagant display and gorgeous fixtures. To have a comfortable home, and pleasant family occupants, was his ardent desire; — in both he was successful, until the interposition of Providence robbed him of his most cherished flowers.

The many virtues of his wife, were not unappreciated in the circle of their acquaintance. As a wife, she was a devoted one; as a mother, none was ever more affectionate. The guardianship she exercised over the household during Mr. Fillmore's absence, engaged in public duty, could not have been more faithful, or attended with happier results. Her gentleness and devotion befitted her admirably for the position she occupied. She was anxious at all times to promote that domestic happiness which she knew was so congenial to her husband's feelings, and to make home the abode of those joys he so highly prized. In consequence of Mr. Fillmore's frequent absence, the entire management of the home affairs, especially the training of their children, necessarily devolved upon her. These duties she discharged with the successful devotion of a wife and a mother.

Meek and mild to a fault, unobtrusive in her deportment, all who knew her loved her for her purity of soul. Quiet and unostentatious, she charmed with her simplicity. Possessing these traits of character, she was most happily moulded to the feelings of Mr. Fillmore, and well caculated to promote gentle cheerfulness around the domestic hearth. Her efforts to make home happy by an exemplification of these traits, were faithfully continued until her death. With such congenial spirits as these to mingle, no purer joys belonged to man than were Mr. Fillmore's in the midst of his domestic circle. These he treasures as the genuine happiness of his life — the Sabbath of his soul.

Mr. Fillmore as a philanthropist, if philanthropy means a love for our species, has no superior. The greatness of his heart can not resist the touching appeals of humanity, come they from whom, or in whatsoever shape they may. He is essentially a feeling man in every sense of the word. The actions of his past life have been illustrative of these attributes of his nature. The peculiar sensibility of his nature, has been evinced in all his actions from earliest boyhood. The active sympathy he manifested for the sufferers of the Emerald Isle, shows he has a soul susceptible of entire sway to the promptings of true benevolence. No man can be for an hour in his presence, without becoming impressed with the belief that he loves his fellow men; he manifests it in all his actions; it is legibly written on his countenance; it beams with mildest radiance from his eye; it speaks in the tones of his voice; and glows in the chambers of his soul. The

deserver of alms can never say he applied in vain to Mr.
Fillmore for relief. His heart beats a warm response
to the dictates of charity, and is overwhelmed with grief
at the distress of a suffering fellow creature.

The susceptibility of his nature to the deepest grief—
the intensest agony — is evidenced by the overwhelming
sorrow in which he was thrown, by the domestic afflictions elsewhere related in this book. It is not my purpose to open those wounds afresh, or to intrude upon the
ashes of his loved ones. To him they were jewels of the
heart, worn closely round it every day; when they were
torn from his bosom, the intensity of his feelings seemed
to consume the vitality of existence, and the portals of
the tomb to close every avenue to happiness. Lost to
the tender condolence of friends, in the voyage of mournful retrospection, he communed with the visions of the
by-gone, and lived alone in a world of memory.

Insensible to the offerings of friendship, he mused
upon the "loved and the lost," and in the mantle of misery
"mourned the pale ashes of his hopes." The beauteous
gems of his home had ceased to gladden, and left him
alone on the Sahara of his hopes, to mourn the departed.
Such bereavements as these, unstring the stoutest hearts
not chilled to every impulse; but to one of Mr. Fillmore's
feelings, it was the pierce of an icicle—the bitterness of
misery. The wounds were deep and lasting, and though
he has regained his wonted serenity, they are still un-
healed. But, susceptible as are his feelings, Mr. Fillmore
is not a man of impulse. The feelings of sympathy
with, and love for, his fellow men do not have to be

excited or aroused in his bosom by pathetic appeals. As
a part of his nature they exist there, and are always
ready to manifest themselves. He never forgets the
kindness of a friend ; and, if he had one, he would never
forget the injuries of an enemy. As a man of feeling,
he manifests this attribute of his nature, in the daily
walks of life.

He feels deeply wounded over the wrongs of his country, as well as those of his fellow men. In 1849–50,
when the old ship of state was about to strand on the
rock of disunion, he manifested the deepest concern. To
his friends he expressed himself as feeling willing to make
any personal sacrifice, could it avail in conciliating the
elements of discord, and cementing the bonds of union.
To this feeling, humane nature of Mr. Fillmore is attributable the great esteem in which he is held by his neighbors and friends. This esteem can not properly be
called popularity. It is worthy a higher appellation. It
is an absolute admiration on the part of the citizens of all
parties for the intrinsic virtues of the man.

As to Mr. Fillmore's character as a neighbor, those
with whom he has lived the longest, and spent the greater
portion of his life, can bear the best attestation. Let
the generous Buffalonians, who love him so well, and love
to do him honor, speak out under this head, and not one
among her many voices would say aught against him.
Mr. Fillmore's is not one of those characters to which
"distance lends enchantment." No distance is so great that
its intervention would keep him from being admired, but
the nearer the approach to Buffalo, the more attractive

he becomes, until in the city and his county, his name
becomes an embodiment of the purest patriotism. The
fact, that not a man among those who are acquainted with
him, even though he differ with him in politics, can say
aught against him, shows the enviable position he occupies in the midst of his people, and how highly he is
esteemed as a neighbor. The love Mr. Fillmore has for
his neighbors has always been peculiarly manifest. Often,
while absent, in the discharge of his official duty, in letters to his friends, he expressed anxiety to be in their
midst. From Europe he frequently wrote, contrasting
the ceremonial formalities of court with the social life of
his fellow citizens, and expressing his anxiety to mingle
with his neighbors and his friends. At Liverpool, when
the vessel was almost ready to bear him home, and he
was about "turning from a foreign strand," his bosom
swelled with delight at the prospect of meeting his
friends.

On his arrival in Buffalo, the position he occupied in
the hearts of the people as a man and a neighbor, became
truly manifest. The mutual joy, the outburst of enthusiasm from the assembled thousands who welcomed their
neighbor home, told his valued worth. The greetings
and gratulations of rich and poor, official and peasant,
wholly divested of formality, showed the unbounded joy
they experienced at seeing him again in their midst. The
offices of honor and responsibility to the elevation of
which he has always received the cordial support of the
city of Buffalo and Erie county, show that as a neighbor
and a citizen he occupies an elevated position in their

esteem. No man has natural qualities better adapted to the discharge of duties as a neighbor, than has Mr. Fillmore. Kind, liberal, and generous, his intercourse is marked with a great desire to render himself agreeable, and to make those happy around him. To all those neighborhood courtesies, Mr. Fillmore is particularly careful to devote due attention. Living on terms of unrestricted sociability with his neighbors, his intercourse is entirely free and easy, accompanied frequently with kind pleasantries, of a neighborhood, home-like nature. Mr. Fillmore is known by almost the entire population of the city of Buffalo, and is beloved by all. In the recent demonstration of his welcome, all classes and all parties engaged in the reception of their fellow citizen. Old men were overjoyed and thronged to the stand, prepared to give a welcome. Ladies of all ages mingled in the occasion, and with a thousand handkerchiefs waved their welcome. Men of all parties harmonized on an occasion at which all were equally gratified. Little girls ran joyously to him with boquets, as if to "strew his way with flowers." One thing is worthy of note. The young men of Buffalo, and in the entire state of New York, *all* admire Mr. Fillmore. There has never been a man who has taken a greater hold upon the affections of the young men of a state than has Mr. Fillmore upon those of New York. The place Henry Clay occupied in the hearts of the young men of the noble state of Kentucky, is equaled only by that occupied by Mr. Fillmore in the hearts of the young men of New York.

But the high esteem for Mr. Fillmore on the part
17*

of young men is not confined to the state of New York, it prevades over the entire Union. This is a significant fact, and should be hailed as a good indication, as showing that the young men of the country place a higher estimate upon virtue and patriotism than upon the leaders of party factions. It shows a disposition on the part of young men to make moral worth the basis of their good opinions, and to emulate a virtuous example, set in a career of usefulness and honor.

Mr. Fillmore's love of home is a prominent trait of his character. He loves his home better than any place else, and the friendship of his neighbors better than the plaudits of the great. He has mingled in public life, because he conceived it his duty to do so, when his personal inclinations would have kept him under "the vine and shadow of his own fig-tree." In his absence in the services of his country, his desires to experience the solid joys of home, and to be in the bosom of his family have amounted to the deepest yearnings, and he looked forward to the conclusions of his labors, when no barrier would interpose between him and his loved ones, with fondest anticipations.

The pride he took in the city of his adoption, in her growing prosperity and increasing commerce, and the successful operation of her well conducted educational systems, are evidences of his love of home. In the rising generation, especially the young men of that city, he feels the deepest solicitude, and encourages every enterprise tending to their elevation. He is a member of the Young Men's Association, whose objects are to infuse a literary taste throughout society, and promote the facilities of reading. The enjoyments he feels in the social intercourse of his neighbors and friends are, compared to every other, of a transcendent nature. The city of Buffalo is the cradle of his fame, where his young aspirations were rocked into maturity, and he doats on her citizens and her home associations with the fervor of filial affection. The city of his adoption, and the home of his heart, he is proud of her proverbial refinement, and the high-toned generosity of her children. Sensible of the many manifestations of regard for him on the part of her citizens, he feels bound to them by the golden cord of friendship. Coming in their midst a poor and penniless boy, they took him to their bosoms with parental solicitude and made him the recipient of their confidence and esteem. Of these kindnesses he is not forgetful, but treasures them as a boon of friendship's offering, and in the enjoyment of free intercourse with his friends, he feels he has vindicators of his name.

A resident of the city for a quarter of a century, he watched the development of her resources with pride, and cheerfully assisted in her progress. The friends of his early career for his neighbors, in the quietude of repose he would love to glide down the stream of life, till gathered to the grave of his fathers. In the shades of his Buffalo home, he wishes to pass the declivity of age, among his friends, and repose at last by the treasures of his heart — the loved of his youth. This love of home, on the part of Mr. Fillmore, no distance can damp, no gorgeous displays of power and pomp can change or suppress. His friends, with whom he has mingled so long, and whose devotion has been evinced by an unchanging fidelity to his fortunes through his whole career, are so associated with his feelings, that they have become as a part of himself. And his home, so long the bower of his heart, the Eden of his joys, though deprived of its fairest ornaments, is still the sanctuary of his repose — the asylum of his heart. Around his home and in the midst of his friends, stands the Ararat of his fortunes — rests the ark of his joys — and blooms the olive of his love.

The recent reception extended to Mr. Fillmore was replete with incidents illustrative of this trait of character. As the large procession moved on to the tune of "Home, Sweet Home," and banners were streaming a welcome across the streets of the city, "This is my own, my native land," was traceable upon his countenance, full of emotional joy. He was overwhelmed with feelings of gladness. The friends of his early career flocked around him — the wives and daughters of his old neighbors smiled him "Welcome!"

In his response to the address of welcome, the depth of his feelings almost choked his utterance. The expression that he had, often, in his travels over the old world, longed to be in the city of Buffalo, and on the shores of Lake Erie showed his love of home. The expression that he valued that spontaneous reception by his fellow citizens, more than such an one as Queen Victoria elicited in the city of Paris, showed the high estimate he placed upon the good will of his neighbors and his friends. The deep feelings he could not suppress when the procession halted, to the

notes of " Sweet Home," at his own door, showed how
hallowed to him by the tenderest associations, and how
enshrined in his bosom was that loved spot of the past.
When he entered its lone portals, and met no loved smile
there that used to give so dear a greeting — no girlhood
joy to twine a fond embrace, we can but imagine how,
" gush after gush," the fountain of feeling rolled its
mighty waves into the deep bosom of the past, and hovered around the most pleasing recollections of its horizon.
No heart beats a warmer response to cherished reminiscences than does his.   One of his first impulses on step-
ping from the Atlantic, upon his native soil, was to thank
God that he was a freeman, and stood in no need of pass-
ports.   More than a king, or a potentate, he was a son
of Columbia, with the stars and stripes waving over his
head, and treading a soil unpolluted by the impress of
tyranny.

His addresses to his fellow-citizens, who gave him receptions of welcome at every point, from his landing in
New York, until his arrival in Buffalo, are replete with
patriotism, and a spirit elevated by the love of home.
To the " sea of upturned faces " that met him at every
point, he returned a response, showing the happiness he
experienced on being again in the midst of his fellow
freemen, and upon the soil of his home-land.   He has
always loved his home, but by its contrast with the down-
trodden of other lands, he learned, if possible, to appreciate it more highly.

Mr. Fillmore, as a husband, presents himself to our
view in the light of a model.   From the time of his

marriage, in 1826, up to the time of his first great domestic affliction, he was the kindest of husbands. The peculiar adaptation of his temperament to the enjoyment of domestic happiness, and the exalted purity of his virtue could not have made him otherwise. During his residence at Aurora, before success began to crown his efforts to any great degree, and prosperity began to smile in his pathway, he maintained an equanimity of feeling and cheerfulness, and manifested the greatest devotion as a husband. He felt the responsibilities resting upon him were of the heaviest nature, and was exceedingly faithful in their performance. He was never from home except on business, the prosecution of which was to promote its interests, and immediately on his release from such duties he would hasten to it. Mr. Fillmore's devotion to his wife was almost excessive. She was the idol of his being, and seemed interwoven in every ligament of his feelings. To her he was kind and tender to a fault. Looking to the family circle of his home for the purest rays of his happiness, he regarded his wife as the source from whence they must emanate, and cherished her as a part of his being. Regarding virtuous purity as worthy his warmest admiration, he beheld its impersonation in his wife, and did homage at its shrine. Possessing the highest appreciation for the opposite sex, in the many virtues and mild gentleness of his wife he saw exemplified all that was lovely in woman, and was tenderly solicitous of her comfort. Thus careful to render her happy, and watchful of her welfare, they lived a life of conjugal felicity, unmoved by the slightest sign of indifference or neglect. He was is kind solicitude up to the time of her

, as a parent, has pursued a course that
so be known to be admired. He has had but
two children, a son and a daughter, but on these he
doted with paternal fondness. Mr. Fillmore has a fondness for children and they a fondness for him. One of
the most pleasing incidents of the occasion of his recent
reception in Buffalo was connected with the children.
Quite a number of fair young girls presented him
bunches of flowers, at the stand. When the last one of
the number came to present her's, by some mishap, she
dropped it. With all the pleasantry of a parent, he
drew her to him and kissed her in the kindest manner.
He loves children, and regarding them as but men of a
smaller growth, he manifests a great interest in their welfare and moral culture. In training his children to lessons of early duty, he pursued a course, while it produced
the most implicit obedience, endeared him to them in the
purest love. He was never harsh and reproachful in
correction or reproof. In impressing a sense of right and
wrong upon their minds, he would, with earnestness, point
out the proper course for them, and tell the importance
of a correct deportment. He showed to them the beauty
of an even course, and the deformity of a reckless one.
He gave them to understand the sure rewards of a virtuous life, and the equally certain punishments of a
vicious one. He was careful to set an example he would
love to have them follow, and demonstrated by practice
what he taught by precept. He desired to make home

an agreeable place, that his children might always look to it for their most pleasing recollections. Knowing it to be of vital importance, he was careful to set for his children that glorious example they would be proud to contemplate. He was careful to rear them to habits of industry and usefulness. He always felt that duties of a high order devolved upon every one, and wished his children to be useful members of society. For his children, no man ever manifested a greater paternal solicitude than he. Over their early education he exercised great personal supervision, and was extremely careful to supplant all mistaken views with correct ones. He sent them to good schools, and gave them excellent educations. He trained them to habits of regular industry, and gave them clear conceptions of duty. His labors and his solicitude were rewarded. They grew up, possessed of accomplishments, and universally beloved. His daughter, at the time of her death, in 1853, possessed not only a highly cultivated intellect and the knowledge of those fine arts that so much adorn a lady, but she was a proficient in many useful lessons of life. She had made great proficiency in drawing, music, etc., indicating an active mind and a correct taste.

He now has but one child, M. P. Fillmore, a young lawyer in Buffalo. In the discharge of every duty as a parent, Mr. Fillmore has been faithful. His son and himself compose the entire family, over whose interests he presided and exercised guardianship with successful fidelity. The chain is broken that bound it together in such harmonious felicity for a number of years. It was

a golden one. Its links were love and happiness. When
"life's fitful fever" is over, and the remaining links are
passed, may it be reunited in a better sphere.

The residence of Mr. Fillmore, on Franklin Street, in
the city of Buffalo, is in one of the most beautiful parts
of the city. Like its proprietor, it is plain and unostentatious. It is a two-story white building, exceedingly neat
and handsome. The entrance is into a hall, with a suit
of rooms below and above. Its rooms are very neatly,
but not gorgeously furnished. Everything in and about
his dwelling displays a taste of the correctest simplicity
and order. In front of the residence is a row of trees
arranged with the happiest design, that look pleasingly
cheerful. The yard is decorated with shrubbery taste-
fully arranged, and cultivated with great care. The
grounds embracing his yard and garden are not extensive,
but sufficiently so for all purposes of convenience and
comfort. Plain, but exceedingly neat, upon the door-
plate is seen " M. Fillmore," to whose domicil the friend,
the citizen, and the stranger is ever welcome. From his
residence, it is but a short and a very pleasant walk to
the placid waters of Lake Erie. It is in every respect
adapted to the quiet, home-like temperament of Mr. Fillmore. One of his door neighbors is Judge N. K. Hall,
former post-master-general during Mr. Fillmore's administration. Between them a long and friendly intimacy
has existed of the most disinterested nature. His home,
like himself, bears the aspect of quiet cheerfulness and
order, wholly divested of everything like display.

This has been Mr. Fillmore's home for a number of

years, and the scene of the most generous hospitalities. There his friends, in the sacredness of his domestic circle, always met the most cordial greetings, and were the recipients of the kindest generosity. To the good and the great, the rich and the poor, the peasant and the man of rank, its hospitalities are extended with free good-will. Go there, and a kind reception awaits you. Among his books or papers, or with some of his numerous friends, he spends the greater portion of his time there, ready to extend a cordial greeting to the friend or the visitor.

In manners, while Mr. Fillmore displays no studied formalities, his natural kindness makes him a most agreeable companion. We often see men whom the world esteem as great, and they often fall infinitely below the position we had assigned them in our conceptions. A rigid stiffness, indicative of feelings of superiority, seems to manifest itself in their looks and their entire manners, that assumes to themselves an elevation at least commensurate with, and often above, that assigned them by the people. But between true greatness and its assumption, there is a very wide distinction. Between the man who drinks the cup of adulation till his brain grows dizzy, and with arrogant assumption concludes he is great, and the one who is really so above the effect of his fellow men's plaudits, there is a wide difference. While the one looks down upon his fellow men from the elevation of his own conceptions, and indicates a superiority of feeling not justifiable from any real merits, the other, with feelings of gratitude, looks upon his fellow men as his brothers, and regards their happiness as a part of his own. Mr.

Fillmore is an impersonation of true greatness.   And if we have been disappointed by those we presumed great falling below our conceptions, we are apt to be equally so in the contraction of Mr. Fillmore's acquaintance, for he is sure to rise above them. The plainness of his person and attire, the easy dignity of his address, will elicit the esteem of all.   His manners, though divested of all ceremonial formalities, are extremely dignified. It is not that assumptive dignity, however, that repels with its formal arrogance.   While it elevates and commands the greatest respect, it divests you of all embarrassment, and charms with its winning amiability.   It is a dignity of the soul. He meets his friends with a smile that, like a ray from the sunshine of his bosom, melts the feelings into social communion.   He extends his hand of welcome with all the cordiality of a true friend, and talks over the general topics of the day with cheerfulness and freedom. His manners are marked with the plainest simplicity, entirely divested of all semblance of affectation, and indicative of true refinement.   His natural courtesy, while it exhibits a polished exterior, indicates a yet higher polish of the soul.   The extreme freedom, ease, and sociability, his nature, forbid all satiety and uncomfortable embarrassments.

There is a uniformity about the manners of Mr. Fillmore that is strikingly manifest.   In the white house, in the city, among his friends, in the quiet seclusion of home, mingling with his fellow citizens, or among the crowned heads of Europe, he is the same plain, unostentatious, amiable, and polished gentleman.

In regard to Mr. Fillmore's habits, they have, in every particular, been most unexceptionable. He has led a life of extreme regularity. He has never embarked in any enterprise with an active zeal that abated before it was successfully completed. He never pursued his studies in his boyhood with great zeal one day, and trifled his time the next. With systematic earnestness he applied himself, and continued their prosecution with unabated industry. " Let no day pass without one line," he has exemplified as his motto. His regularity has been displayed in every department of his business. In the domestic duties of his home, the exactest regularity was always manifest, and the history of a day was the history of a year, unless an incidental interference prevented.

Order he regards as indispensable to success, and of the first importance in business. Nothing he ever performs is done in an indifferent, hasty manner. Regarding it an object worth doing at all, he regards it as being worth doing well, and performs it with neatness and correctness. From his earliest boyhood he observed the strictest punctuality, and complied with his promises just as he made them, when not unavoidably prevented. Living within his means, he contracted no debts ; and promises he made in every other respect were sure to be complied with. So strict was his punctuality, that in his earliest career he had the confidence of all, and was proverbial for the certainty with which he performed his promises.

No hastily and badly performed duty can claim him for its executor, for he does everything in a proper manner, and with neatness. His penmanship is neat and regular, with no blots upon his manuscript. His manners are uniform — the same to-day they were yesterday. His whole character, in fact, is impressed with the most even consistency.

Of Mr. Fillmore's industry I scarcely need speak. He has never eaten the bread of idleness. From child-hood he has been an active laborer. He is, essentially, an industrious man. No one ever pursued a profession with more energetic activity than did he. He was from youth an early riser, and began the duties of the day at an early hour. Having in the beginning of his life to sustain himself with the labor of his own hands, habits of regular industry were acquired in youth. When he commenced his profession, he applied himself with zealous activity to master its intricacies, and after he got into practice, the business of his office received the most persevering attention. He did not embark in his profession from any inducement to lead an easy life, but with a determined spirit to render himself useful. If a pro-fessional life forms a bed of ease for some men, Mr. Fill-more has not been one of those men. His life has been one of triumphant success, but it has not been one of ease. Far the greater portion of his life has been spent in active labor, either in professional engagements, or in a public capacity. His industrial habits have always been exhibited about his home in the happiest manner. It is his nature to be actively engaged in either mental or physical labor.

After he began to be successful in his career, and not

necessitated to do so, he labored with his own hands. In his garden, with the spade or the hoe, he superintended the laborers, and assisted in its arrangement and tillage. Out in the early morning air, with his gardening utensils, he loved to sow his seed, and plant his vegetation. To Mr. Fillmore, there is a morality in labor. Regarding idleness as the parent of misery, and a direct violation of duty itself, he has shunned it as an Upasian vale to his hopes. " Thou shalt earn thy bread by the sweat of thy brow," he has thoroughly comprehended, and has complied with the enactment to the fullest extent. Man, as having relative duties to perform, the neglect of which would prove him recreant to his race, he regards as morally bound to labor.

As a result of his industry, Mr. Fillmore presents himself to our view a statesman of extraordinary capacity and world-wide renown. Mr. Fillmore has always been the most temperate of men in every respect. According to apostolic injunction, he is " temperate in all things." From intoxicating drinks he has abstained entirely, during his whole life. He was never tempted, in his younger days, by the lure of the wine cup. His family, back to John Fillmore, his great-grandfather — and the father of all by that name in America — were remarkable for their sobriety. So strictly has he adhered to this principle of abstinence, that he is scarcely acquainted with anything of that nature.

The lessons of his boyhood, and the principles which were impressed upon his mind, in connection with his subsequent high-toned resolves, kept him aloof from the sway of all such vices. Extremely cautious to preserve a correct deportment, and to establish a character of moral rectitude, he never was thrown amid the evil influences of corrupt associations. The effects of this regular, temperate life, are most happily felt. He has always enjoyed almost uinterrupted good health, and a buoyancy of feeling unknown to the epicure, or the wine bibber.

In his diet he is plain and simple. He is not fastidious in regard to dress or diet. His attire is always neat, but exceedinly plain and citizen-like. He has never used tobacco, in any shape or form; from the strict adherence to his temperate principles, he has been entirely free from the effects and expenditures of this pernicious practice. In boyhood, he never indulged in a single habit of this nature. He has never sworn an oath, or used language in the least profane. From his example let little boys learn lessons of temperance and industry, and profit by putting them in practice.

As regards Mr. Fillmore's moral character, it is of an elevated nature. In childhood he was more moral than most children; in youth his morality was remarkable for its strictness; in manhood it was unexceptionable, and now braced by the moral culture of years, it presents itself to our view in noble proportions, without blemish.

Mr. Fillmore, as a statesman, has left his character upon the institutions of his country, and impressed it upon the tablets of the American mind. He is decisive, patriotic, and conservative. As a statesman, shunning all Machavelian artifice, he sees the wide distinction between a patriot and a politician, and spurns the schemes of the one with the moral purity of the other. The purity of his character as a statesman stands above the men of his day and reminds us of our illustrious Washington.

It is a little remarkable, that since the author has been engaged on these pages, he has received numerous letters from different sections of the country, in every one of which occur the enviable words " OUR PUREST STATES-MAN," applied to Mr. Fillmore. Mr. Fillmore, as a man, possesses the attributes of God's true noblemen.

We are now at the conclusion of our labors. We have endeavored faithfully to record the career of a patriot. Of the manner in which the task is performed, the reader must judge. If, in conclusion, the author of these pages should be the means of casting a ray of light along the dark path traveled by struggling youth in adversity — if he should dispel a cloud of despair from the horizon of impoverished worth — if he should thrill a single heart that bleeds under the chill blast of penury with hopeful pulsations — if he should light a smile upon the pale and fevered brow of friendless genius — if he should dry a burning tear that drops from the fount of orphaned ambition — and if, in the example of one so noble as the subject of these pages, the struggling youth may see a light to guide his steps — he will feel rewarded.